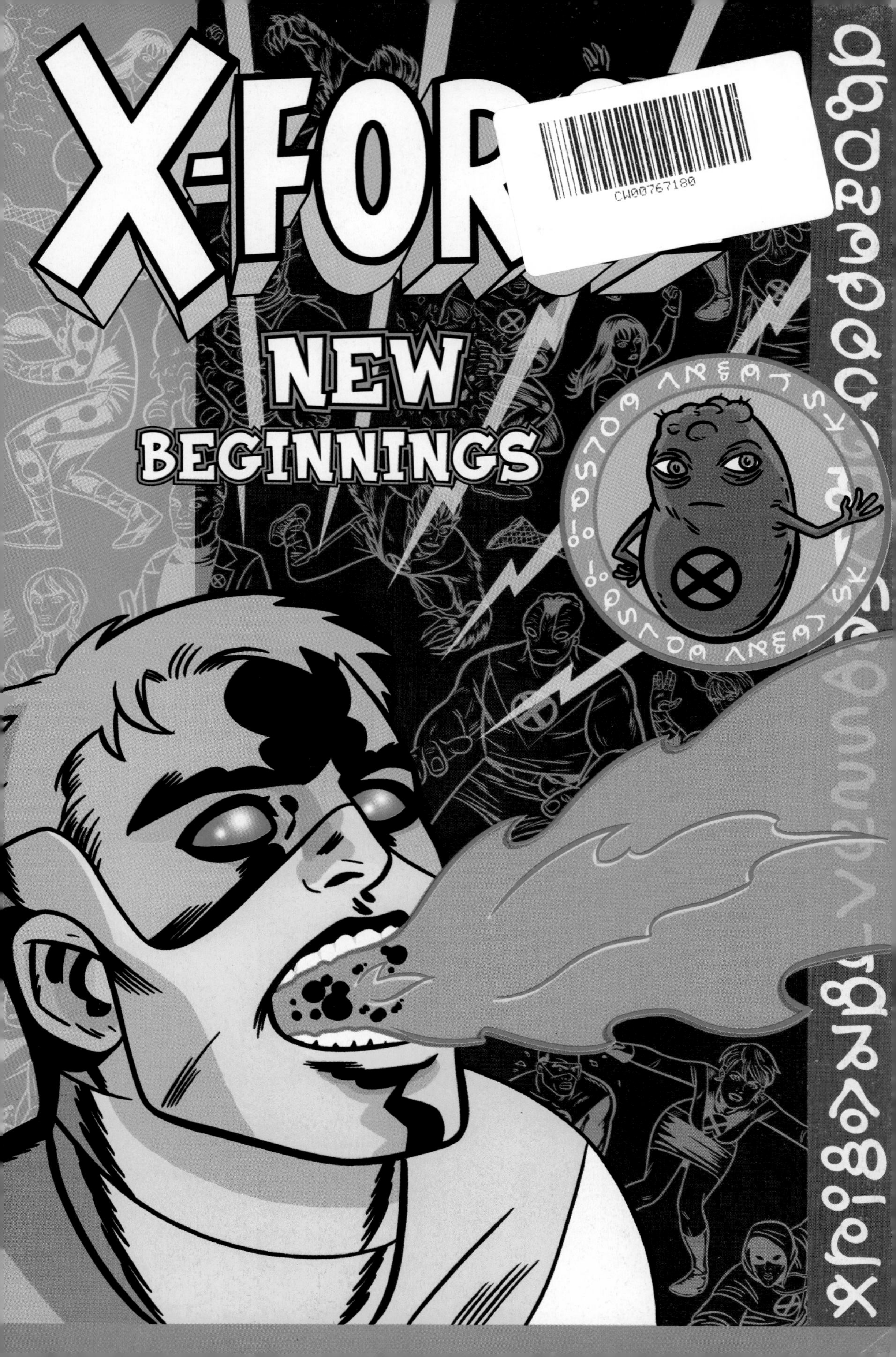
X-FOR
NEW BEGINNINGS

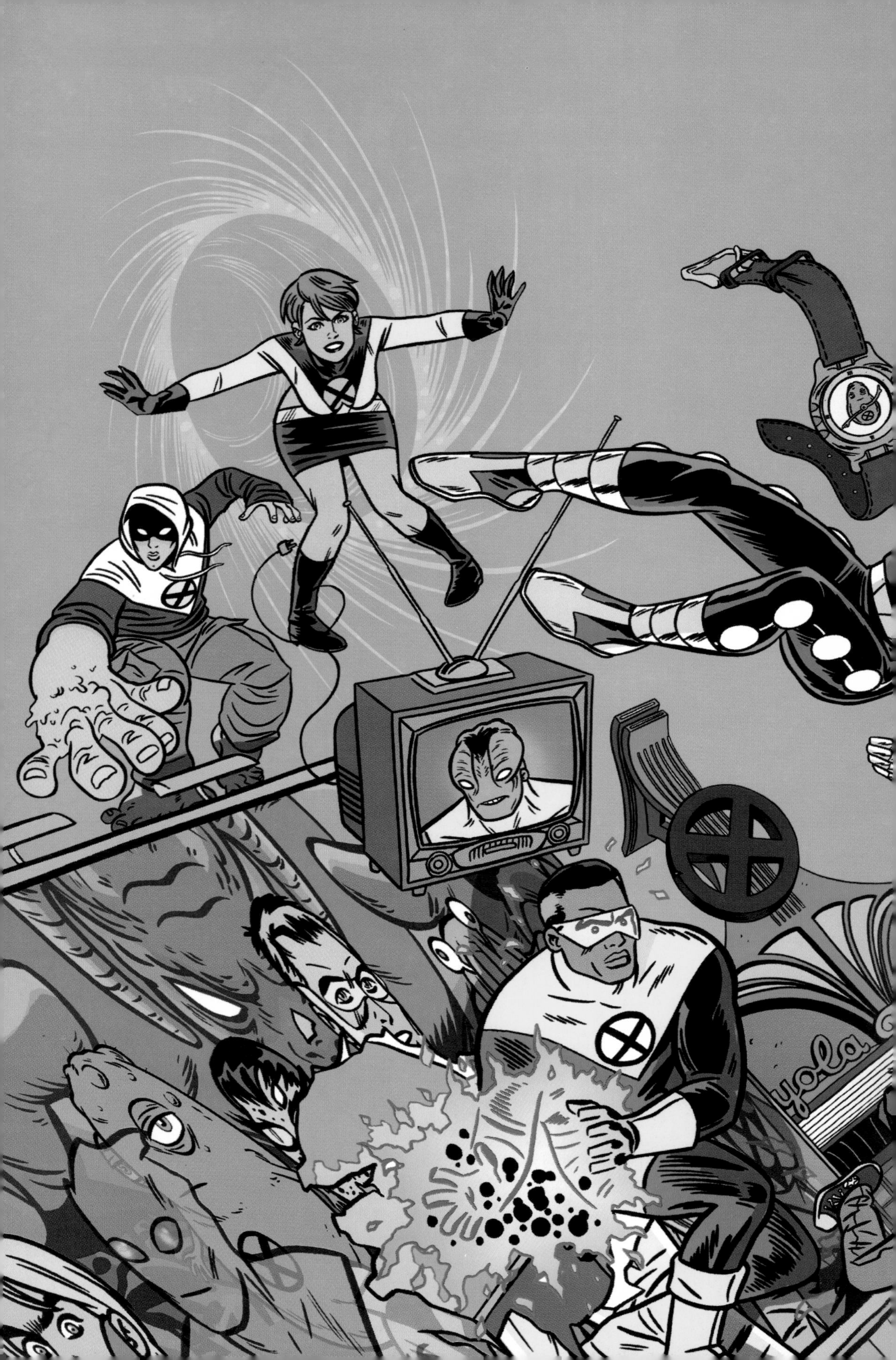

X-FORCE: NEW BEGINNINGS

PETER MILLIGAN
WRITER

MIKE ALLRED
ARTIST

LAURA ALLRED
COLORIST & SEPARATOR

DOC ALLRED & BLAMBOT
LETTERER

AXEL ALONSO
ORIGINAL EDITOR

MATTY RYAN
BOOK DESIGN

BEN ABERNATHY
COLLECTIONS EDITOR

BOB GREENBERGER
DIRECTOR– PUBLISHING OPERATIONS

JESSICA SCHWARTZ
PRODUCTION ASSISTANT

STEFANO PERRONE, JR.
MANUFACTURING REPRESENTATIVE

JOE QUESADA
EDITOR IN CHIEF

BILL JEMAS
PRESIDENT

X-FORCE ® NEW BEGINNINGS. Contains material originally published in magazine form as X-FORCE # 116-120. First Printing, October 2001. ISBN # 0-7851-0819-X. GST. #R127032852. Published by MARVEL COMICS, a division of MARVEL ENTERTAINMENT GROUP, INC. OFFICE OF PUBLICATION: 10 EAST 40th STREET, NEW YORK, NY 10016. Copyright © 2001 Marvel Characters, Inc. No similarity between any of the names, characters, persons, and/or institutions in this publication with those of any living or dead person or institutions is intended, and any such similarity which may exist is purely coincidental. This publication may not be sold except by authorized dealers and is sold subject to the conditions that it shall not be sold or distributed with any part of its cover or markings removed, nor in a mutilated condition. X-FORCE (including all prominent characters featured in this publication and the distinctive likenesses thereof) is a trademark of MARVEL CHARACTERS, INC. Printed in Canada. PETER CUNEO, Chief Executive Officer; AVI ARAD, Chief Creative Officer; GUI KARYO, Chief Information Officer; BOB GREENBERGER, Director – Publishing Operations; STAN LEE, Chairman Emeritus.

10 9 8 7 6 5 4 3 2 1

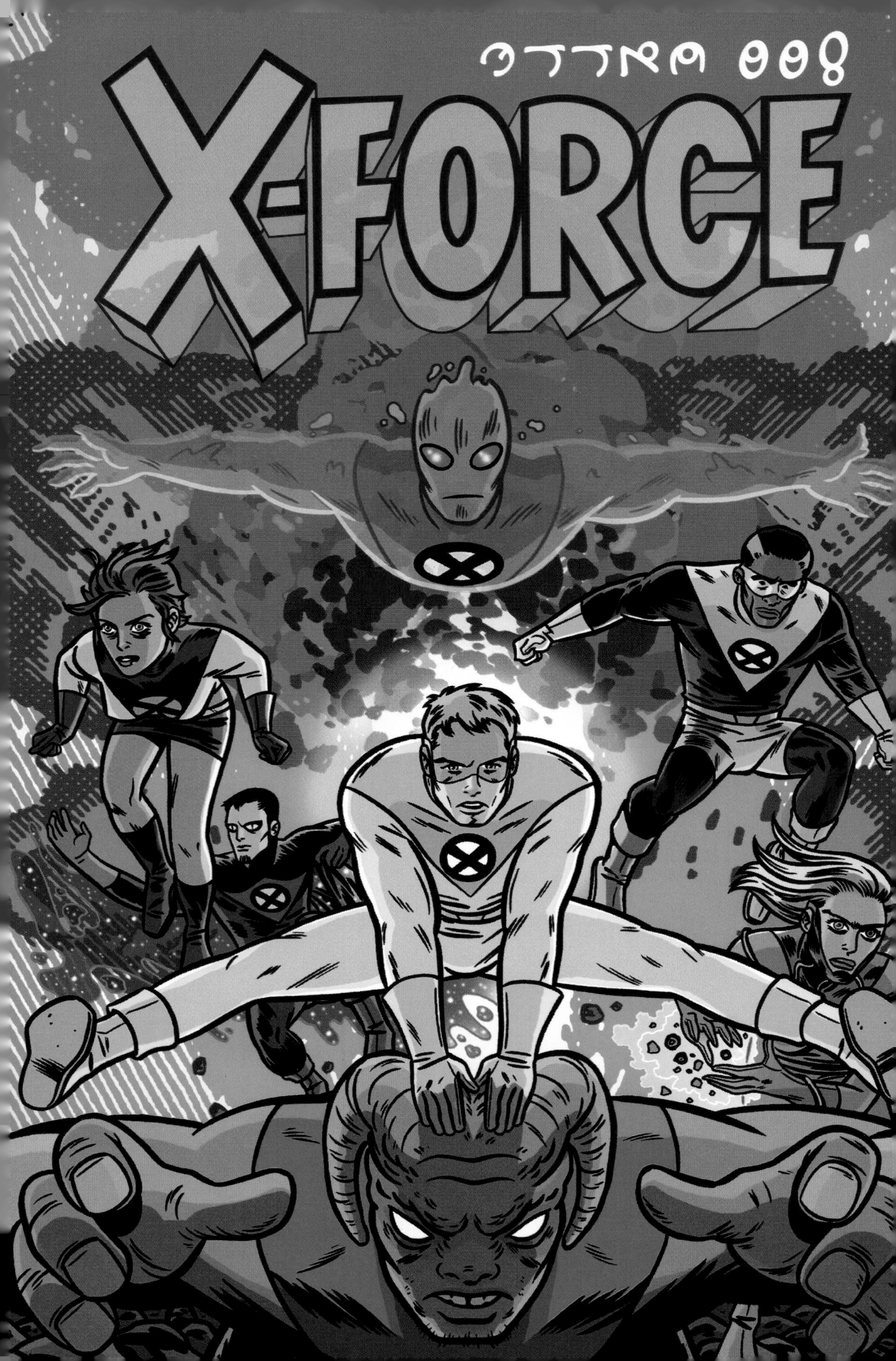
X-FORCE

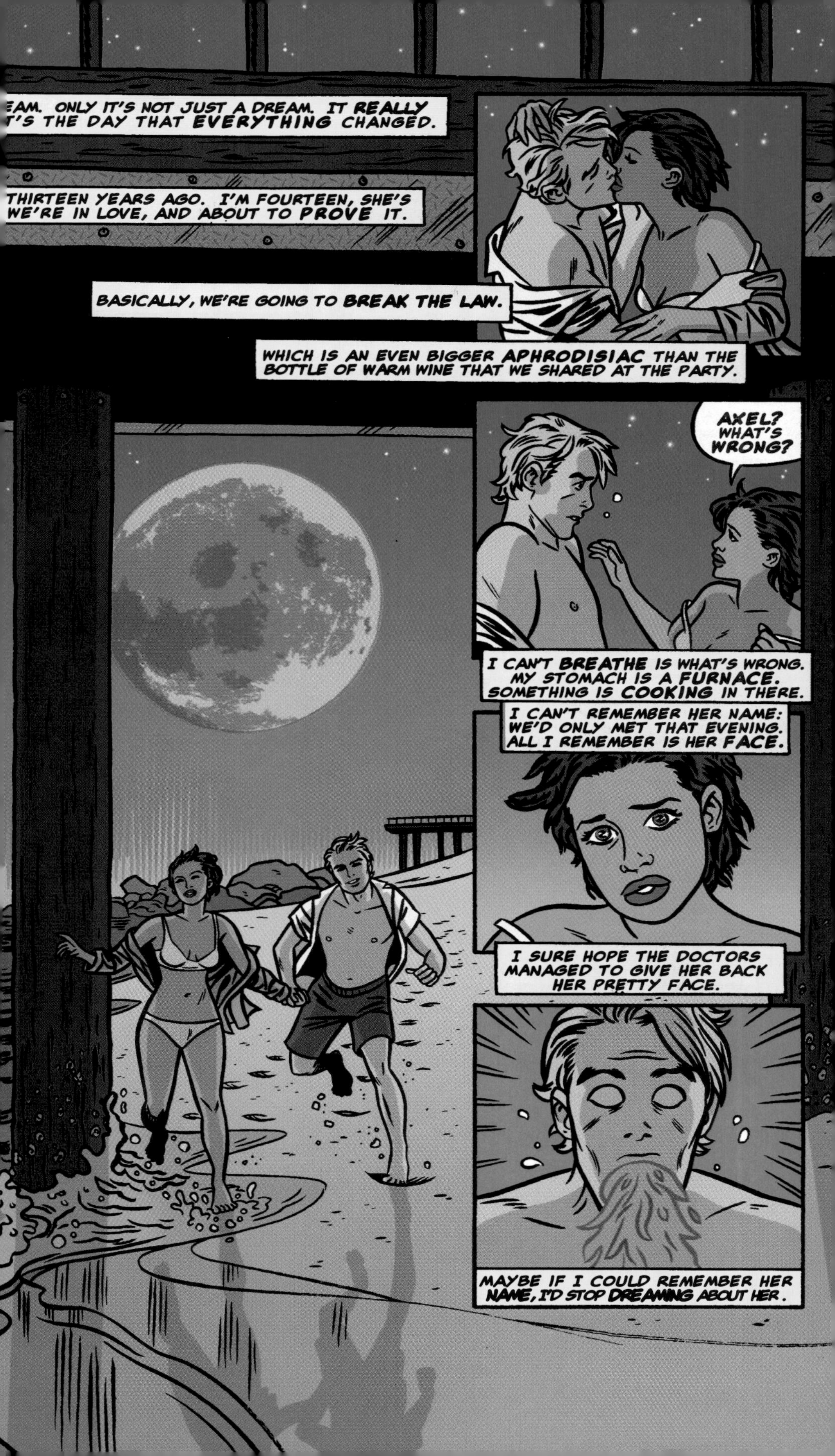
EAM. ONLY IT'S NOT JUST A DREAM. IT REALLY
T'S THE DAY THAT EVERYTHING CHANGED.
THIRTEEN YEARS AGO. I'M FOURTEEN, SHE'S
WE'RE IN LOVE, AND ABOUT TO PROVE IT.
BASICALLY, WE'RE GOING TO BREAK THE LAW.
WHICH IS AN EVEN BIGGER APHRODISIAC THAN THE BOTTLE OF WARM WINE THAT WE SHARED AT THE PARTY.
AXEL? WHAT'S WRONG?
I CAN'T BREATHE IS WHAT'S WRONG. MY STOMACH IS A FURNACE. SOMETHING IS COOKING IN THERE.
I CAN'T REMEMBER HER NAME: WE'D ONLY MET THAT EVENING. ALL I REMEMBER IS HER FACE.
I SURE HOPE THE DOCTORS MANAGED TO GIVE HER BACK HER PRETTY FACE.
MAYBE IF I COULD REMEMBER HER NAME, I'D STOP DREAMING ABOUT HER.

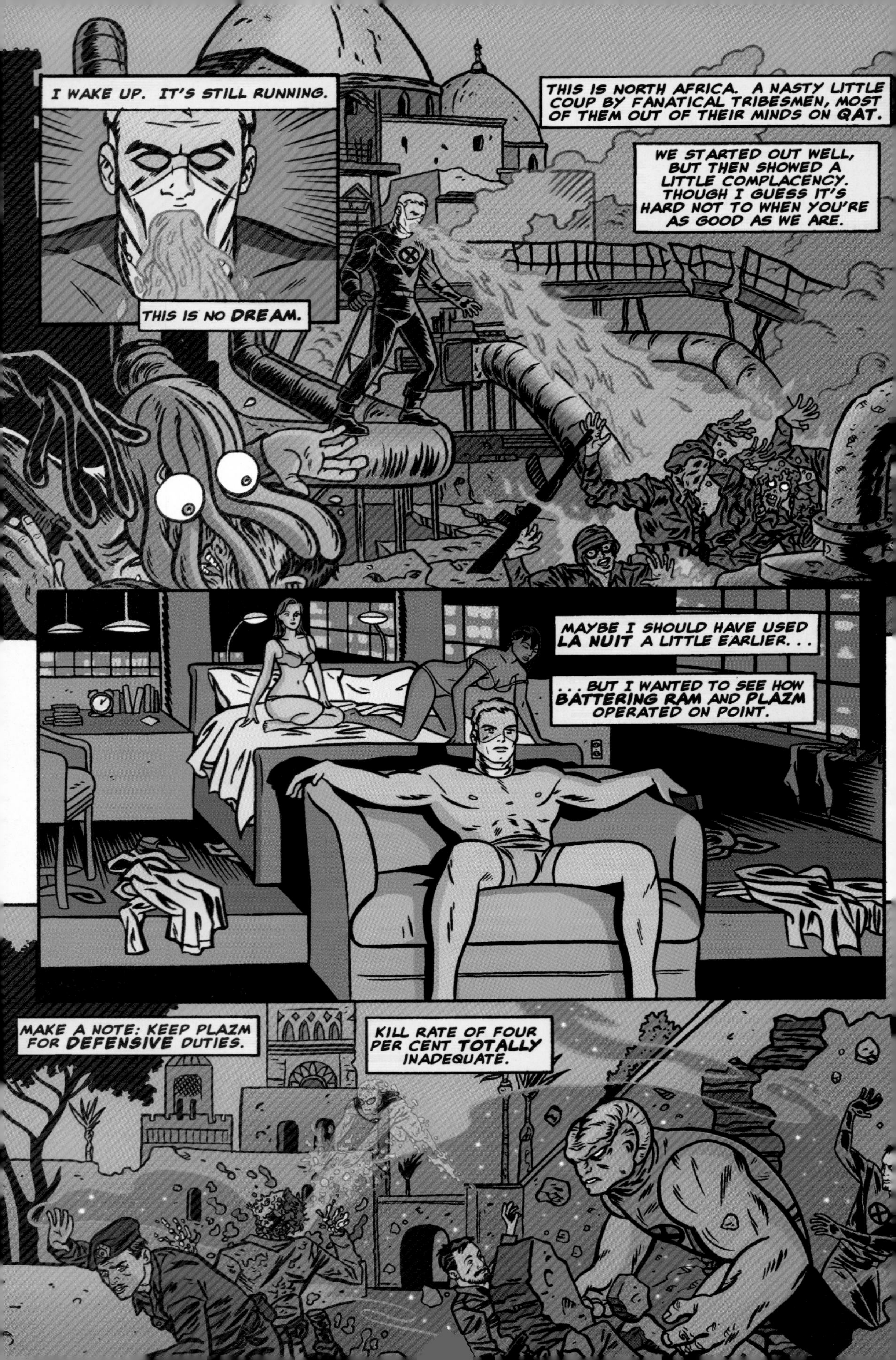
I WAKE UP. IT'S STILL RUNNING.
THIS IS NO DREAM.
THIS IS NORTH AFRICA. A NASTY LITTLE COUP BY FANATICAL TRIBESMEN, MOST OF THEM OUT OF THEIR MINDS ON QAT.
WE STARTED OUT WELL, BUT THEN SHOWED A LITTLE COMPLACENCY. THOUGH I GUESS IT'S HARD NOT TO WHEN YOU'RE AS GOOD AS WE ARE.
MAYBE I SHOULD HAVE USED LA NUIT A LITTLE EARLIER. . .
. . . BUT I WANTED TO SEE HOW BATTERING RAM AND PLAZM OPERATED ON POINT.
MAKE A NOTE: KEEP PLAZM FOR DEFENSIVE DUTIES.
KILL RATE OF FOUR PER CENT TOTALLY INADEQUATE.

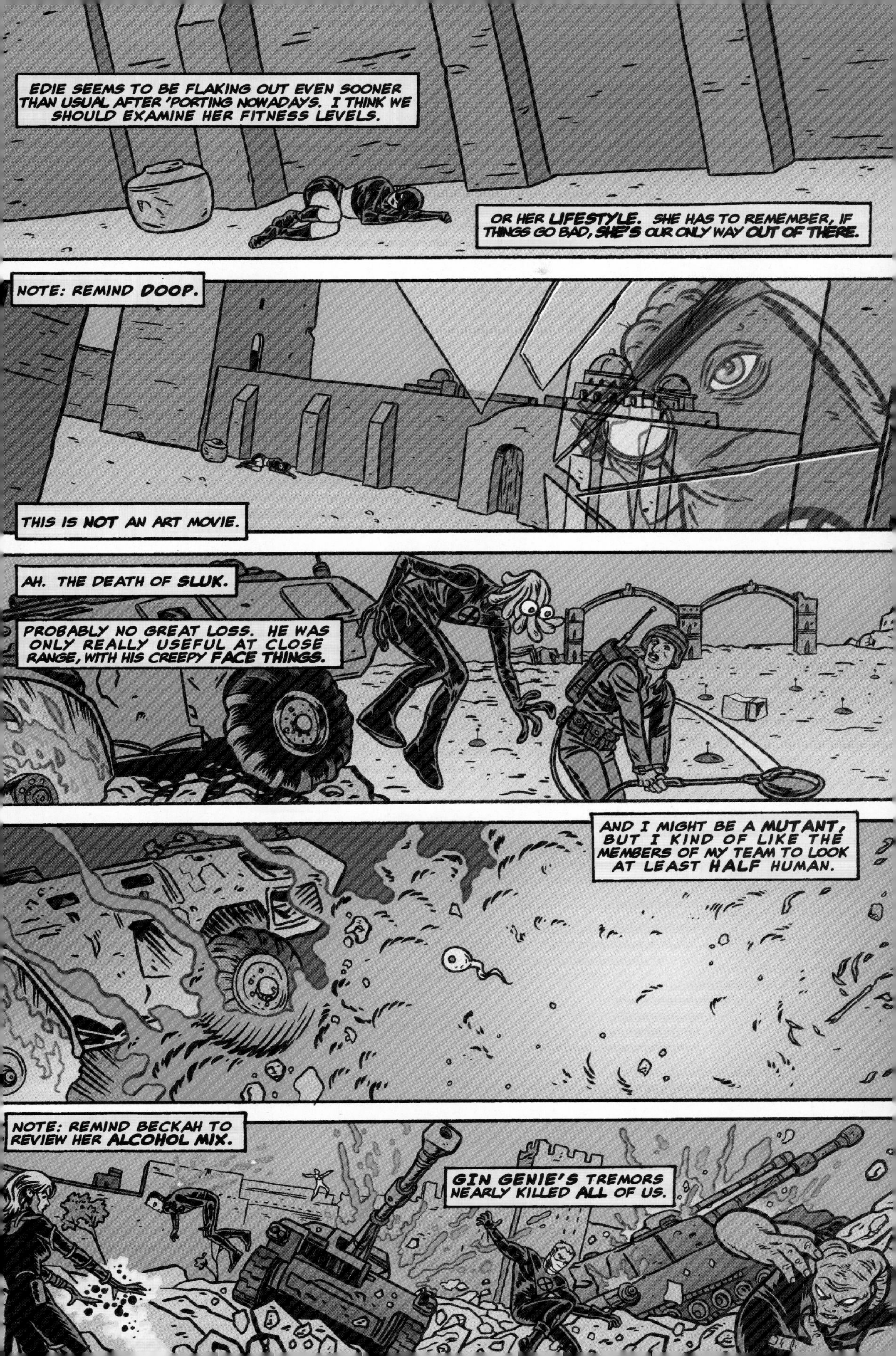
EDIE SEEMS TO BE FLAKING OUT EVEN SOONER THAN USUAL AFTER 'PORTING NOWADAYS. I THINK WE SHOULD EXAMINE HER FITNESS LEVELS.
OR HER LIFESTYLE. SHE HAS TO REMEMBER, IF THINGS GO BAD, SHE'S OUR ONLY WAY OUT OF THERE.
NOTE: REMIND DOOP.
THIS IS NOT AN ART MOVIE.
AH. THE DEATH OF SLUK.
PROBABLY NO GREAT LOSS. HE WAS ONLY REALLY USEFUL AT CLOSE RANGE, WITH HIS CREEPY FACE THINGS.
AND I MIGHT BE A MUTANT, BUT I KIND OF LIKE THE MEMBERS OF MY TEAM TO LOOK AT LEAST HALF HUMAN.
NOTE: REMIND BECKAH TO REVIEW HER ALCOHOL MIX.
GIN GENIE'S TREMORS NEARLY KILLED ALL OF US.

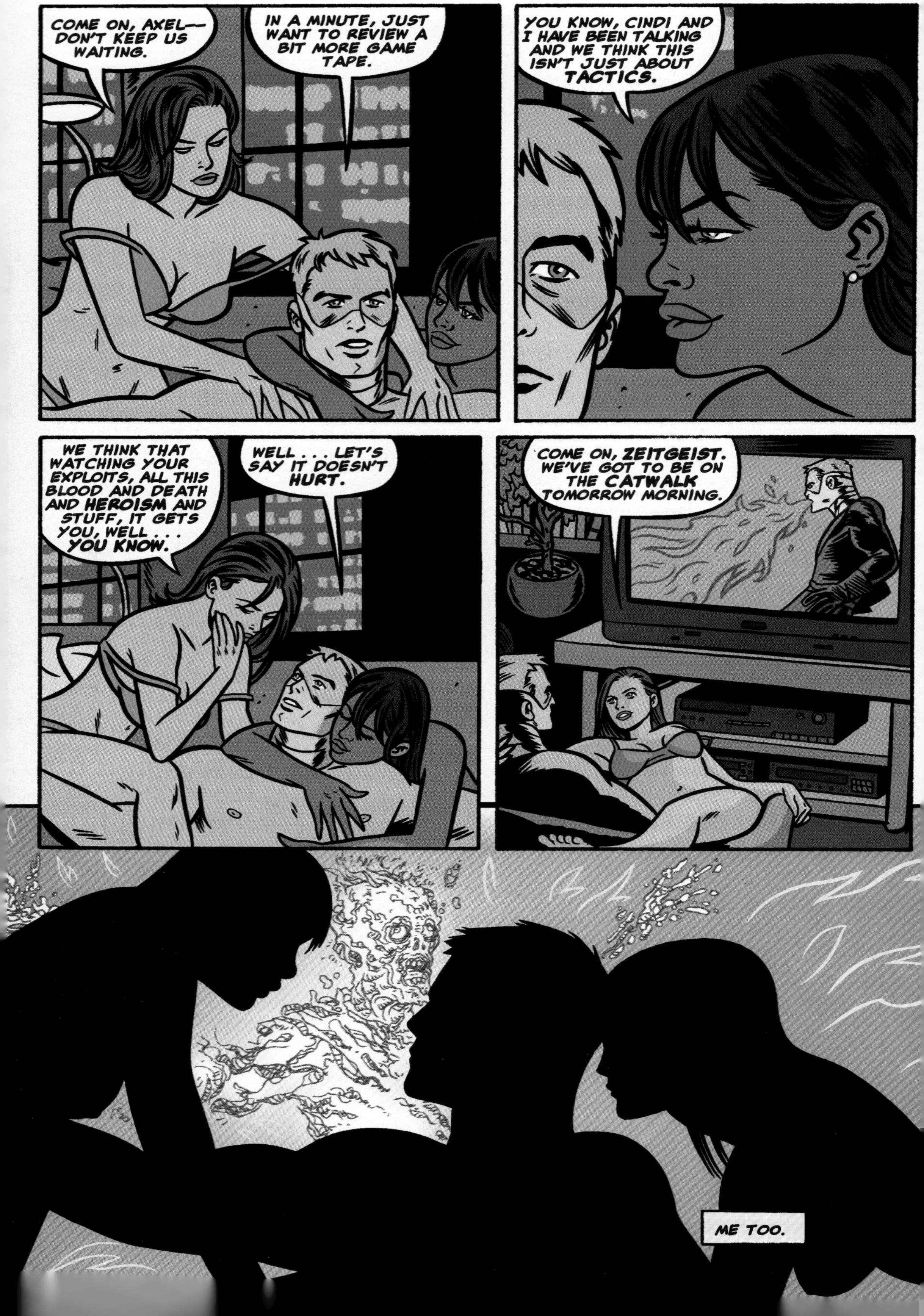
COME ON, AXEL— DON'T KEEP US WAITING.
IN A MINUTE, JUST WANT TO REVIEW A BIT MORE GAME TAPE.
YOU KNOW, CINDI AND I HAVE BEEN TALKING AND WE THINK THIS ISN'T JUST ABOUT TACTICS.
WE THINK THAT WATCHING YOUR EXPLOITS, ALL THIS BLOOD AND DEATH AND HEROISM AND STUFF, IT GETS YOU, WELL . . . YOU KNOW.
WELL . . . LET'S SAY IT DOESN'T HURT.
COME ON, ZEITGEIST. WE'VE GOT TO BE ON THE CATWALK TOMORROW MORNING.
ME TOO.

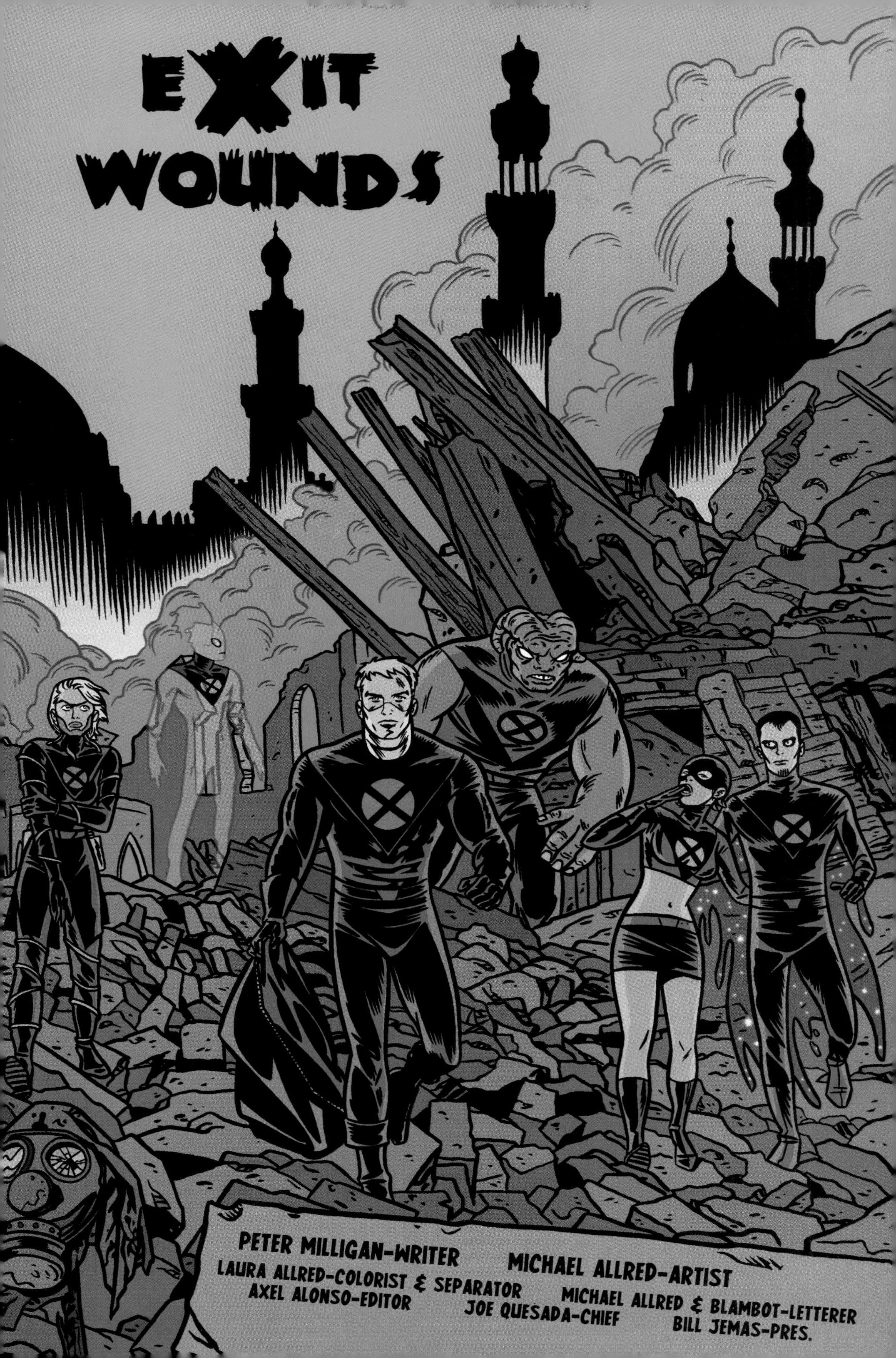
EXIT
WOUNDS
PETER MILLIGAN-WRITER
MICHAEL ALLRED-ARTIST
LAURA ALLRED-COLORIST & SEPARATOR
AXEL ALONSO-EDITOR
MICHAEL ALLRED & BLAMBOT-LETTERER
JOE QUESADA-CHIEF
BILL JEMAS-PRES.

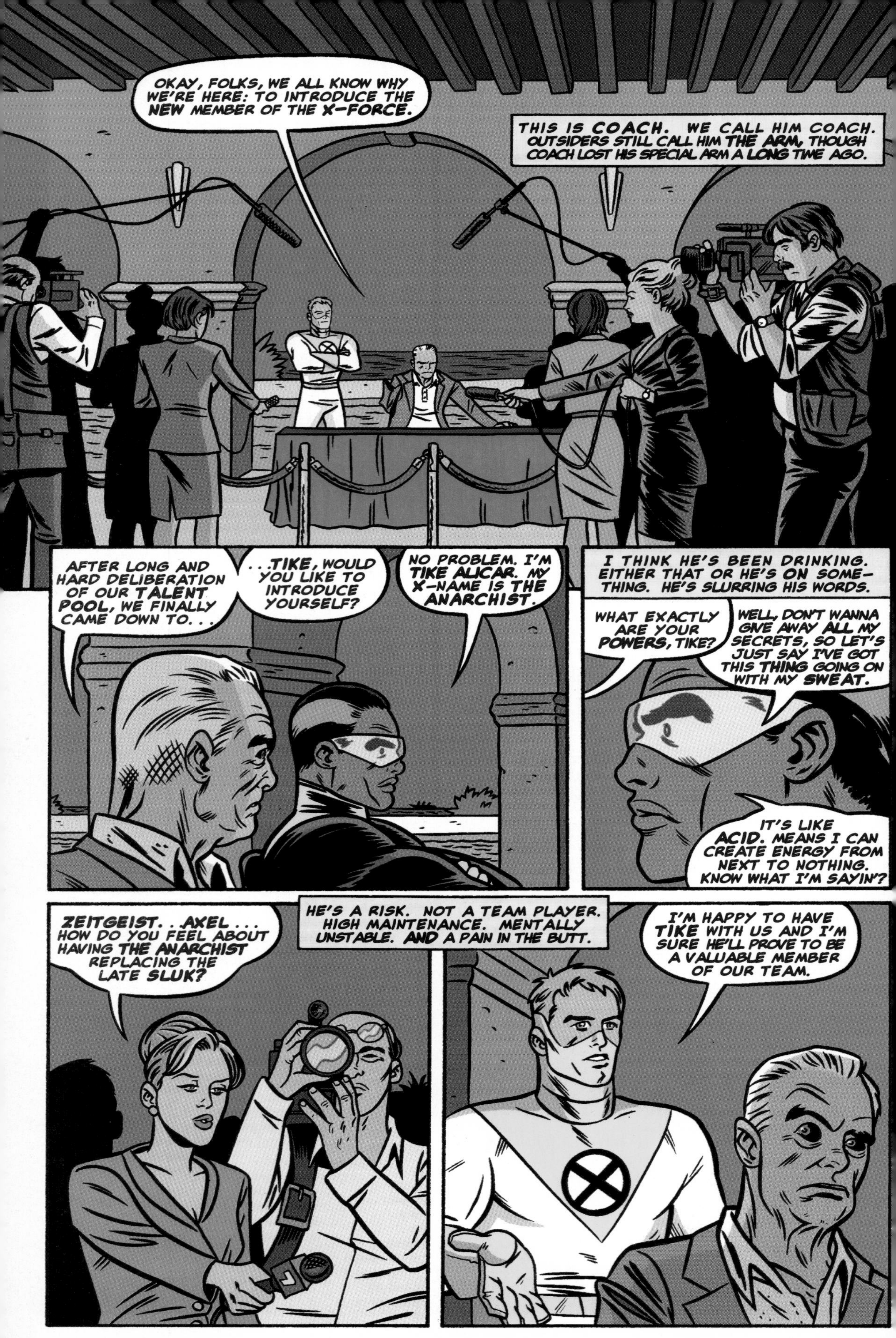
OKAY, FOLKS, WE ALL KNOW WHY WE'RE HERE: TO INTRODUCE THE NEW MEMBER OF THE X-FORCE.
THIS IS COACH. WE CALL HIM COACH. OUTSIDERS STILL CALL HIM THE ARM, THOUGH COACH LOST HIS SPECIAL ARM A LONG TIME AGO.
AFTER LONG AND HARD DELIBERATION OF OUR TALENT POOL, WE FINALLY CAME DOWN TO...
...TIKE, WOULD YOU LIKE TO INTRODUCE YOURSELF?
NO PROBLEM. I'M TIKE ALICAR. MY X-NAME IS THE ANARCHIST.
I THINK HE'S BEEN DRINKING. EITHER THAT OR HE'S ON SOMETHING. HE'S SLURRING HIS WORDS.
WHAT EXACTLY ARE YOUR POWERS, TIKE?
WELL, DON'T WANNA GIVE AWAY ALL MY SECRETS, SO LET'S JUST SAY I'VE GOT THIS THING GOING ON WITH MY SWEAT.
IT'S LIKE ACID. MEANS I CAN CREATE ENERGY FROM NEXT TO NOTHING. KNOW WHAT I'M SAYIN'?
ZEITGEIST...AXEL... HOW DO YOU FEEL ABOUT HAVING THE ANARCHIST REPLACING THE LATE SLUK?
HE'S A RISK. NOT A TEAM PLAYER. HIGH MAINTENANCE. MENTALLY UNSTABLE. AND A PAIN IN THE BUTT.
I'M HAPPY TO HAVE TIKE WITH US AND I'M SURE HE'LL PROVE TO BE A VALUABLE MEMBER OF OUR TEAM.

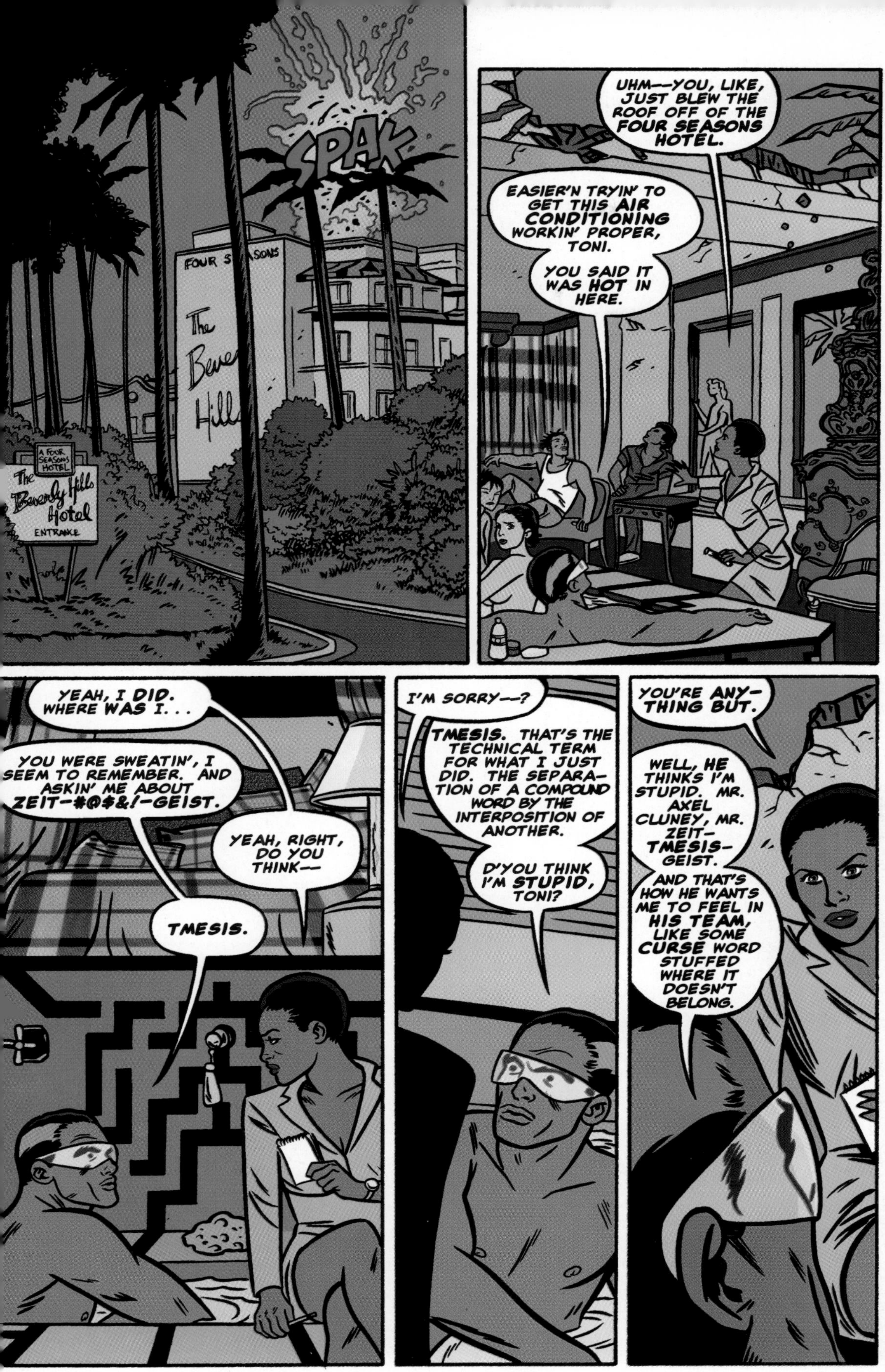
SPAK
A FOUR SEASONS HOTEL
The Beverly Hills Hotel
ENTRANCE
UHM--YOU, LIKE, JUST BLEW THE ROOF OFF OF THE FOUR SEASONS HOTEL.
EASIER'N TRYIN' TO GET THIS AIR CONDITIONING WORKIN' PROPER, TONI.
YOU SAID IT WAS HOT IN HERE.
YEAH, I DID. WHERE WAS I . . .
YOU WERE SWEATIN', I SEEM TO REMEMBER. AND ASKIN' ME ABOUT ZEIT-#@$&!-GEIST.
YEAH, RIGHT, DO YOU THINK--
TMESIS.
I'M SORRY--?
TMESIS. THAT'S THE TECHNICAL TERM FOR WHAT I JUST DID. THE SEPARATION OF A COMPOUND WORD BY THE INTERPOSITION OF ANOTHER.
D'YOU THINK I'M STUPID, TONI?
YOU'RE ANYTHING BUT.
WELL, HE THINKS I'M STUPID. MR. AXEL CLUNEY, MR. ZEIT-TMESIS-GEIST.
AND THAT'S HOW HE WANTS ME TO FEEL IN HIS TEAM, LIKE SOME CURSE WORD STUFFED WHERE IT DOESN'T BELONG.

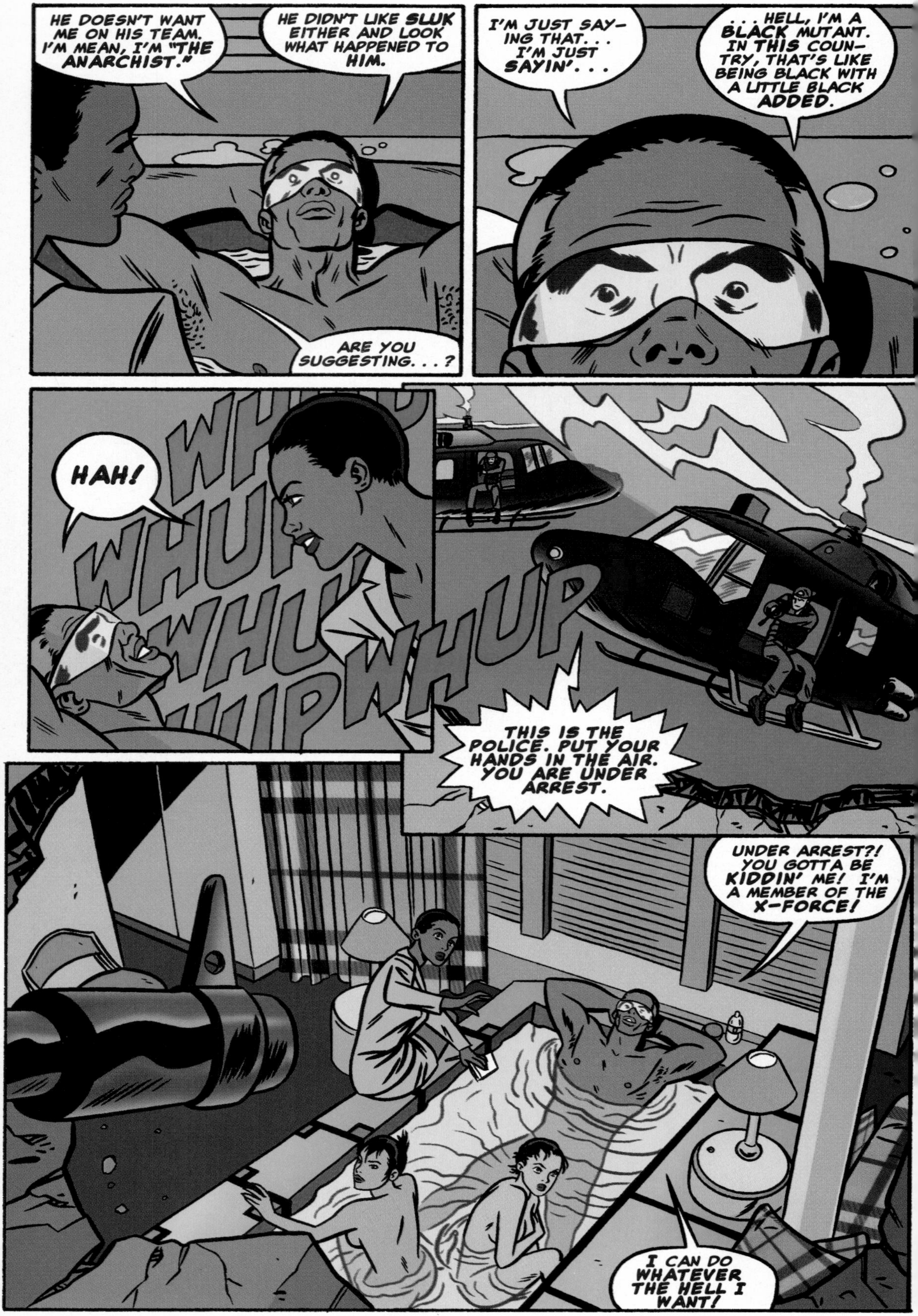

HE DOESN'T WANT ME ON HIS TEAM. I'M MEAN, I'M "THE ANARCHIST."
HE DIDN'T LIKE SLUK EITHER AND LOOK WHAT HAPPENED TO HIM.
ARE YOU SUGGESTING. . . ?
I'M JUST SAY-ING THAT. . . I'M JUST SAYIN'. . .
. . . HELL, I'M A BLACK MUTANT. IN THIS COUN-TRY, THAT'S LIKE BEING BLACK WITH A LITTLE BLACK ADDED.
HAH!
WHUP WHUP WHUP WHUP
THIS IS THE POLICE. PUT YOUR HANDS IN THE AIR. YOU ARE UNDER ARREST.
UNDER ARREST?! YOU GOTTA BE KIDDIN' ME! I'M A MEMBER OF THE X-FORCE!
I CAN DO WHATEVER THE HELL I WANT!

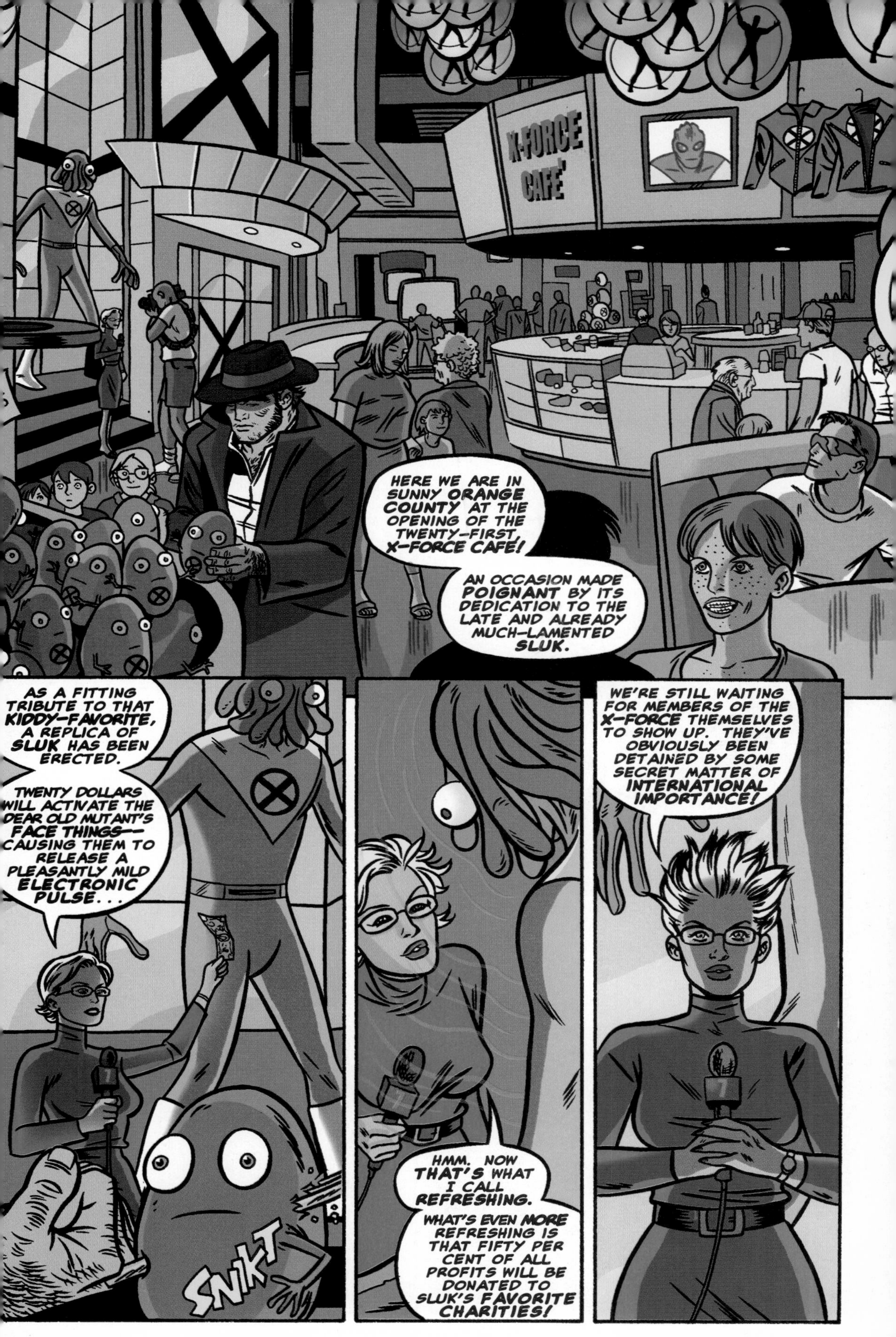
X-FORCE CAFÉ
HERE WE ARE IN SUNNY ORANGE COUNTY AT THE OPENING OF THE TWENTY-FIRST, X-FORCE CAFÉ!
AN OCCASION MADE POIGNANT BY ITS DEDICATION TO THE LATE AND ALREADY MUCH-LAMENTED SLUK.
AS A FITTING TRIBUTE TO THAT KIDDY-FAVORITE, A REPLICA OF SLUK HAS BEEN ERECTED.
TWENTY DOLLARS WILL ACTIVATE THE DEAR OLD MUTANT'S FACE THINGS--CAUSING THEM TO RELEASE A PLEASANTLY MILD ELECTRONIC PULSE...
SNIKT
HMM. NOW THAT'S WHAT I CALL REFRESHING.
WHAT'S EVEN MORE REFRESHING IS THAT FIFTY PER CENT OF ALL PROFITS WILL BE DONATED TO SLUK'S FAVORITE CHARITIES!
WE'RE STILL WAITING FOR MEMBERS OF THE X-FORCE THEMSELVES TO SHOW UP. THEY'VE OBVIOUSLY BEEN DETAINED BY SOME SECRET MATTER OF INTERNATIONAL IMPORTANCE!

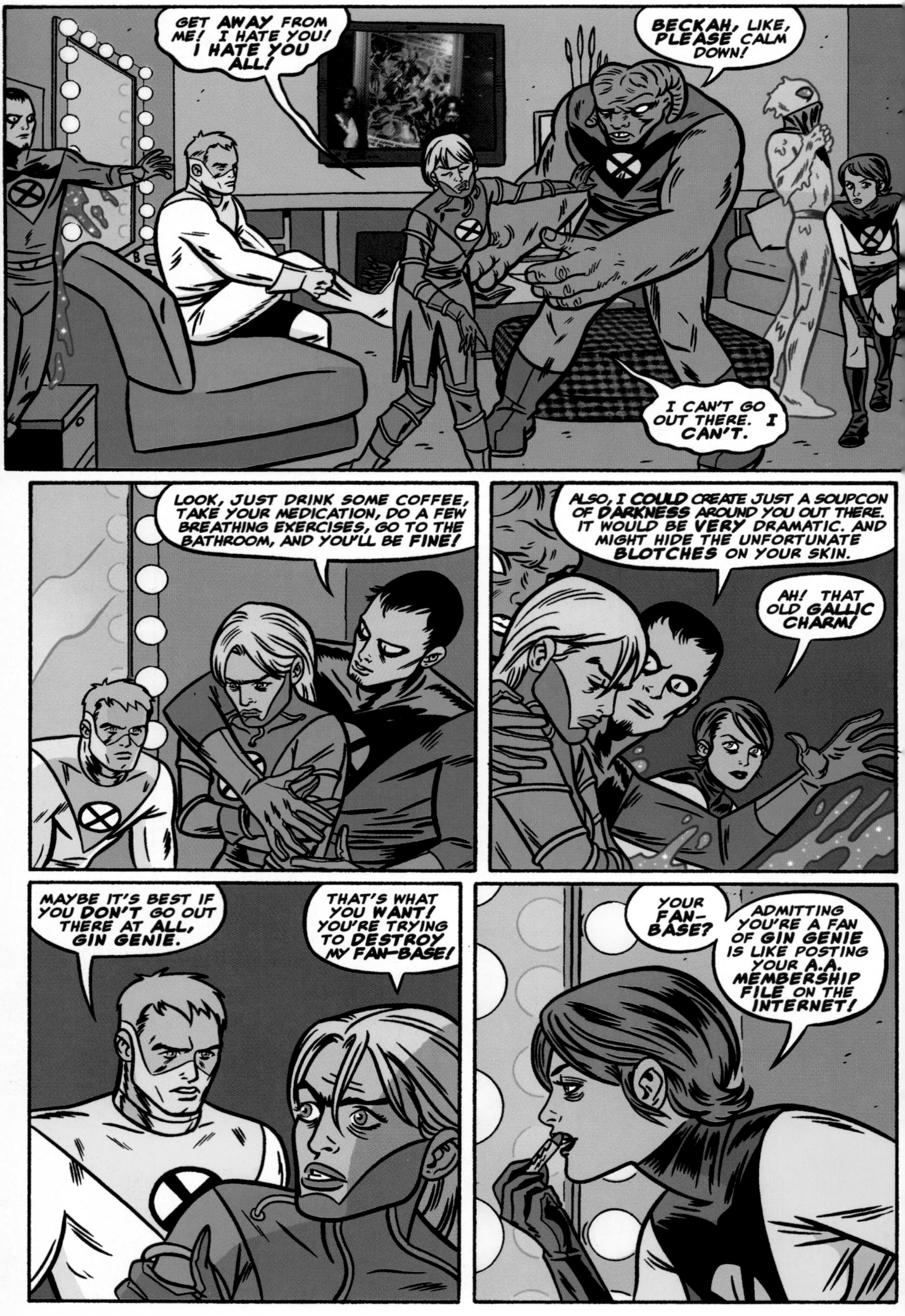
GET AWAY FROM ME! I HATE YOU! I HATE YOU ALL!
BECKAH, LIKE, PLEASE CALM DOWN!
I CAN'T GO OUT THERE. I CAN'T.
LOOK, JUST DRINK SOME COFFEE, TAKE YOUR MEDICATION, DO A FEW BREATHING EXERCISES, GO TO THE BATHROOM, AND YOU'LL BE FINE!
ALSO, I COULD CREATE JUST A SOUPCON OF DARKNESS AROUND YOU OUT THERE. IT WOULD BE VERY DRAMATIC. AND MIGHT HIDE THE UNFORTUNATE BLOTCHES ON YOUR SKIN.
AH! THAT OLD GALLIC CHARM!
MAYBE IT'S BEST IF YOU DON'T GO OUT THERE AT ALL, GIN GENIE.
THAT'S WHAT YOU WANT! YOU'RE TRYING TO DESTROY MY FAN-BASE!
YOUR FAN-BASE?
ADMITTING YOU'RE A FAN OF GIN GENIE IS LIKE POSTING YOUR A.A. MEMBERSHIP FILE ON THE INTERNET!

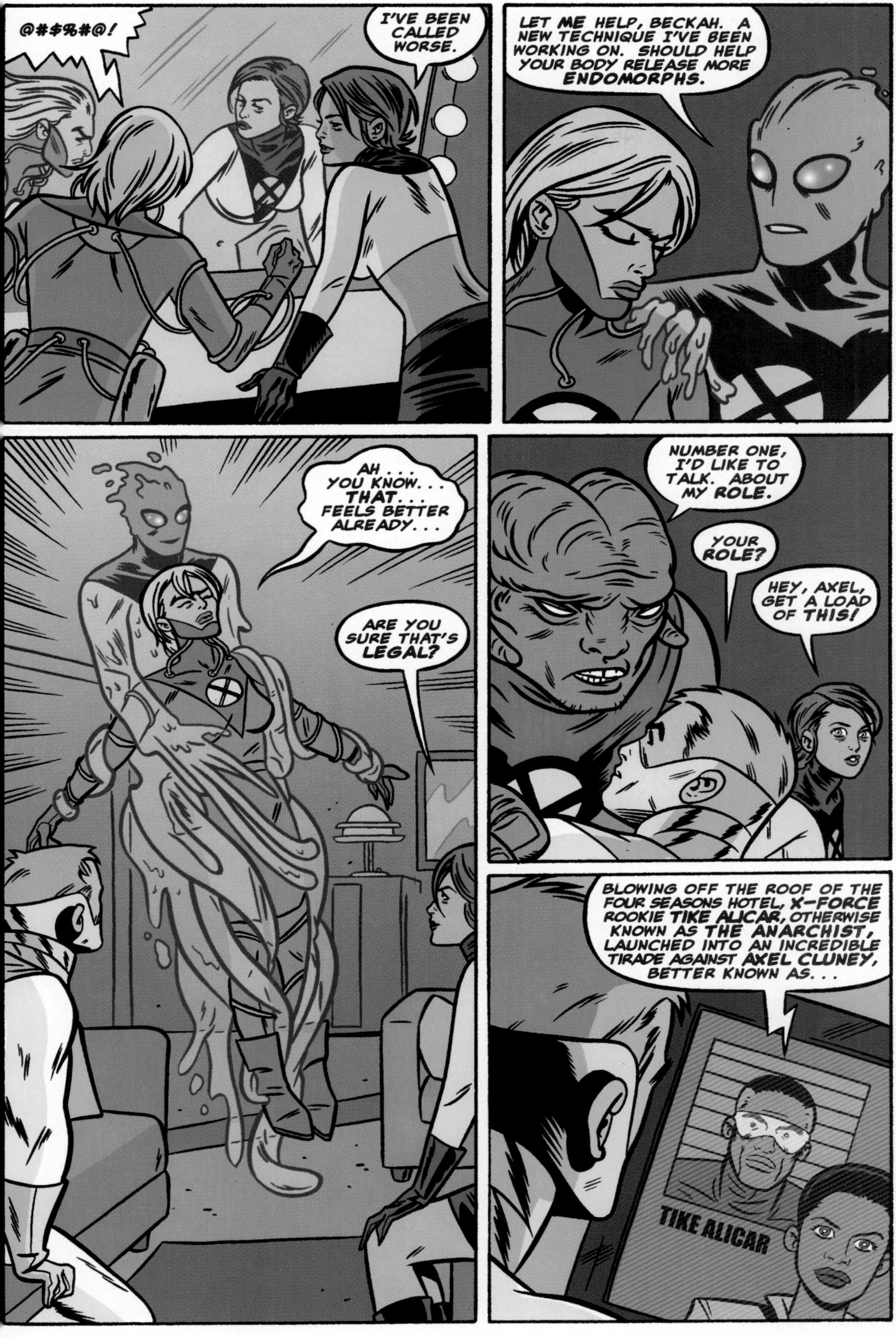
@#$%#@!
I'VE BEEN CALLED WORSE.
LET ME HELP, BECKAH. A NEW TECHNIQUE I'VE BEEN WORKING ON. SHOULD HELP YOUR BODY RELEASE MORE ENDOMORPHS.
AH . . . YOU KNOW. . . THAT. . . FEELS BETTER ALREADY. . .
ARE YOU SURE THAT'S LEGAL?
NUMBER ONE, I'D LIKE TO TALK. ABOUT MY ROLE.
YOUR ROLE?
HEY, AXEL, GET A LOAD OF THIS!
BLOWING OFF THE ROOF OF THE FOUR SEASONS HOTEL, X-FORCE ROOKIE TIKE ALICAR, OTHERWISE KNOWN AS THE ANARCHIST, LAUNCHED INTO AN INCREDIBLE TIRADE AGAINST AXEL CLUNEY, BETTER KNOWN AS. . .
TIKE ALICAR

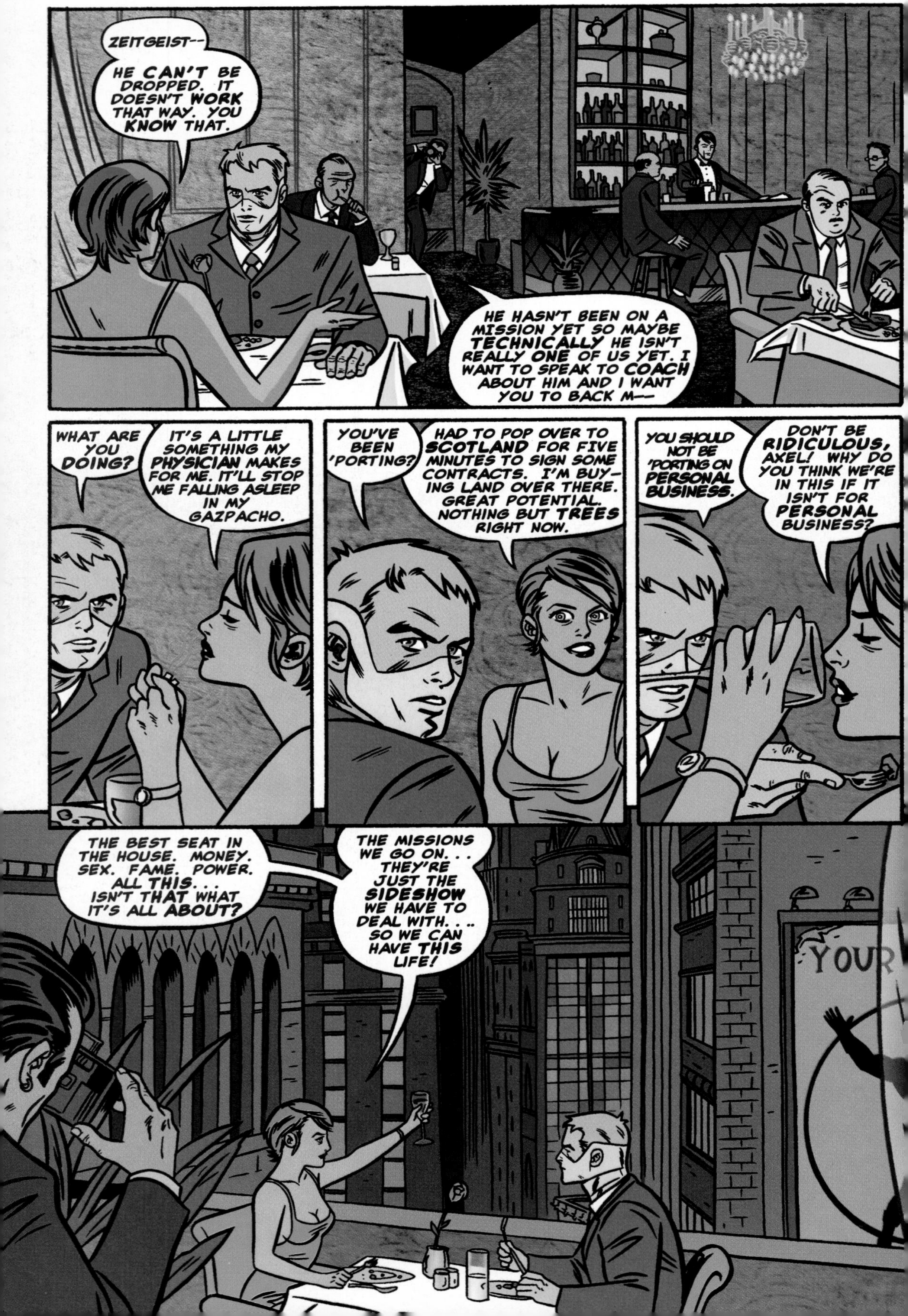
ZEITGEIST--
HE CAN'T BE DROPPED. IT DOESN'T WORK THAT WAY. YOU KNOW THAT.
HE HASN'T BEEN ON A MISSION YET SO MAYBE TECHNICALLY HE ISN'T REALLY ONE OF US YET. I WANT TO SPEAK TO COACH ABOUT HIM AND I WANT YOU TO BACK M--
WHAT ARE YOU DOING?
IT'S A LITTLE SOMETHING MY PHYSICIAN MAKES FOR ME. IT'LL STOP ME FALLING ASLEEP IN MY GAZPACHO.
YOU'VE BEEN 'PORTING?
HAD TO POP OVER TO SCOTLAND FOR FIVE MINUTES TO SIGN SOME CONTRACTS. I'M BUYING LAND OVER THERE. GREAT POTENTIAL. NOTHING BUT TREES RIGHT NOW.
YOU SHOULD NOT BE 'PORTING ON PERSONAL BUSINESS.
DON'T BE RIDICULOUS, AXEL! WHY DO YOU THINK WE'RE IN THIS IF IT ISN'T FOR PERSONAL BUSINESS?
THE BEST SEAT IN THE HOUSE. MONEY. SEX. FAME. POWER. ALL THIS. . . ISN'T THAT WHAT IT'S ALL ABOUT?
THE MISSIONS WE GO ON. . . THEY'RE JUST THE SIDESHOW WE HAVE TO DEAL WITH. . .. SO WE CAN HAVE THIS LIFE!
YOUR

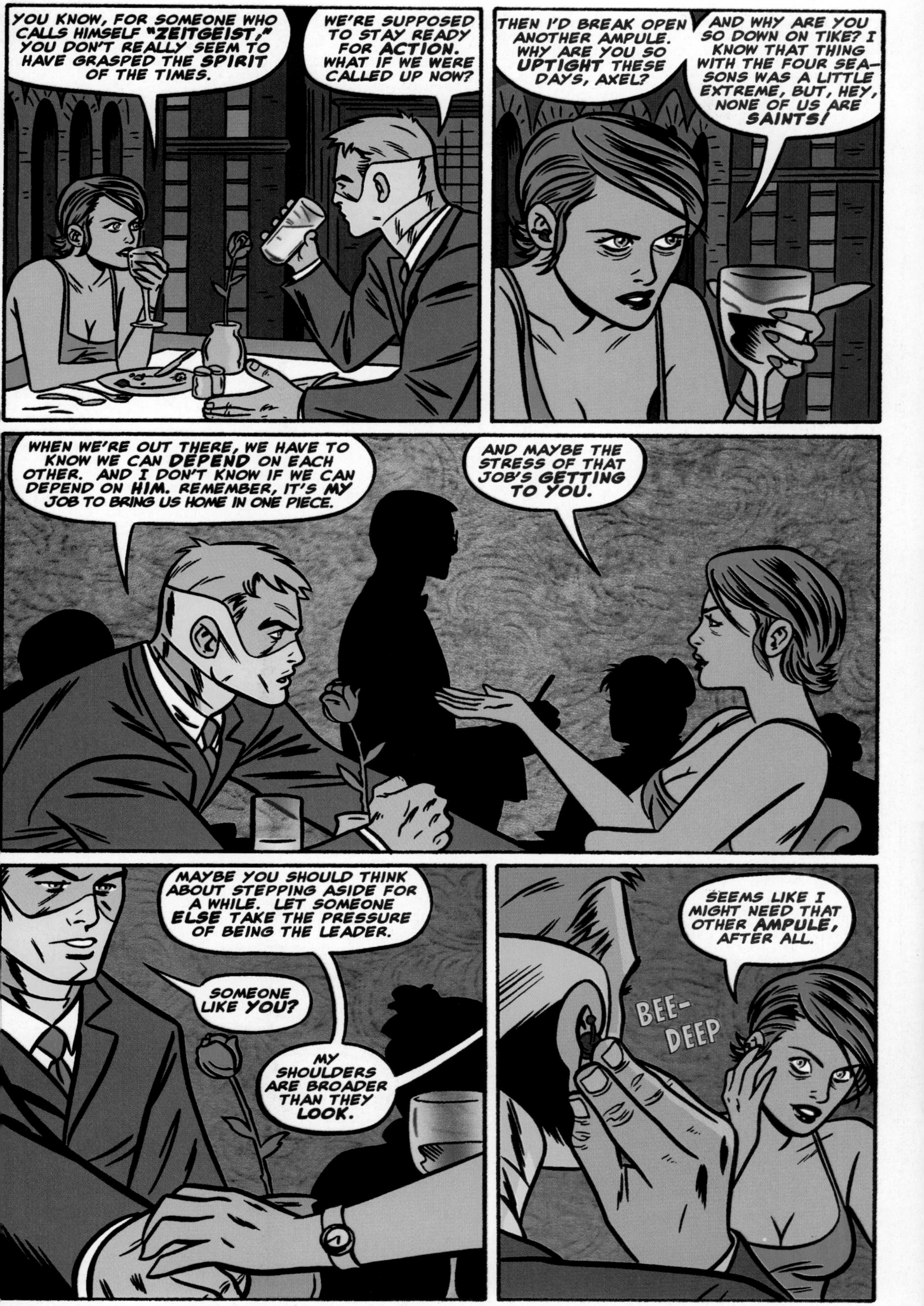
YOU KNOW, FOR SOMEONE WHO CALLS HIMSELF "ZEITGEIST," YOU DON'T REALLY SEEM TO HAVE GRASPED THE SPIRIT OF THE TIMES.
WE'RE SUPPOSED TO STAY READY FOR ACTION. WHAT IF WE WERE CALLED UP NOW?
THEN I'D BREAK OPEN ANOTHER AMPULE. WHY ARE YOU SO UPTIGHT THESE DAYS, AXEL?
AND WHY ARE YOU SO DOWN ON TIKE? I KNOW THAT THING WITH THE FOUR SEASONS WAS A LITTLE EXTREME, BUT, HEY, NONE OF US ARE SAINTS!
WHEN WE'RE OUT THERE, WE HAVE TO KNOW WE CAN DEPEND ON EACH OTHER. AND I DON'T KNOW IF WE CAN DEPEND ON HIM. REMEMBER, IT'S MY JOB TO BRING US HOME IN ONE PIECE.
AND MAYBE THE STRESS OF THAT JOB'S GETTING TO YOU.
MAYBE YOU SHOULD THINK ABOUT STEPPING ASIDE FOR A WHILE. LET SOMEONE ELSE TAKE THE PRESSURE OF BEING THE LEADER.
SOMEONE LIKE YOU?
MY SHOULDERS ARE BROADER THAN THEY LOOK.
BEE-DEEP
SEEMS LIKE I MIGHT NEED THAT OTHER AMPULE, AFTER ALL.

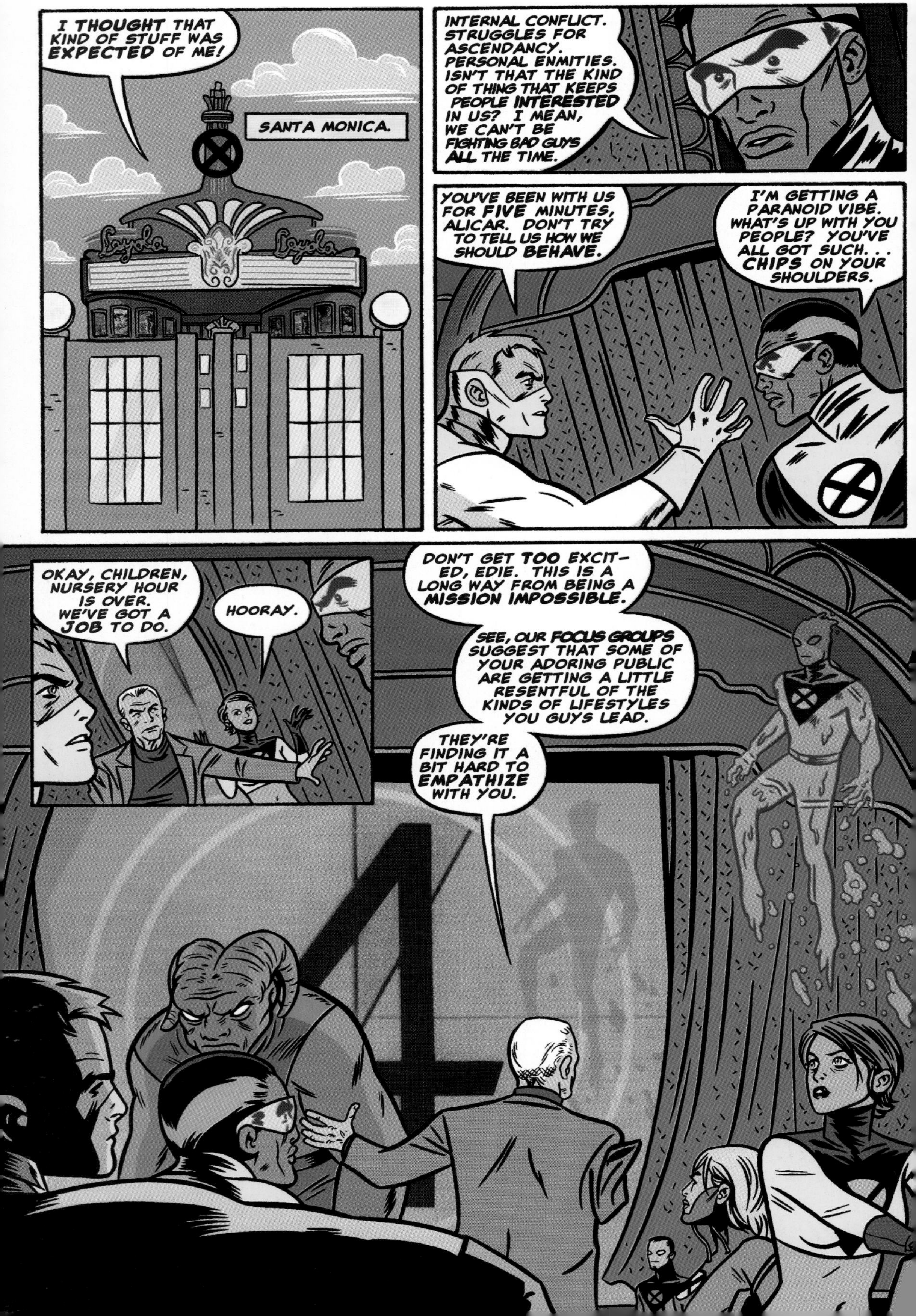
I THOUGHT THAT KIND OF STUFF WAS EXPECTED OF ME!
SANTA MONICA.
INTERNAL CONFLICT. STRUGGLES FOR ASCENDANCY. PERSONAL ENMITIES. ISN'T THAT THE KIND OF THING THAT KEEPS PEOPLE INTERESTED IN US? I MEAN, WE CAN'T BE FIGHTING BAD GUYS ALL THE TIME.
YOU'VE BEEN WITH US FOR FIVE MINUTES, ALICAR. DON'T TRY TO TELL US HOW WE SHOULD BEHAVE.
I'M GETTING A PARANOID VIBE. WHAT'S UP WITH YOU PEOPLE? YOU'VE ALL GOT SUCH. . . CHIPS ON YOUR SHOULDERS.
OKAY, CHILDREN, NURSERY HOUR IS OVER. WE'VE GOT A JOB TO DO.
HOORAY.
DON'T GET TOO EXCIT-ED, EDIE. THIS IS A LONG WAY FROM BEING A MISSION IMPOSSIBLE.
SEE, OUR FOCUS GROUPS SUGGEST THAT SOME OF YOUR ADORING PUBLIC ARE GETTING A LITTLE RESENTFUL OF THE KINDS OF LIFESTYLES YOU GUYS LEAD.
THEY'RE FINDING IT A BIT HARD TO EMPATHIZE WITH YOU.

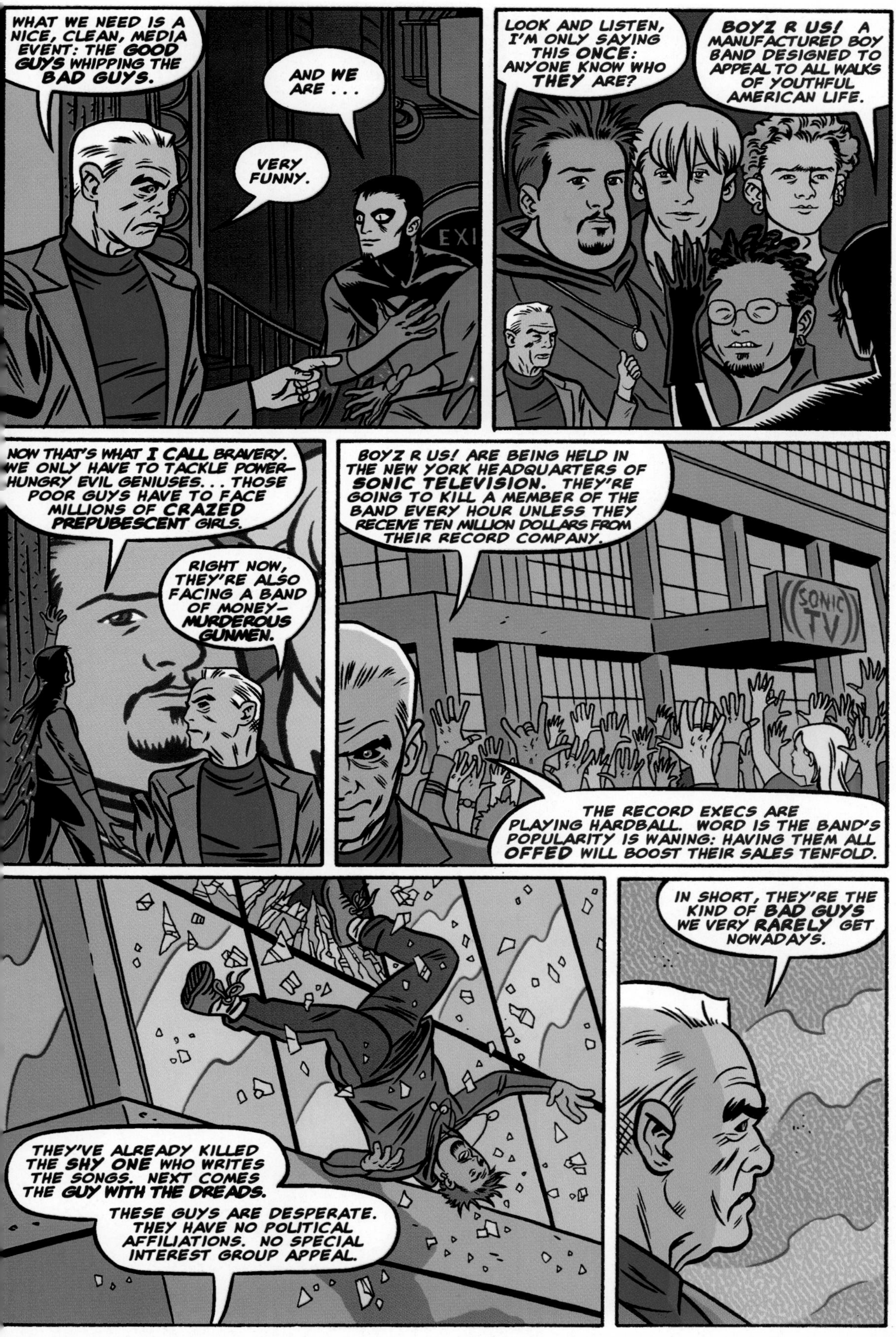
WHAT WE NEED IS A NICE, CLEAN, MEDIA EVENT: THE GOOD GUYS WHIPPING THE BAD GUYS.
AND WE ARE . . .
VERY FUNNY.
LOOK AND LISTEN, I'M ONLY SAYING THIS ONCE: ANYONE KNOW WHO THEY ARE?
BOYZ R US! A MANUFACTURED BOY BAND DESIGNED TO APPEAL TO ALL WALKS OF YOUTHFUL AMERICAN LIFE.
NOW THAT'S WHAT I CALL BRAVERY. WE ONLY HAVE TO TACKLE POWER-HUNGRY EVIL GENIUSES. . . THOSE POOR GUYS HAVE TO FACE MILLIONS OF CRAZED PREPUBESCENT GIRLS.
RIGHT NOW, THEY'RE ALSO FACING A BAND OF MONEY-MURDEROUS GUNMEN.
BOYZ R US! ARE BEING HELD IN THE NEW YORK HEADQUARTERS OF SONIC TELEVISION. THEY'RE GOING TO KILL A MEMBER OF THE BAND EVERY HOUR UNLESS THEY RECEIVE TEN MILLION DOLLARS FROM THEIR RECORD COMPANY.
SONIC TV
THE RECORD EXECS ARE PLAYING HARDBALL. WORD IS THE BAND'S POPULARITY IS WANING: HAVING THEM ALL OFFED WILL BOOST THEIR SALES TENFOLD.
THEY'VE ALREADY KILLED THE SHY ONE WHO WRITES THE SONGS. NEXT COMES THE GUY WITH THE DREADS.
THESE GUYS ARE DESPERATE. THEY HAVE NO POLITICAL AFFILIATIONS. NO SPECIAL INTEREST GROUP APPEAL.
IN SHORT, THEY'RE THE KIND OF BAD GUYS WE VERY RARELY GET NOWADAYS.

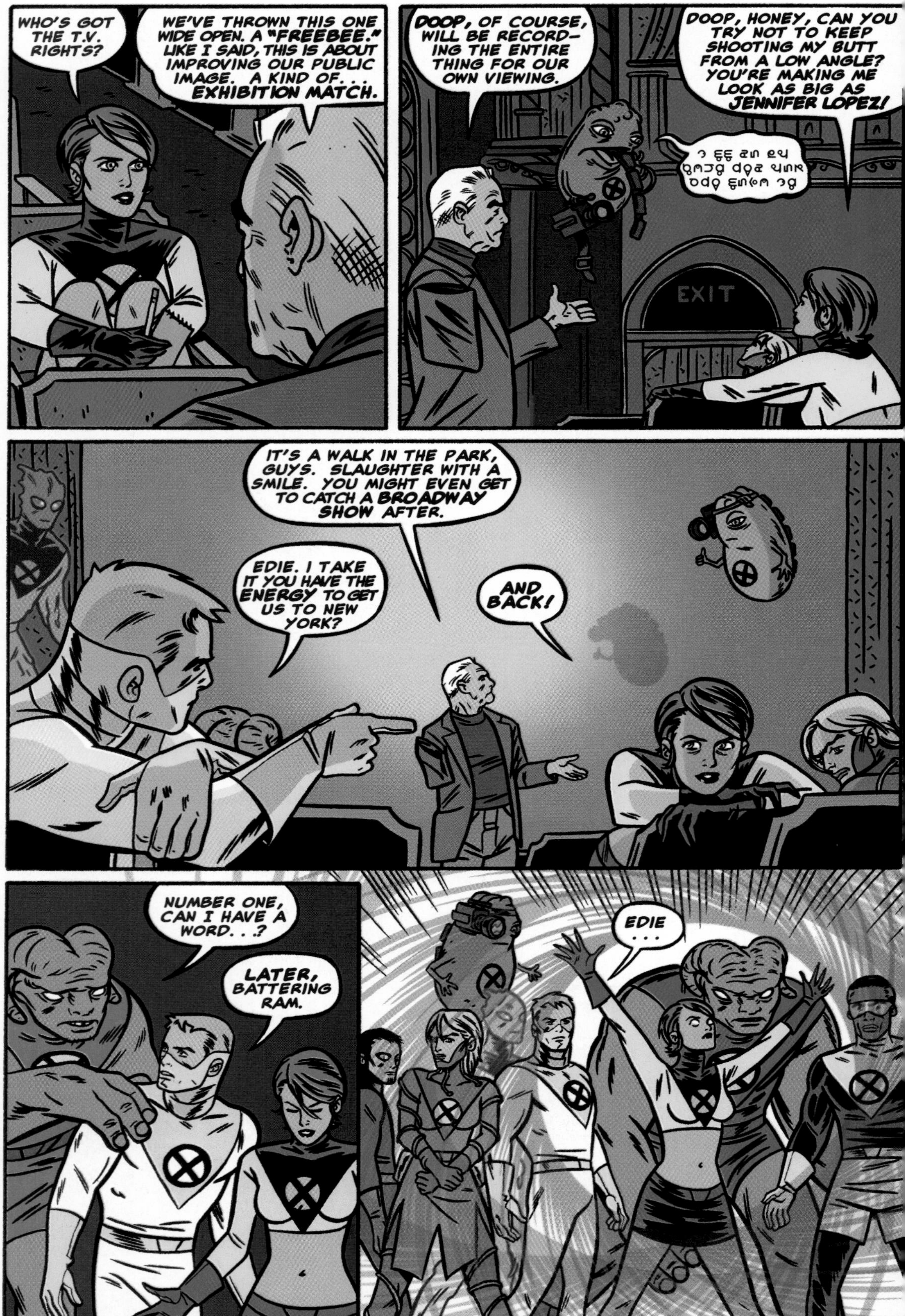
WHO'S GOT THE T.V. RIGHTS?
WE'VE THROWN THIS ONE WIDE OPEN. A "FREEBEE." LIKE I SAID, THIS IS ABOUT IMPROVING OUR PUBLIC IMAGE. A KIND OF. . . EXHIBITION MATCH.
DOOP, OF COURSE, WILL BE RECORDING THE ENTIRE THING FOR OUR OWN VIEWING.
DOOP, HONEY, CAN YOU TRY NOT TO KEEP SHOOTING MY BUTT FROM A LOW ANGLE? YOU'RE MAKING ME LOOK AS BIG AS JENNIFER LOPEZ!
EXIT
IT'S A WALK IN THE PARK, GUYS. SLAUGHTER WITH A SMILE. YOU MIGHT EVEN GET TO CATCH A BROADWAY SHOW AFTER.
EDIE. I TAKE IT YOU HAVE THE ENERGY TO GET US TO NEW YORK?
AND BACK!
NUMBER ONE, CAN I HAVE A WORD. . .?
LATER, BATTERING RAM.
EDIE . . .

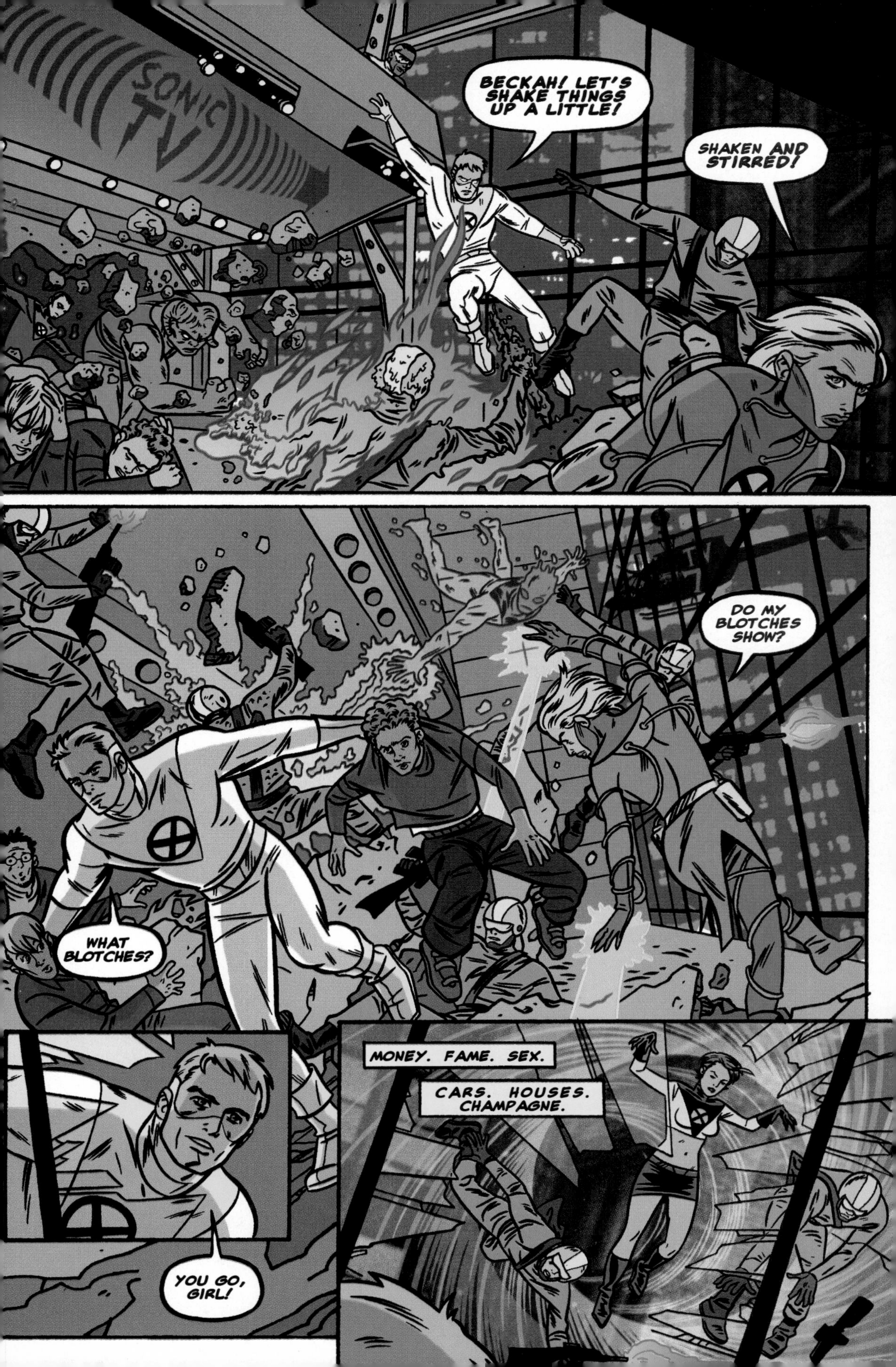
SONIC TV
BECKAH! LET'S SHAKE THINGS UP A LITTLE!
SHAKEN AND STIRRED!
DO MY BLOTCHES SHOW?
WHAT BLOTCHES?
YOU GO, GIRL!
MONEY. FAME. SEX.
CARS. HOUSES. CHAMPAGNE.

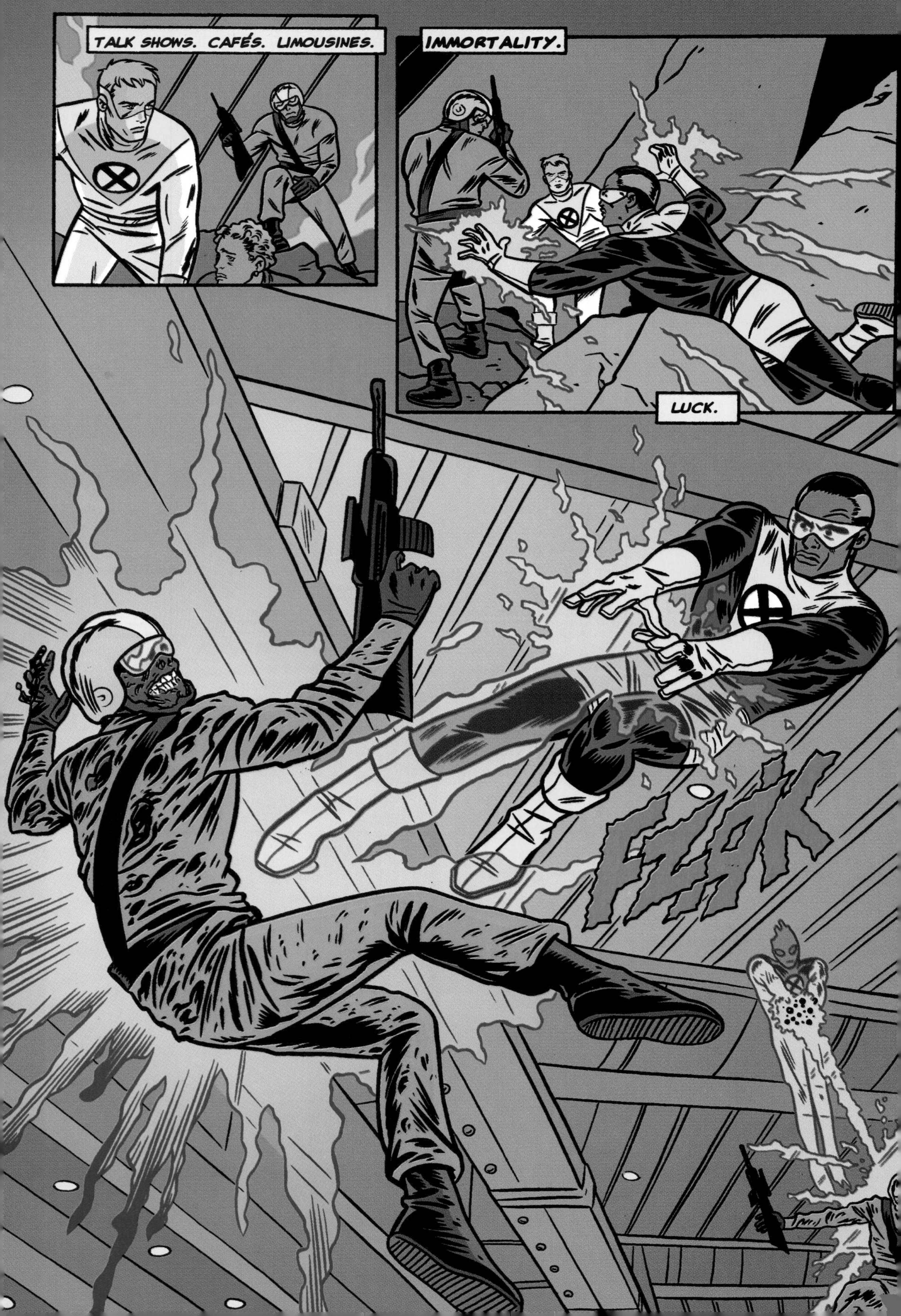
TALK SHOWS. CAFÉS. LIMOUSINES.
IMMORTALITY.
LUCK.
FZAK

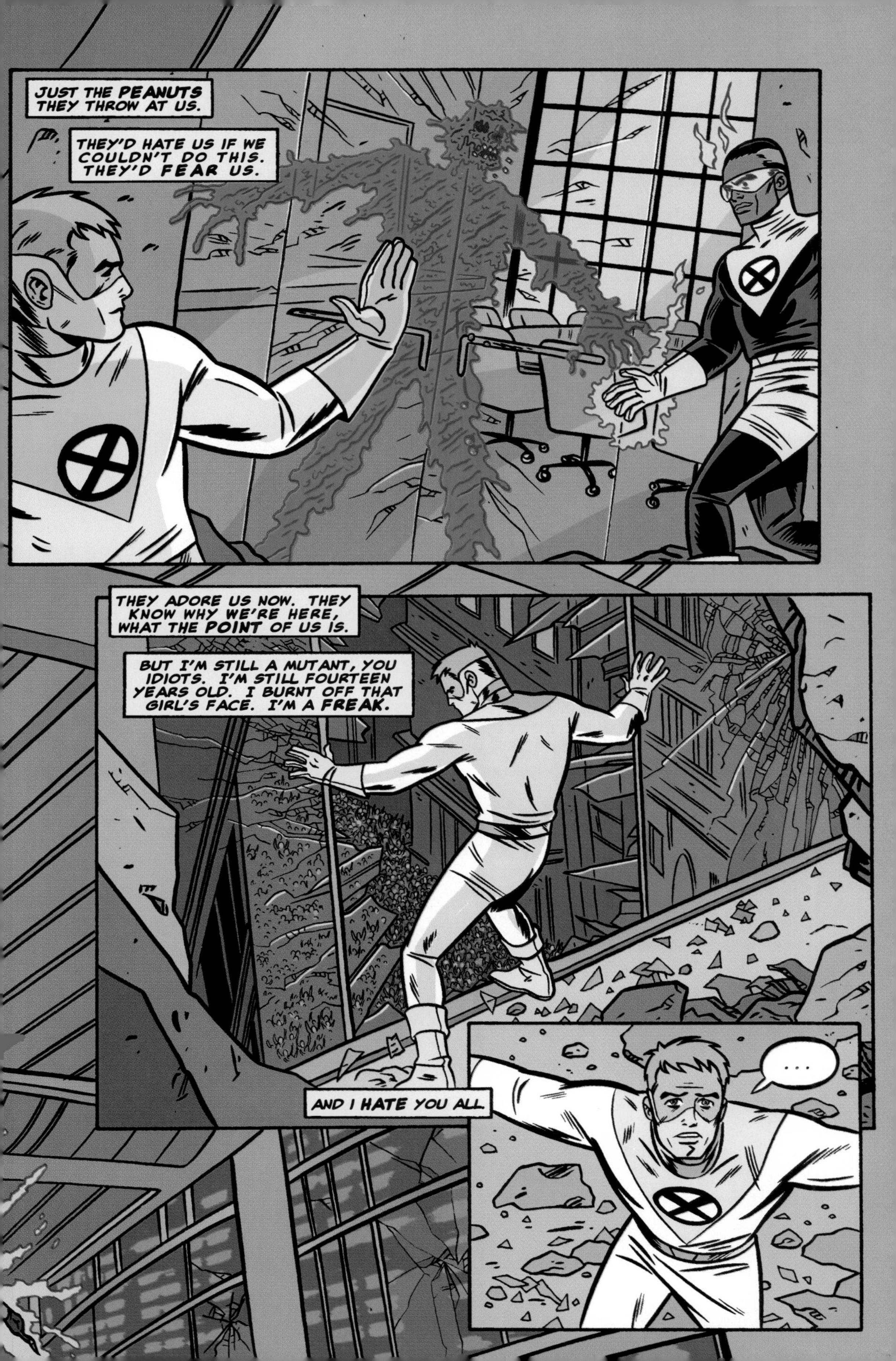
JUST THE PEANUTS THEY THROW AT US.
THEY'D HATE US IF WE COULDN'T DO THIS. THEY'D FEAR US.
THEY ADORE US NOW. THEY KNOW WHY WE'RE HERE, WHAT THE POINT OF US IS.
BUT I'M STILL A MUTANT, YOU IDIOTS. I'M STILL FOURTEEN YEARS OLD. I BURNT OFF THAT GIRL'S FACE. I'M A FREAK.
AND I HATE YOU ALL.
...

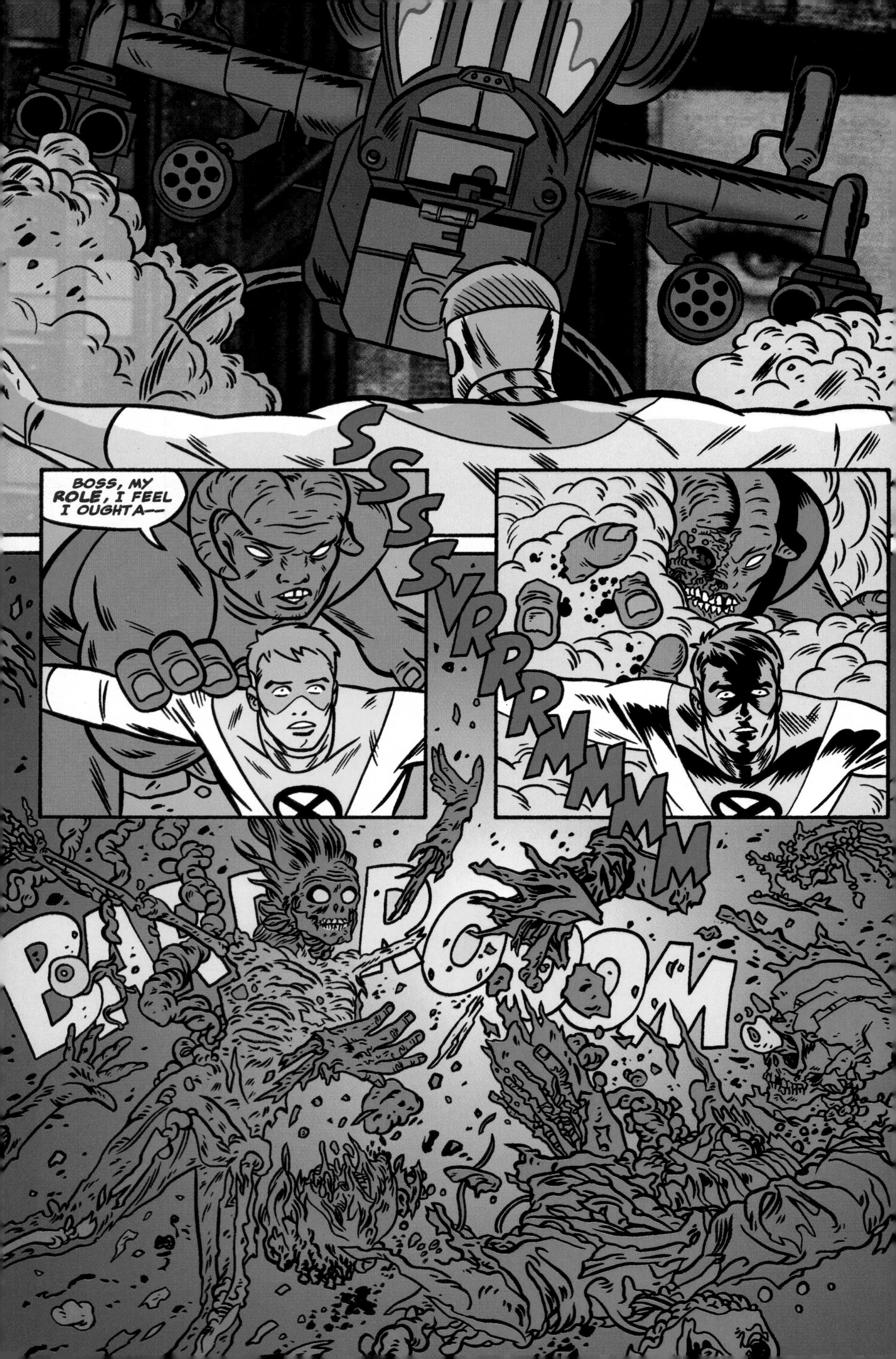
SSSSSVRRRRMMMMMM
BOSS, MY ROLE, I FEEL I OUGHTA--

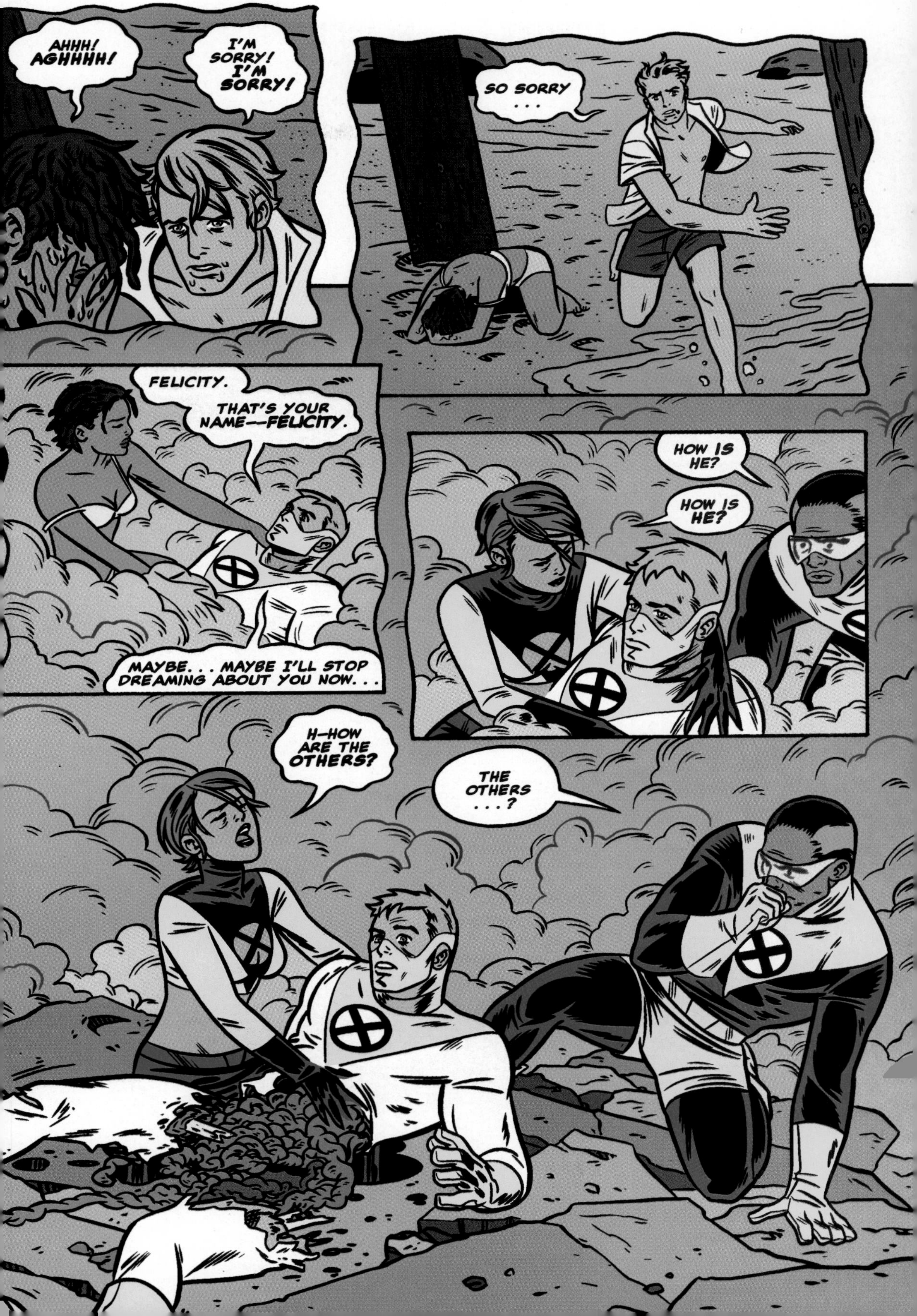
AHHH! AGHHHH!
I'M SORRY! I'M SORRY!
SO SORRY . . .
FELICITY.
THAT'S YOUR NAME--FELICITY.
MAYBE... MAYBE I'LL STOP DREAMING ABOUT YOU NOW...
HOW IS HE?
HOW IS HE?
H-HOW ARE THE OTHERS?
THE OTHERS . . .?

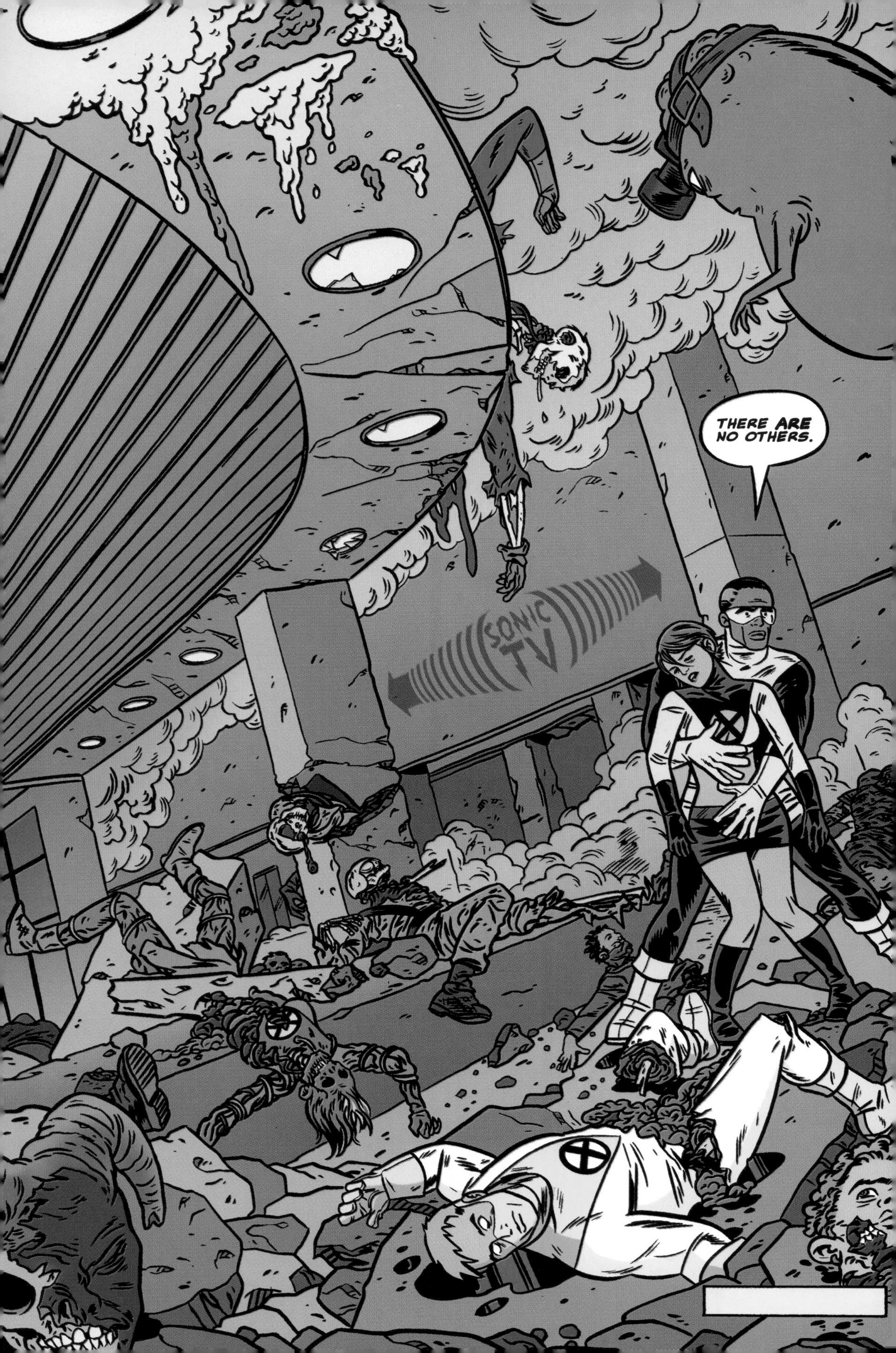
THERE ARE NO OTHERS.
SONIC TV

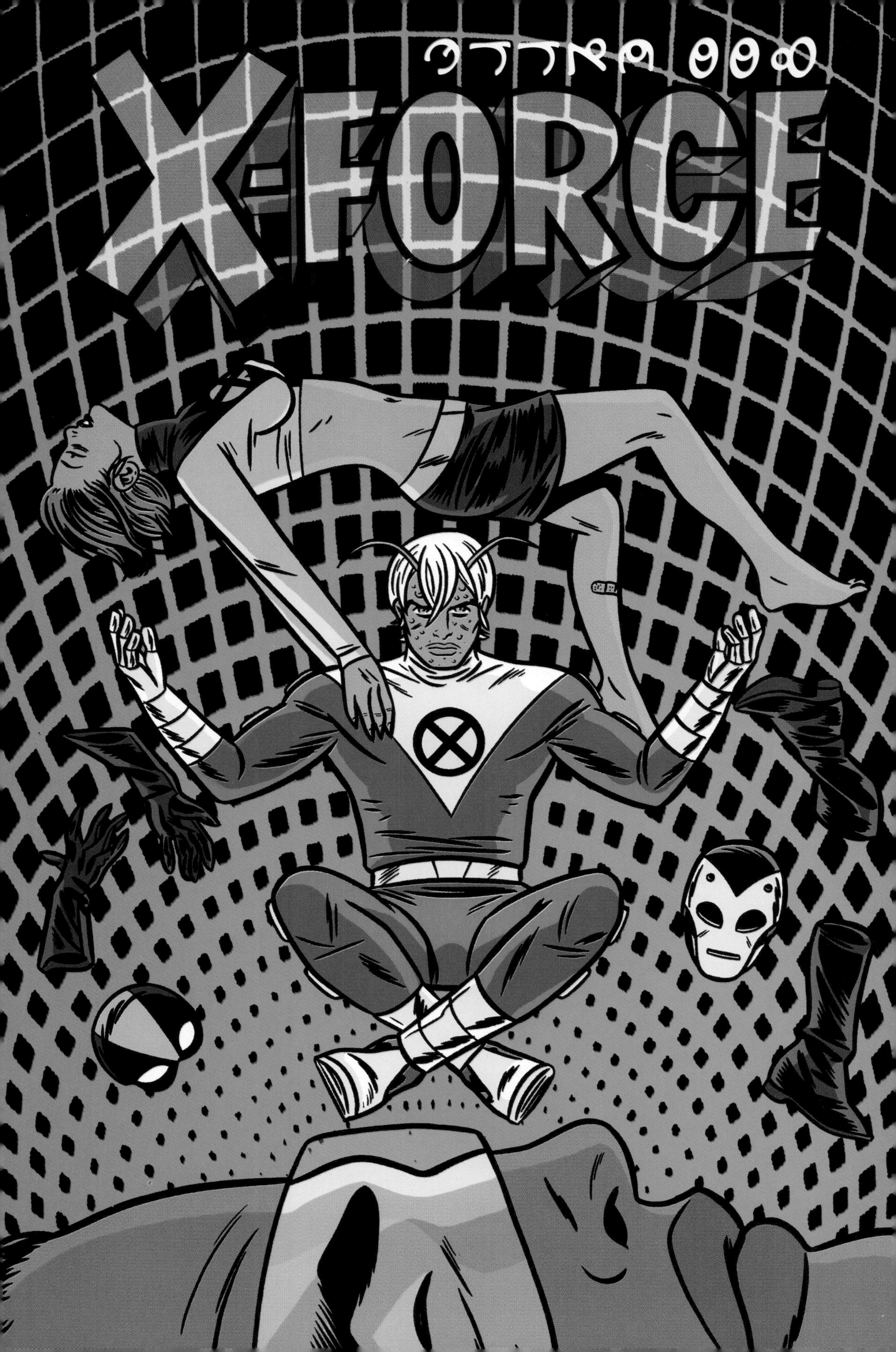
X-FORCE

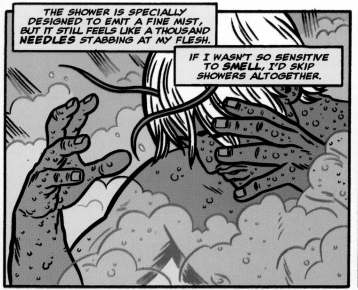

THE SHOWER IS SPECIALLY DESIGNED TO EMIT A FINE MIST, BUT IT STILL FEELS LIKE A THOUSAND NEEDLES STABBING AT MY FLESH.

IF I WASN'T SO SENSITIVE TO SMELL, I'D SKIP SHOWERS ALTOGETHER.

TO THINK I USED TO LIVE WITHOUT THE SUIT.

MY MIND HAS GROWN LAZY. THE DISCIPLINES I USED TO PROTECT MYSELF WITH, RUSTY.

EXAMPLE:

A BLUEBOTTLE FLY'S SLUGGISH TRAJECTORY ACROSS THE ROOM CREATES AN UNPLEASANT VIBRATION DOWN MY SPINE.

BUT NOW I'M SLIPPING IT ON, MY ARMOR AND SHIELD, MUMBLING MY DAILY PRAYER OF THANKS TO PROFESSOR X.

PEPARING FOR MY OTHER DAILY RITUAL.

MY FRIEND, WHO'LL BE WAITING FOR ME AT THE END OF THE DAY.

WHRRRRR

EVER FAITHFUL. THE ONLY THING THAT MAKES SENSE OF THE HOURS AND THE PAIN.

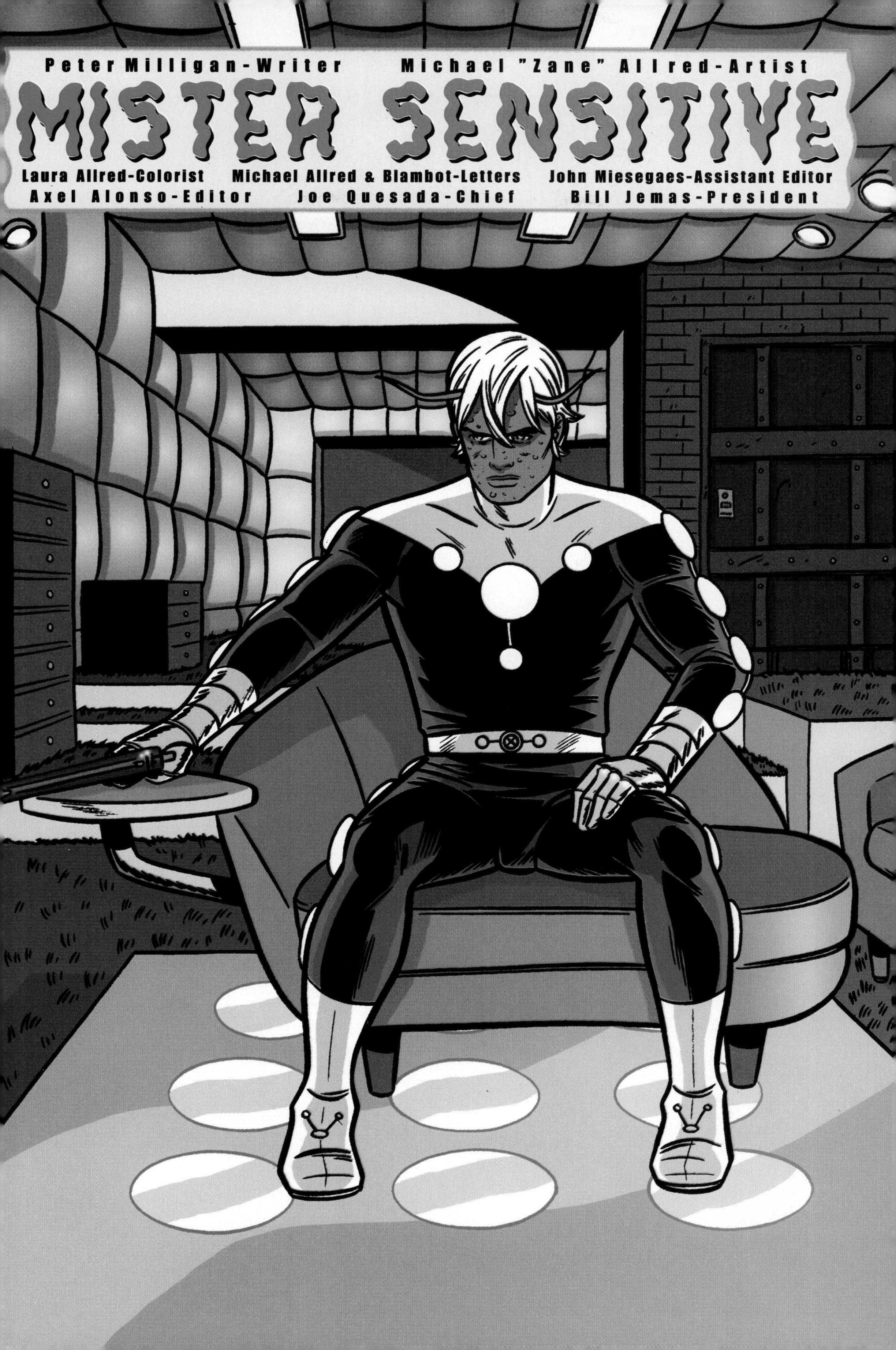
Peter Milligan-Writer
Michael "Zane" Allred-Artist
MISTER SENSITIVE
Laura Allred-Colorist
Michael Allred & Blambot-Letters
John Miesegaes-Assistant Editor
Axel Alonso-Editor
Joe Quesada-Chief
Bill Jemas-President

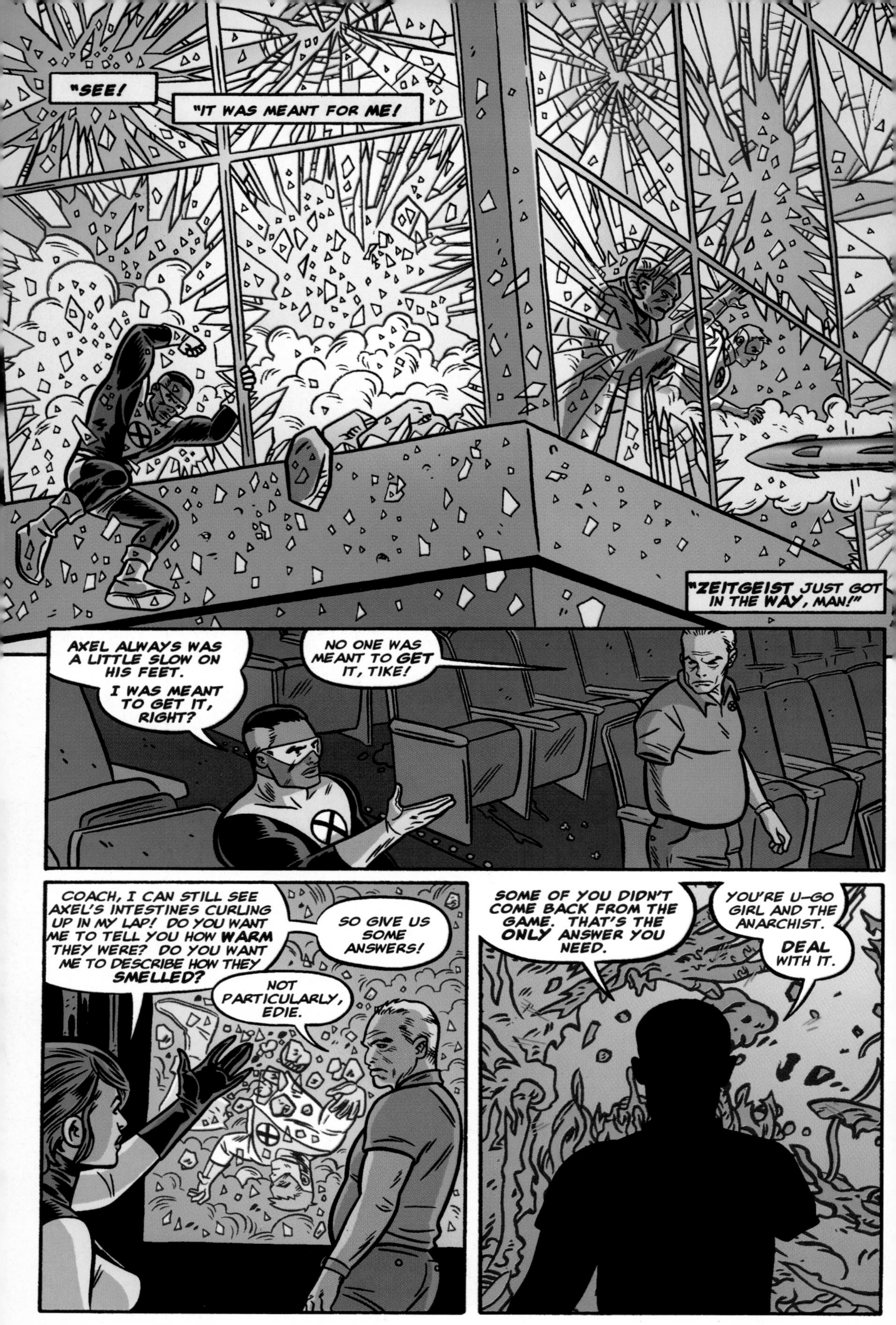
"SEE!
"IT WAS MEANT FOR ME!
"ZEITGEIST JUST GOT IN THE WAY, MAN!"
AXEL ALWAYS WAS A LITTLE SLOW ON HIS FEET.
I WAS MEANT TO GET IT, RIGHT?
NO ONE WAS MEANT TO GET IT, TIKE!
COACH, I CAN STILL SEE AXEL'S INTESTINES CURLING UP IN MY LAP! DO YOU WANT ME TO TELL YOU HOW WARM THEY WERE? DO YOU WANT ME TO DESCRIBE HOW THEY SMELLED?
SO GIVE US SOME ANSWERS!
NOT PARTICULARLY, EDIE.
SOME OF YOU DIDN'T COME BACK FROM THE GAME. THAT'S THE ONLY ANSWER YOU NEED.
YOU'RE U-GO GIRL AND THE ANARCHIST.
DEAL WITH IT.

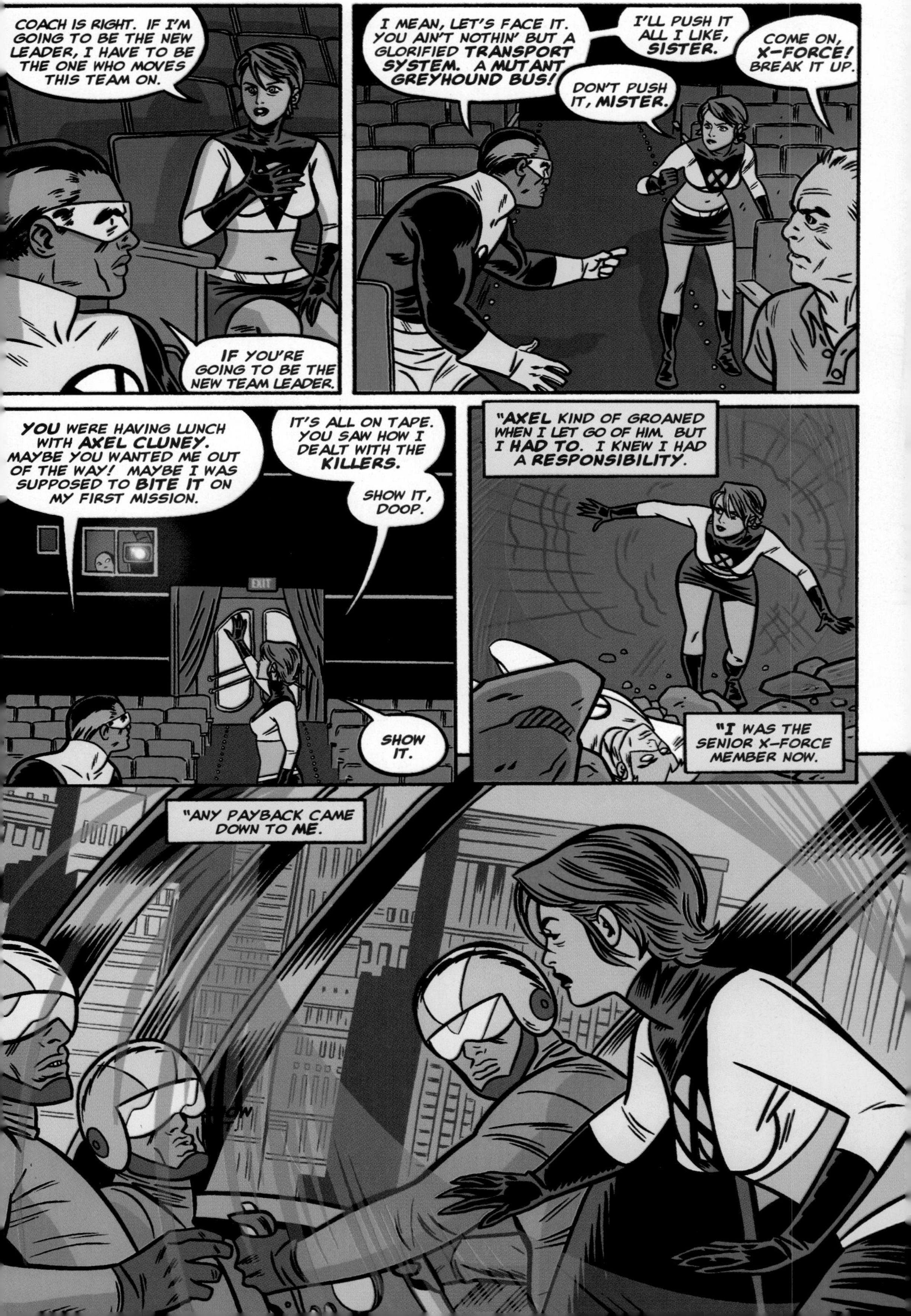
COACH IS RIGHT. IF I'M GOING TO BE THE NEW LEADER, I HAVE TO BE THE ONE WHO MOVES THIS TEAM ON.
IF YOU'RE GOING TO BE THE NEW TEAM LEADER.
I MEAN, LET'S FACE IT. YOU AIN'T NOTHIN' BUT A GLORIFIED TRANSPORT SYSTEM. A MUTANT GREYHOUND BUS!
DON'T PUSH IT, MISTER.
I'LL PUSH IT ALL I LIKE, SISTER.
COME ON, X-FORCE! BREAK IT UP.
YOU WERE HAVING LUNCH WITH AXEL CLUNEY. MAYBE YOU WANTED ME OUT OF THE WAY! MAYBE I WAS SUPPOSED TO BITE IT ON MY FIRST MISSION.
IT'S ALL ON TAPE. YOU SAW HOW I DEALT WITH THE KILLERS.
SHOW IT, DOOP.
EXIT
SHOW IT.
"AXEL KIND OF GROANED WHEN I LET GO OF HIM. BUT I HAD TO. I KNEW I HAD A RESPONSIBILITY.
"I WAS THE SENIOR X-FORCE MEMBER NOW.
"ANY PAYBACK CAME DOWN TO ME.

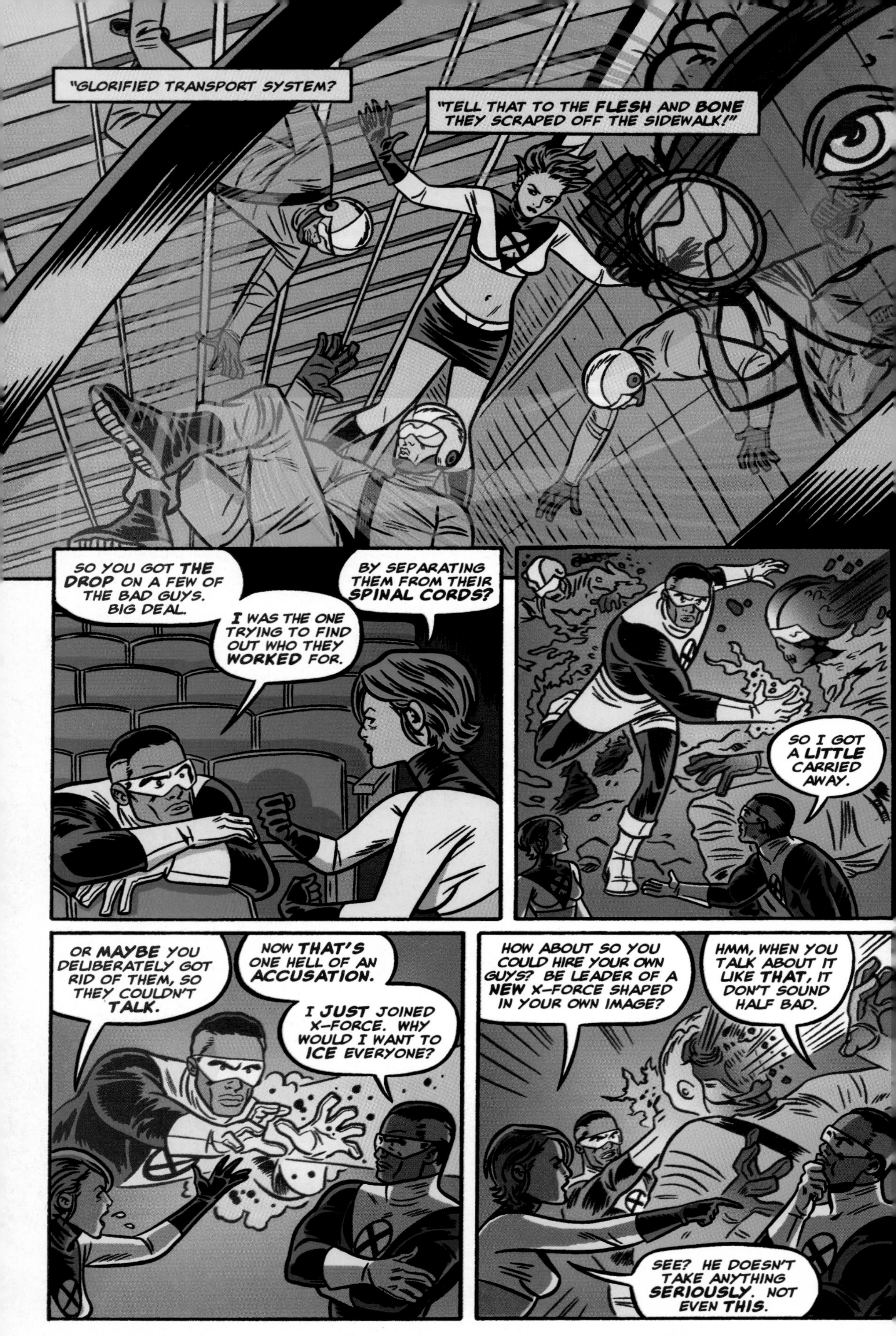
"GLORIFIED TRANSPORT SYSTEM?
"TELL THAT TO THE FLESH AND BONE THEY SCRAPED OFF THE SIDEWALK!"
SO YOU GOT THE DROP ON A FEW OF THE BAD GUYS. BIG DEAL.
BY SEPARATING THEM FROM THEIR SPINAL CORDS?
I WAS THE ONE TRYING TO FIND OUT WHO THEY WORKED FOR.
SO I GOT A LITTLE CARRIED AWAY.
OR MAYBE YOU DELIBERATELY GOT RID OF THEM, SO THEY COULDN'T TALK.
NOW THAT'S ONE HELL OF AN ACCUSATION.
I JUST JOINED X-FORCE. WHY WOULD I WANT TO ICE EVERYONE?
HOW ABOUT SO YOU COULD HIRE YOUR OWN GUYS? BE LEADER OF A NEW X-FORCE SHAPED IN YOUR OWN IMAGE?
HMM, WHEN YOU TALK ABOUT IT LIKE THAT, IT DON'T SOUND HALF BAD.
SEE? HE DOESN'T TAKE ANYTHING SERIOUSLY. NOT EVEN THIS.

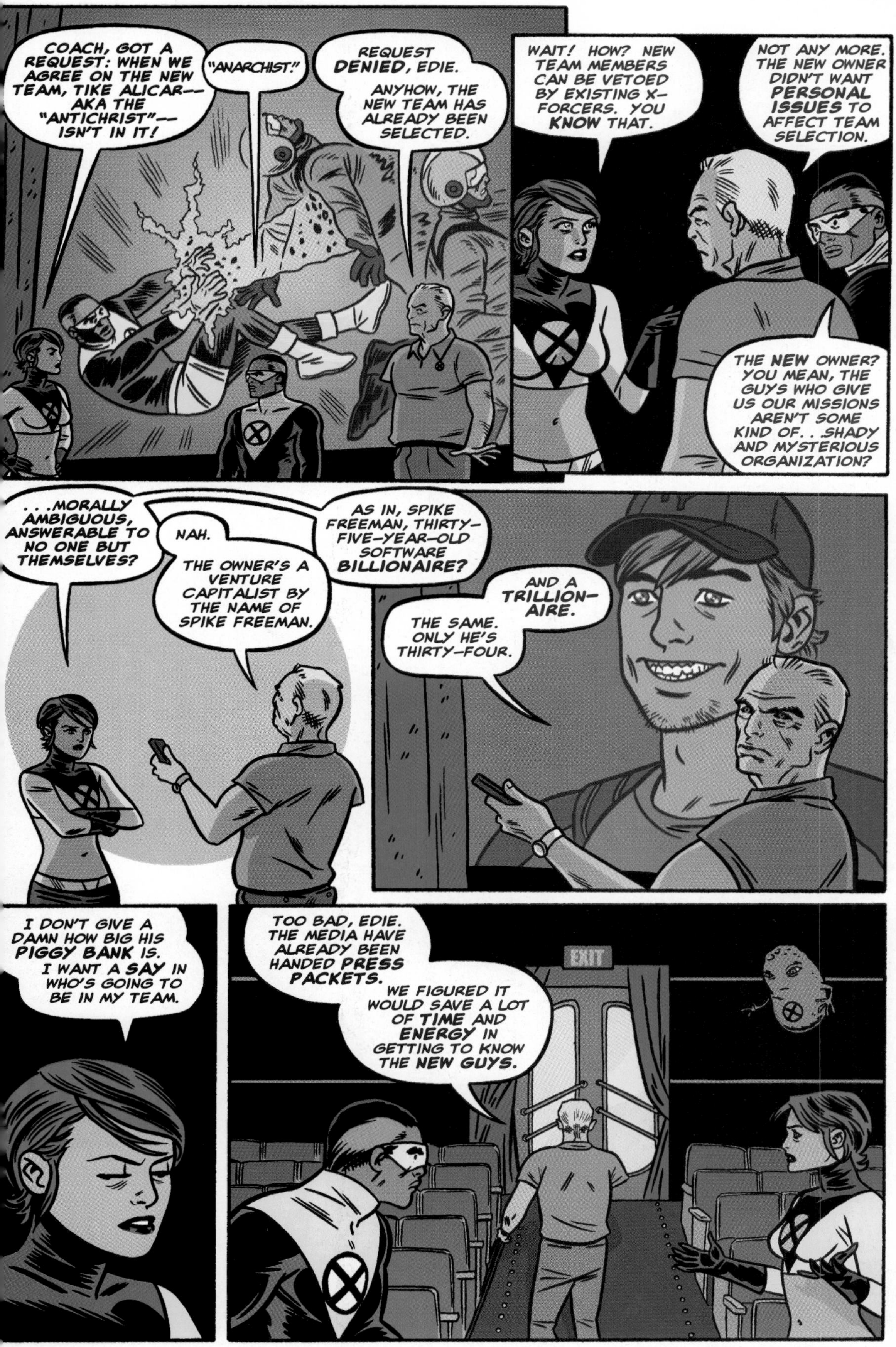
COACH, GOT A REQUEST: WHEN WE AGREE ON THE NEW TEAM, TIKE ALICAR--AKA THE "ANTICHRIST"--ISN'T IN IT!
"ANARCHIST!"
REQUEST DENIED, EDIE.
ANYHOW, THE NEW TEAM HAS ALREADY BEEN SELECTED.
WAIT! HOW? NEW TEAM MEMBERS CAN BE VETOED BY EXISTING X-FORCERS. YOU KNOW THAT.
NOT ANY MORE. THE NEW OWNER DIDN'T WANT PERSONAL ISSUES TO AFFECT TEAM SELECTION.
THE NEW OWNER? YOU MEAN, THE GUYS WHO GIVE US OUR MISSIONS AREN'T SOME KIND OF. . .SHADY AND MYSTERIOUS ORGANIZATION?
. . .MORALLY AMBIGUOUS, ANSWERABLE TO NO ONE BUT THEMSELVES?
NAH.
THE OWNER'S A VENTURE CAPITALIST BY THE NAME OF SPIKE FREEMAN.
AS IN, SPIKE FREEMAN, THIRTY-FIVE-YEAR-OLD SOFTWARE BILLIONAIRE?
AND A TRILLION-AIRE.
THE SAME. ONLY HE'S THIRTY-FOUR.
I DON'T GIVE A DAMN HOW BIG HIS PIGGY BANK IS.
I WANT A SAY IN WHO'S GOING TO BE IN MY TEAM.
TOO BAD, EDIE. THE MEDIA HAVE ALREADY BEEN HANDED PRESS PACKETS.
WE FIGURED IT WOULD SAVE A LOT OF TIME AND ENERGY IN GETTING TO KNOW THE NEW GUYS.
EXIT

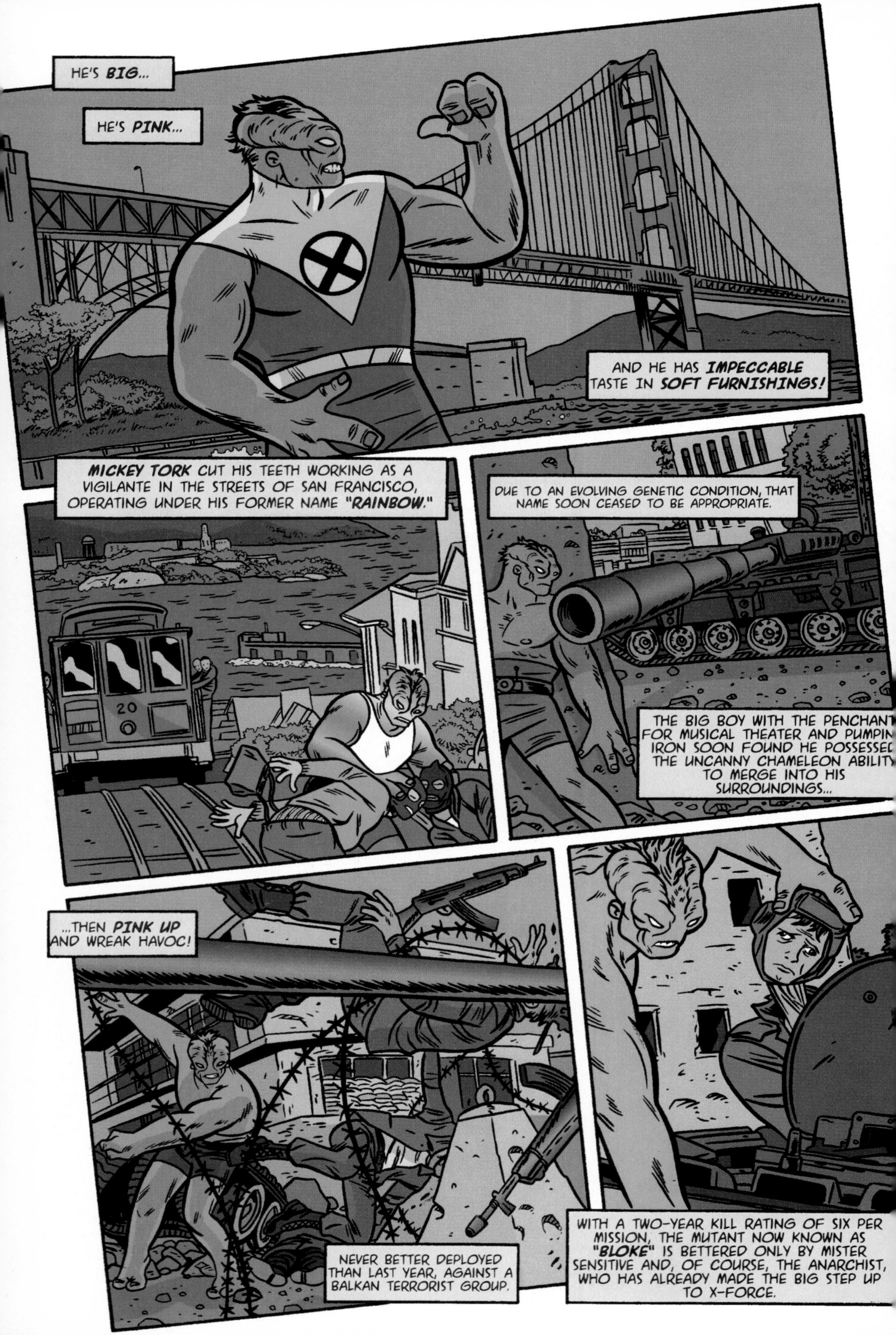

HE'S **BIG**...
HE'S **PINK**...
AND HE HAS **IMPECCABLE** TASTE IN **SOFT FURNISHINGS!**
MICKEY TORK CUT HIS TEETH WORKING AS A VIGILANTE IN THE STREETS OF SAN FRANCISCO, OPERATING UNDER HIS FORMER NAME "**RAINBOW.**"
20
DUE TO AN EVOLVING GENETIC CONDITION, THAT NAME SOON CEASED TO BE APPROPRIATE.
THE BIG BOY WITH THE PENCHANT FOR MUSICAL THEATER AND PUMPIN IRON SOON FOUND HE POSSESSE THE UNCANNY CHAMELEON ABILIT TO MERGE INTO HIS SURROUNDINGS...
...THEN **PINK UP** AND WREAK HAVOC!
NEVER BETTER DEPLOYED THAN LAST YEAR, AGAINST A BALKAN TERRORIST GROUP.
WITH A TWO-YEAR KILL RATING OF SIX PER MISSION, THE MUTANT NOW KNOWN AS "**BLOKE**" IS BETTERED ONLY BY MISTER SENSITIVE AND, OF COURSE, THE ANARCHIST, WHO HAS ALREADY MADE THE BIG STEP UP TO X-FORCE.

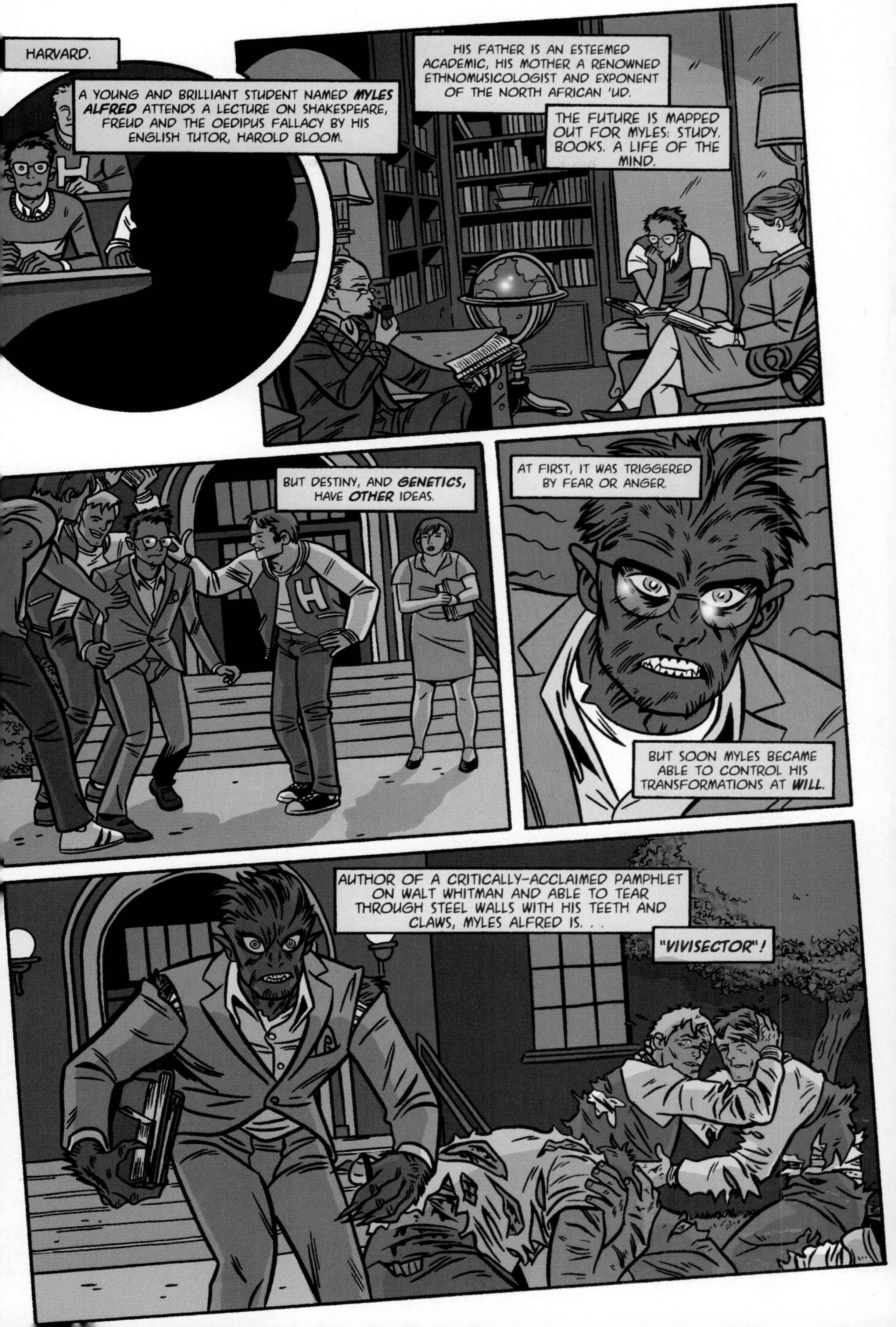
HARVARD.
A YOUNG AND BRILLIANT STUDENT NAMED MYLES ALFRED ATTENDS A LECTURE ON SHAKESPEARE, FREUD AND THE OEDIPUS FALLACY BY HIS ENGLISH TUTOR, HAROLD BLOOM.
HIS FATHER IS AN ESTEEMED ACADEMIC, HIS MOTHER A RENOWNED ETHNOMUSICOLOGIST AND EXPONENT OF THE NORTH AFRICAN 'UD.
THE FUTURE IS MAPPED OUT FOR MYLES: STUDY. BOOKS. A LIFE OF THE MIND.
BUT DESTINY, AND GENETICS, HAVE OTHER IDEAS.
AT FIRST, IT WAS TRIGGERED BY FEAR OR ANGER.
BUT SOON MYLES BECAME ABLE TO CONTROL HIS TRANSFORMATIONS AT WILL.
AUTHOR OF A CRITICALLY-ACCLAIMED PAMPHLET ON WALT WHITMAN AND ABLE TO TEAR THROUGH STEEL WALLS WITH HIS TEETH AND CLAWS, MYLES ALFRED IS. . .
"VIVISECTOR"!

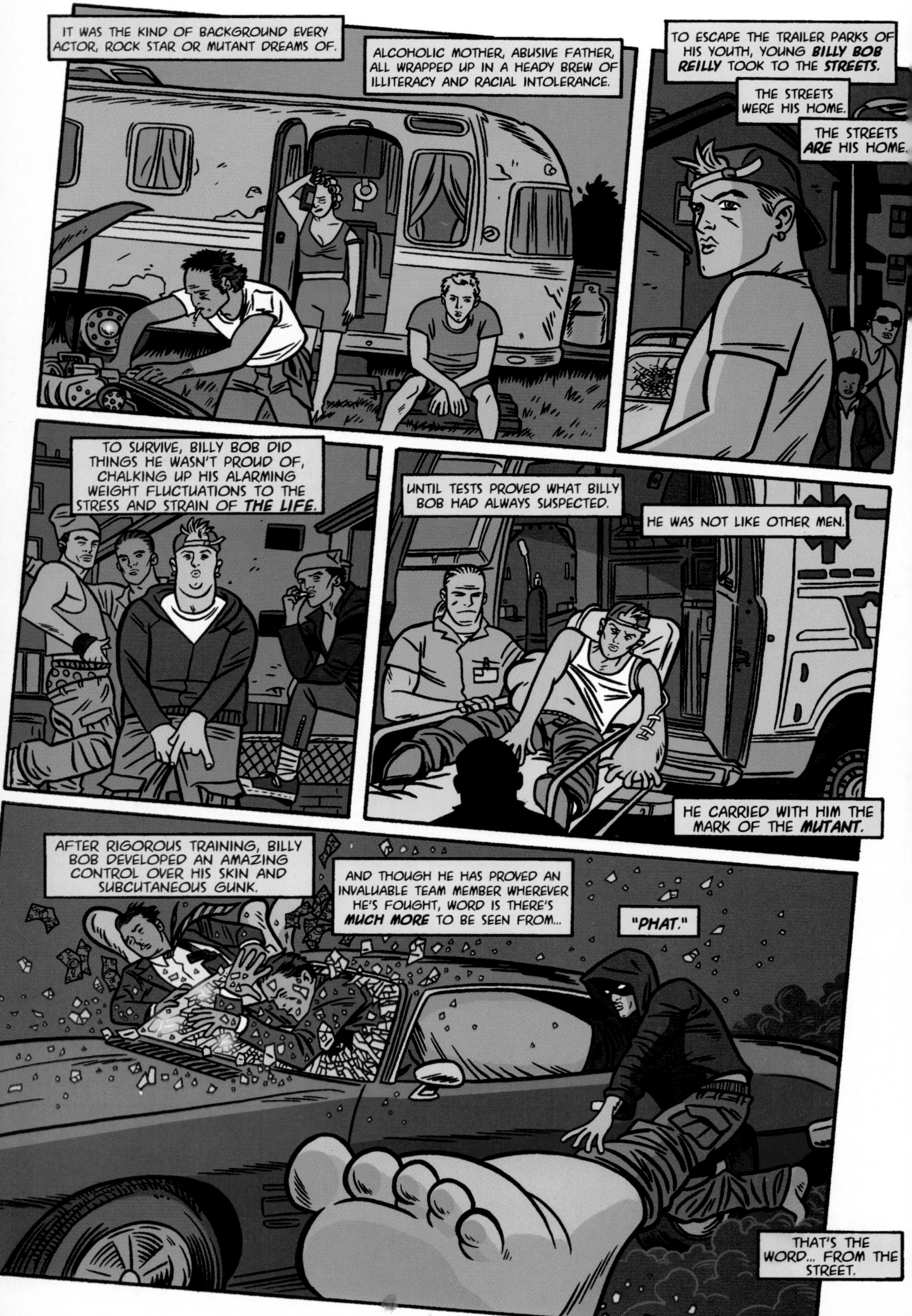
IT WAS THE KIND OF BACKGROUND EVERY ACTOR, ROCK STAR OR MUTANT DREAMS OF.
ALCOHOLIC MOTHER, ABUSIVE FATHER, ALL WRAPPED UP IN A HEADY BREW OF ILLITERACY AND RACIAL INTOLERANCE.
TO ESCAPE THE TRAILER PARKS OF HIS YOUTH, YOUNG BILLY BOB REILLY TOOK TO THE STREETS.
THE STREETS WERE HIS HOME.
THE STREETS ARE HIS HOME.
TO SURVIVE, BILLY BOB DID THINGS HE WASN'T PROUD OF, CHALKING UP HIS ALARMING WEIGHT FLUCTUATIONS TO THE STRESS AND STRAIN OF THE LIFE.
UNTIL TESTS PROVED WHAT BILLY BOB HAD ALWAYS SUSPECTED.
HE WAS NOT LIKE OTHER MEN.
HE CARRIED WITH HIM THE MARK OF THE MUTANT.
AFTER RIGOROUS TRAINING, BILLY BOB DEVELOPED AN AMAZING CONTROL OVER HIS SKIN AND SUBCUTANEOUS GUNK.
AND THOUGH HE HAS PROVED AN INVALUABLE TEAM MEMBER WHEREVER HE'S FOUGHT, WORD IS THERE'S MUCH MORE TO BE SEEN FROM...
"PHAT."
THAT'S THE WORD... FROM THE STREET.

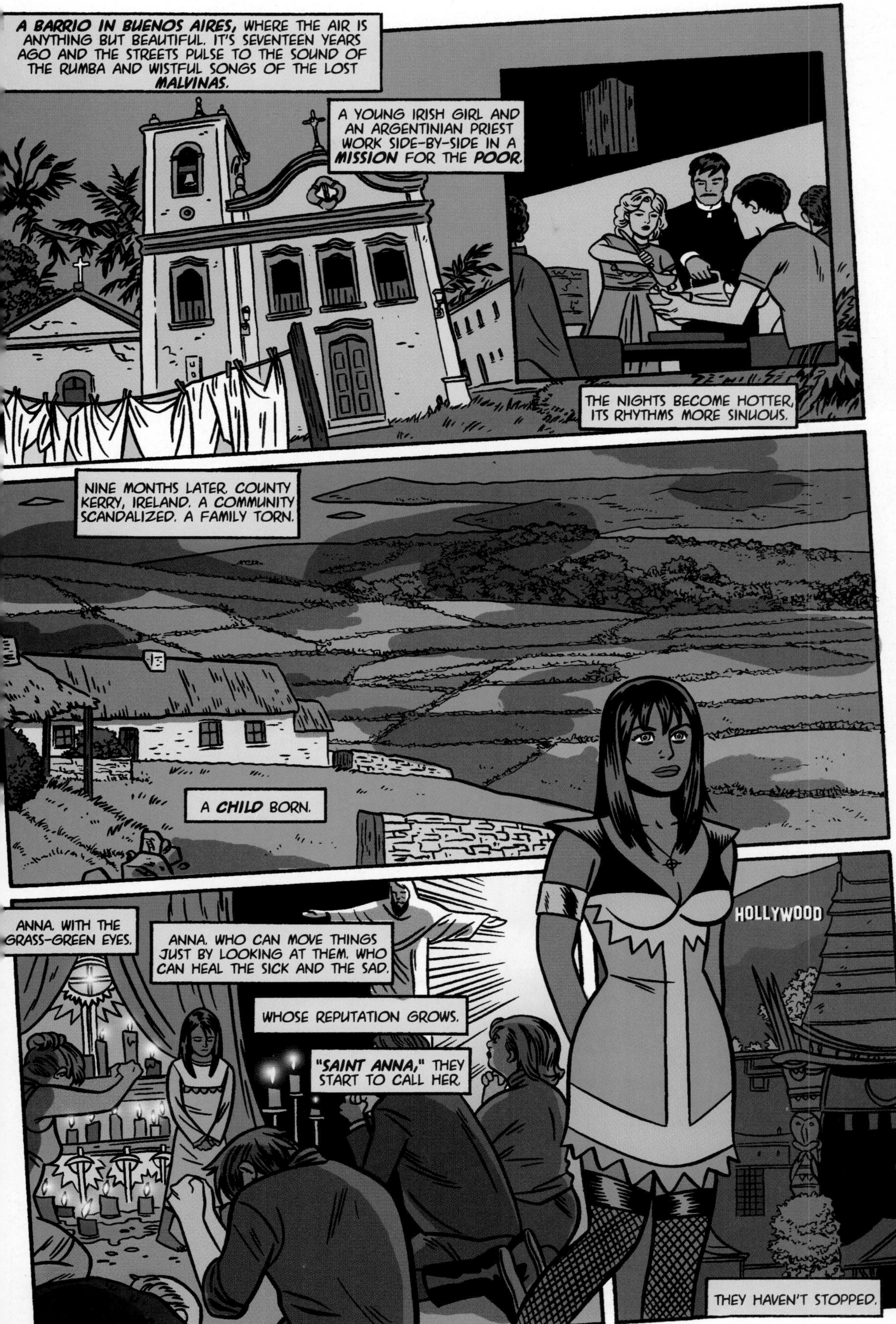
A BARRIO IN BUENOS AIRES, WHERE THE AIR IS ANYTHING BUT BEAUTIFUL. IT'S SEVENTEEN YEARS AGO AND THE STREETS PULSE TO THE SOUND OF THE RUMBA AND WISTFUL SONGS OF THE LOST MALVINAS.
A YOUNG IRISH GIRL AND AN ARGENTINIAN PRIEST WORK SIDE-BY-SIDE IN A MISSION FOR THE POOR.
THE NIGHTS BECOME HOTTER, ITS RHYTHMS MORE SINUOUS.
NINE MONTHS LATER, COUNTY KERRY, IRELAND. A COMMUNITY SCANDALIZED. A FAMILY TORN.
A CHILD BORN.
ANNA, WITH THE GRASS-GREEN EYES.
ANNA, WHO CAN MOVE THINGS JUST BY LOOKING AT THEM, WHO CAN HEAL THE SICK AND THE SAD.
WHOSE REPUTATION GROWS.
"SAINT ANNA," THEY START TO CALL HER.
HOLLYWOOD
THEY HAVEN'T STOPPED.

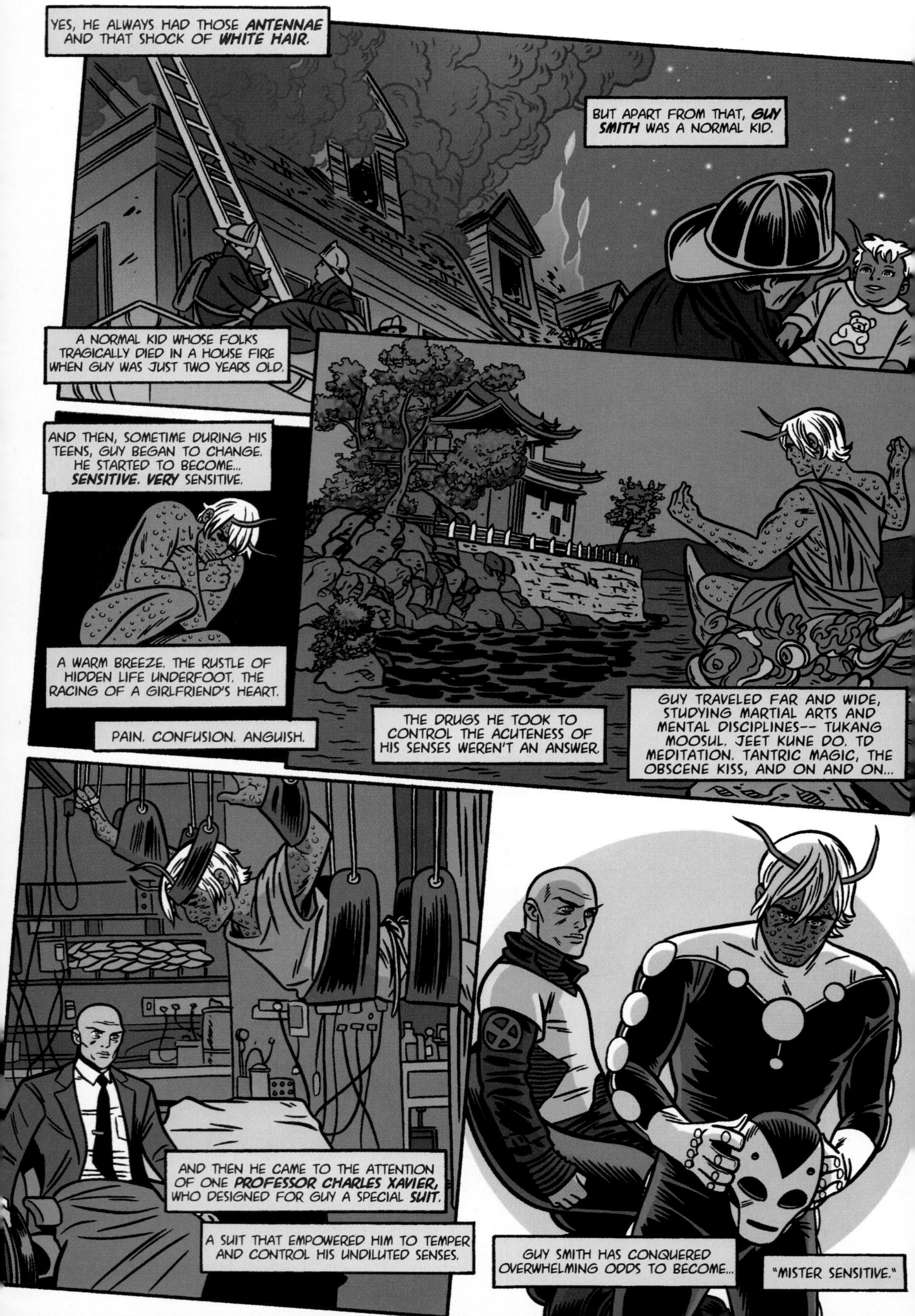
YES, HE ALWAYS HAD THOSE ANTENNAE AND THAT SHOCK OF WHITE HAIR.
BUT APART FROM THAT, GUY SMITH WAS A NORMAL KID.
A NORMAL KID WHOSE FOLKS TRAGICALLY DIED IN A HOUSE FIRE WHEN GUY WAS JUST TWO YEARS OLD.
AND THEN, SOMETIME DURING HIS TEENS, GUY BEGAN TO CHANGE. HE STARTED TO BECOME... SENSITIVE. VERY SENSITIVE.
A WARM BREEZE. THE RUSTLE OF HIDDEN LIFE UNDERFOOT. THE RACING OF A GIRLFRIEND'S HEART.
PAIN. CONFUSION. ANGUISH.
THE DRUGS HE TOOK TO CONTROL THE ACUTENESS OF HIS SENSES WEREN'T AN ANSWER.
GUY TRAVELED FAR AND WIDE, STUDYING MARTIAL ARTS AND MENTAL DISCIPLINES-- TUKANG MOOSUL. JEET KUNE DO. TD MEDITATION. TANTRIC MAGIC, THE OBSCENE KISS, AND ON AND ON...
AND THEN HE CAME TO THE ATTENTION OF ONE PROFESSOR CHARLES XAVIER, WHO DESIGNED FOR GUY A SPECIAL SUIT.
A SUIT THAT EMPOWERED HIM TO TEMPER AND CONTROL HIS UNDILUTED SENSES.
GUY SMITH HAS CONQUERED OVERWHELMING ODDS TO BECOME...
"MISTER SENSITIVE."

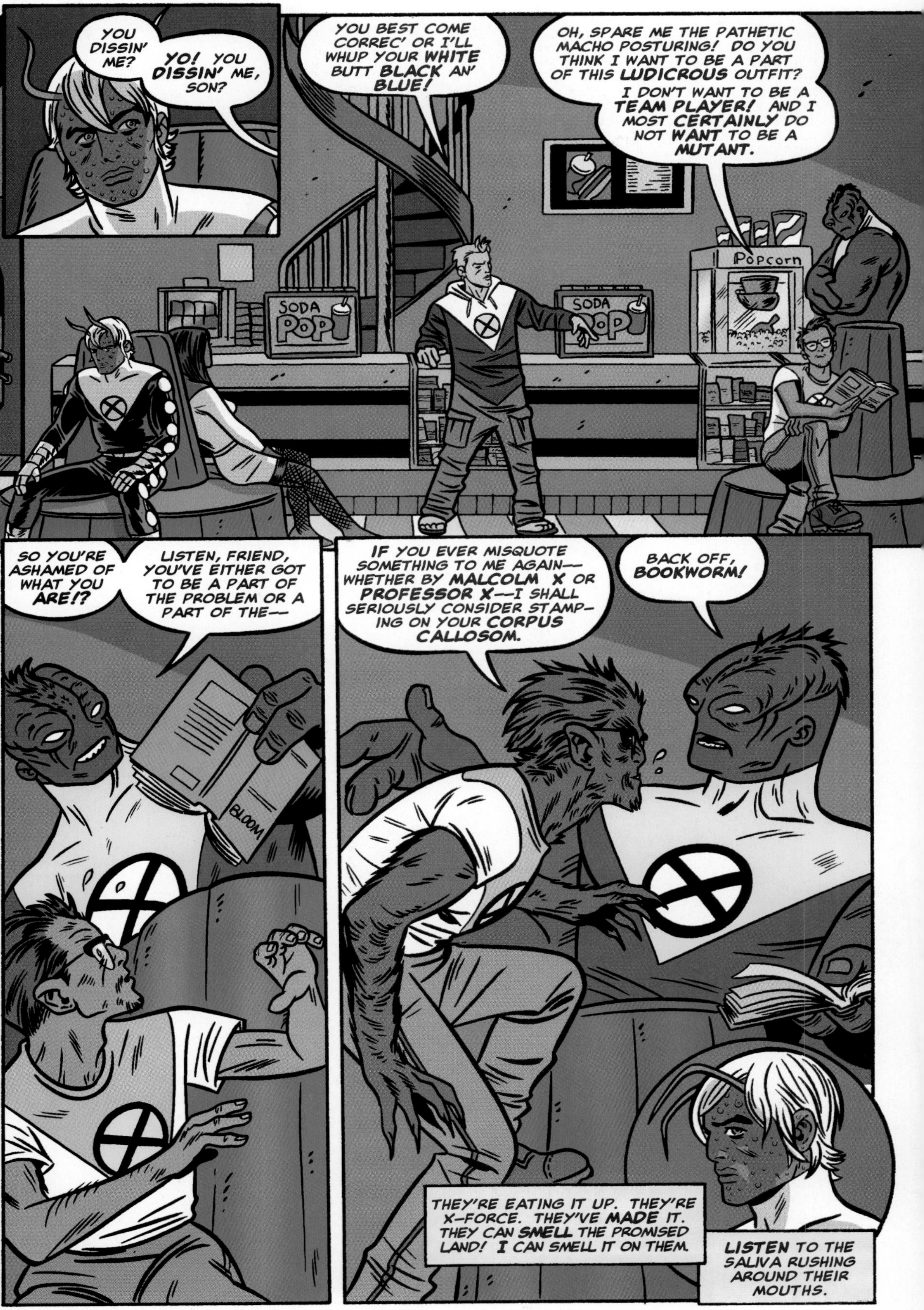

YOU DISSIN' ME?
YO! YOU DISSIN' ME, SON?
YOU BEST COME CORREC' OR I'LL WHUP YOUR WHITE BUTT BLACK AN' BLUE!
OH, SPARE ME THE PATHETIC MACHO POSTURING! DO YOU THINK I WANT TO BE A PART OF THIS LUDICROUS OUTFIT?
I DON'T WANT TO BE A TEAM PLAYER! AND I MOST CERTAINLY DO NOT WANT TO BE A MUTANT.
SODA POP
SODA POP
Popcorn
SO YOU'RE ASHAMED OF WHAT YOU ARE!?
LISTEN, FRIEND, YOU'VE EITHER GOT TO BE A PART OF THE PROBLEM OR A PART OF THE--
BLOOM
IF YOU EVER MISQUOTE SOMETHING TO ME AGAIN-- WHETHER BY MALCOLM X OR PROFESSOR X--I SHALL SERIOUSLY CONSIDER STAMPING ON YOUR CORPUS CALLOSOM.
BACK OFF, BOOKWORM!
THEY'RE EATING IT UP. THEY'RE X-FORCE. THEY'VE MADE IT. THEY CAN SMELL THE PROMISED LAND! I CAN SMELL IT ON THEM.
LISTEN TO THE SALIVA RUSHING AROUND THEIR MOUTHS.

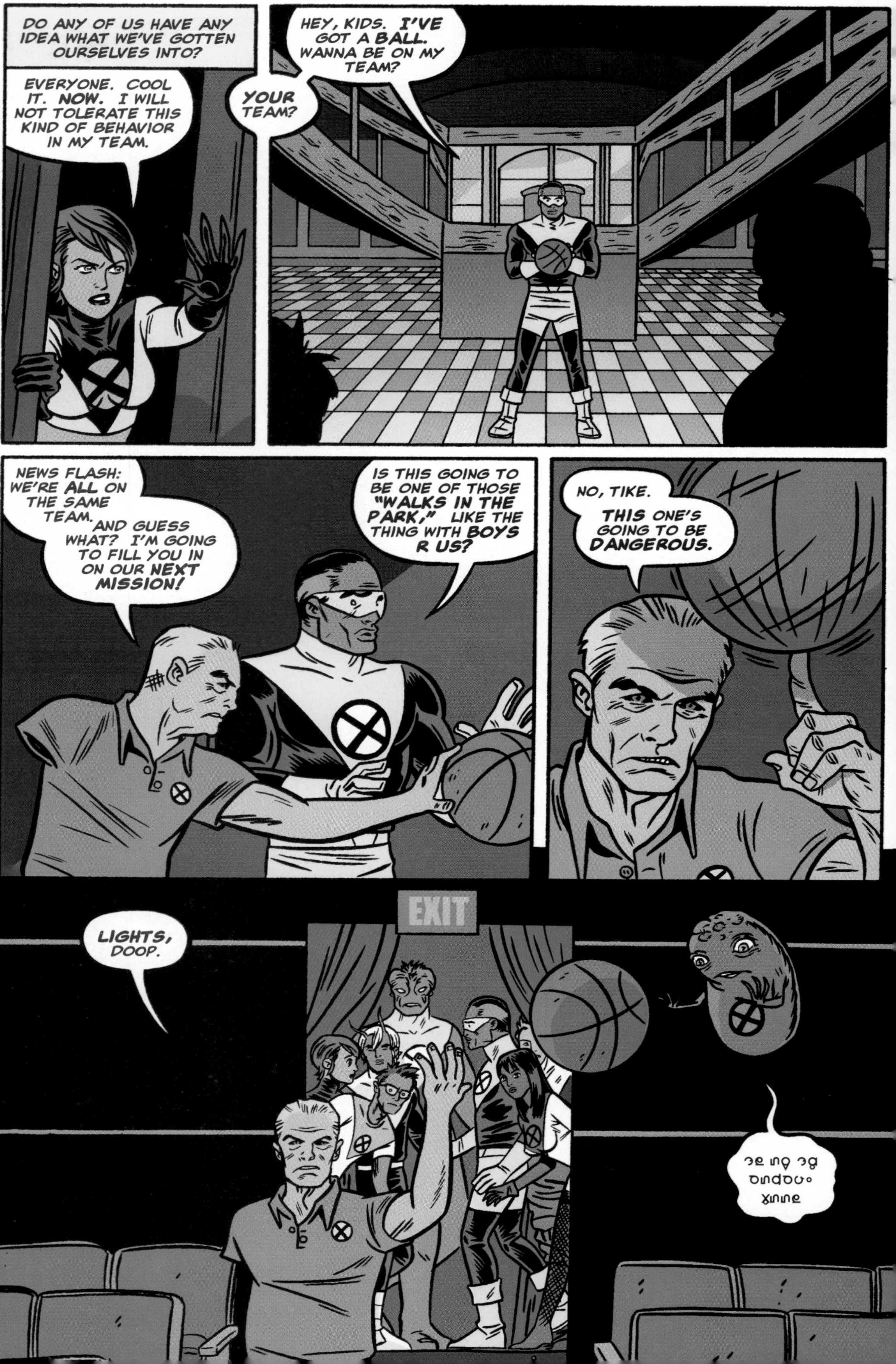
DO ANY OF US HAVE ANY IDEA WHAT WE'VE GOTTEN OURSELVES INTO?
EVERYONE. COOL IT. NOW. I WILL NOT TOLERATE THIS KIND OF BEHAVIOR IN MY TEAM.
YOUR TEAM?
HEY, KIDS. I'VE GOT A BALL. WANNA BE ON MY TEAM?
NEWS FLASH: WE'RE ALL ON THE SAME TEAM.
AND GUESS WHAT? I'M GOING TO FILL YOU IN ON OUR NEXT MISSION!
IS THIS GOING TO BE ONE OF THOSE "WALKS IN THE PARK," LIKE THE THING WITH BOYS R US?
NO, TIKE.
THIS ONE'S GOING TO BE DANGEROUS.
EXIT
LIGHTS, DOOP.

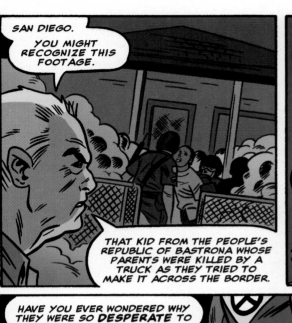

SAN DIEGO.

YOU MIGHT RECOGNIZE THIS FOOTAGE.

THAT KID FROM THE PEOPLE'S REPUBLIC OF BASTRONA WHOSE PARENTS WERE KILLED BY A TRUCK AS THEY TRIED TO MAKE IT ACROSS THE BORDER.

THERE HE IS. POOR LITTLE PACO PEREZ.

THE FEDS RESCUED HIM FOR THE REDS.

SO WHAT'S THAT GOT TO DO WITH US?

HAVE YOU EVER WONDERED WHY THEY WERE SO DESPERATE TO GET LITTLE PACO BACK?

POLITICS?

TO STICK IT TO THE >AHEM< "IMPERIALIST RUNNING DOGS OF THE UNITED STATES"?

THIS IS A CRATER IN SOUTHERN BASTRONA. IT'S HALF A MILE WIDE AND ALMOST AS DEEP.

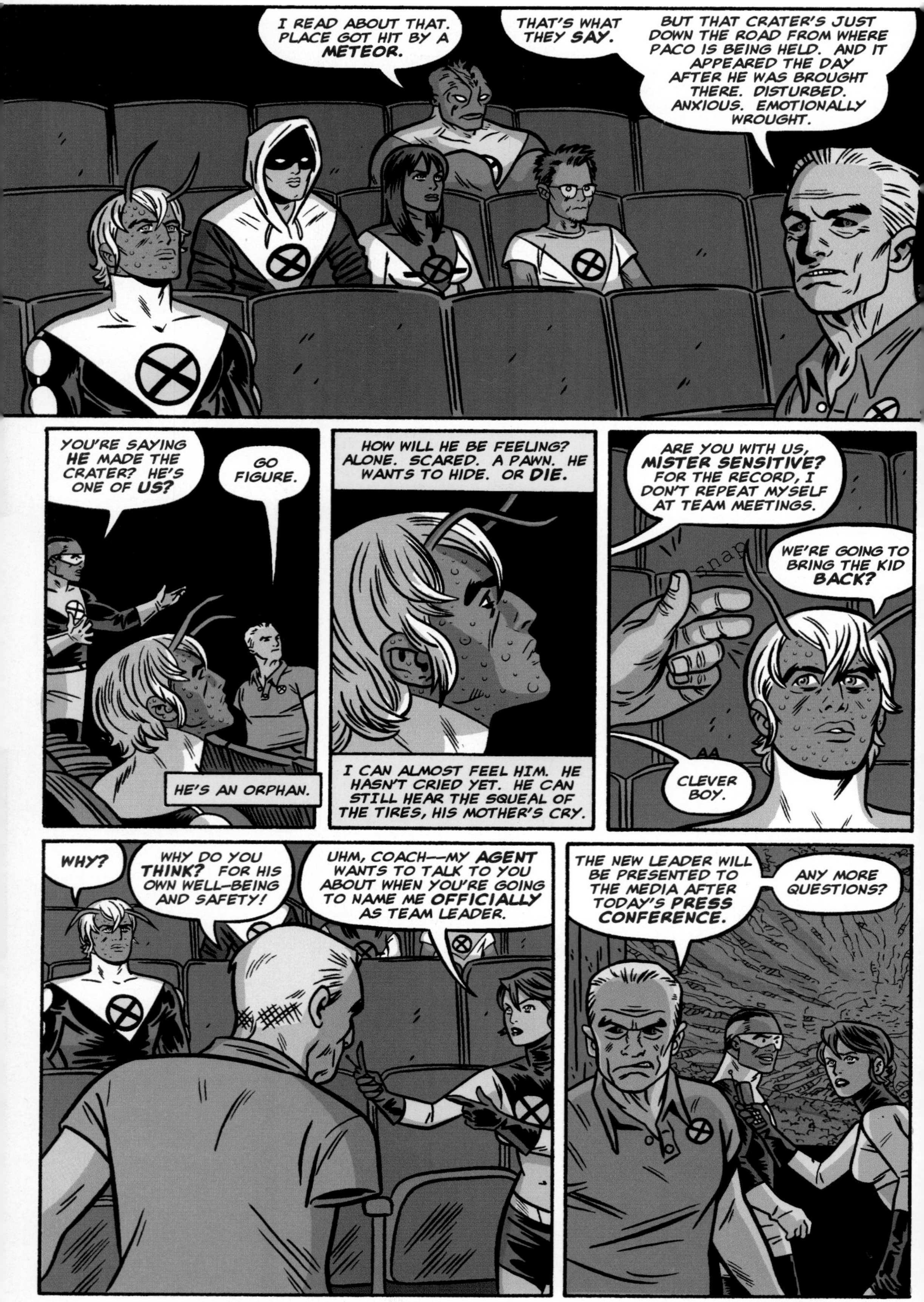

I READ ABOUT THAT. PLACE GOT HIT BY A METEOR.
THAT'S WHAT THEY SAY.
BUT THAT CRATER'S JUST DOWN THE ROAD FROM WHERE PACO IS BEING HELD. AND IT APPEARED THE DAY AFTER HE WAS BROUGHT THERE. DISTURBED. ANXIOUS. EMOTIONALLY WROUGHT.
YOU'RE SAYING HE MADE THE CRATER? HE'S ONE OF US?
GO FIGURE.
HE'S AN ORPHAN.
HOW WILL HE BE FEELING? ALONE. SCARED. A PAWN. HE WANTS TO HIDE. OR DIE.
I CAN ALMOST FEEL HIM. HE HASN'T CRIED YET. HE CAN STILL HEAR THE SQUEAL OF THE TIRES, HIS MOTHER'S CRY.
ARE YOU WITH US, MISTER SENSITIVE? FOR THE RECORD, I DON'T REPEAT MYSELF AT TEAM MEETINGS.
snap
WE'RE GOING TO BRING THE KID BACK?
CLEVER BOY.
WHY?
WHY DO YOU THINK? FOR HIS OWN WELL-BEING AND SAFETY!
UHM, COACH--MY AGENT WANTS TO TALK TO YOU ABOUT WHEN YOU'RE GOING TO NAME ME OFFICIALLY AS TEAM LEADER.
THE NEW LEADER WILL BE PRESENTED TO THE MEDIA AFTER TODAY'S PRESS CONFERENCE.
ANY MORE QUESTIONS?

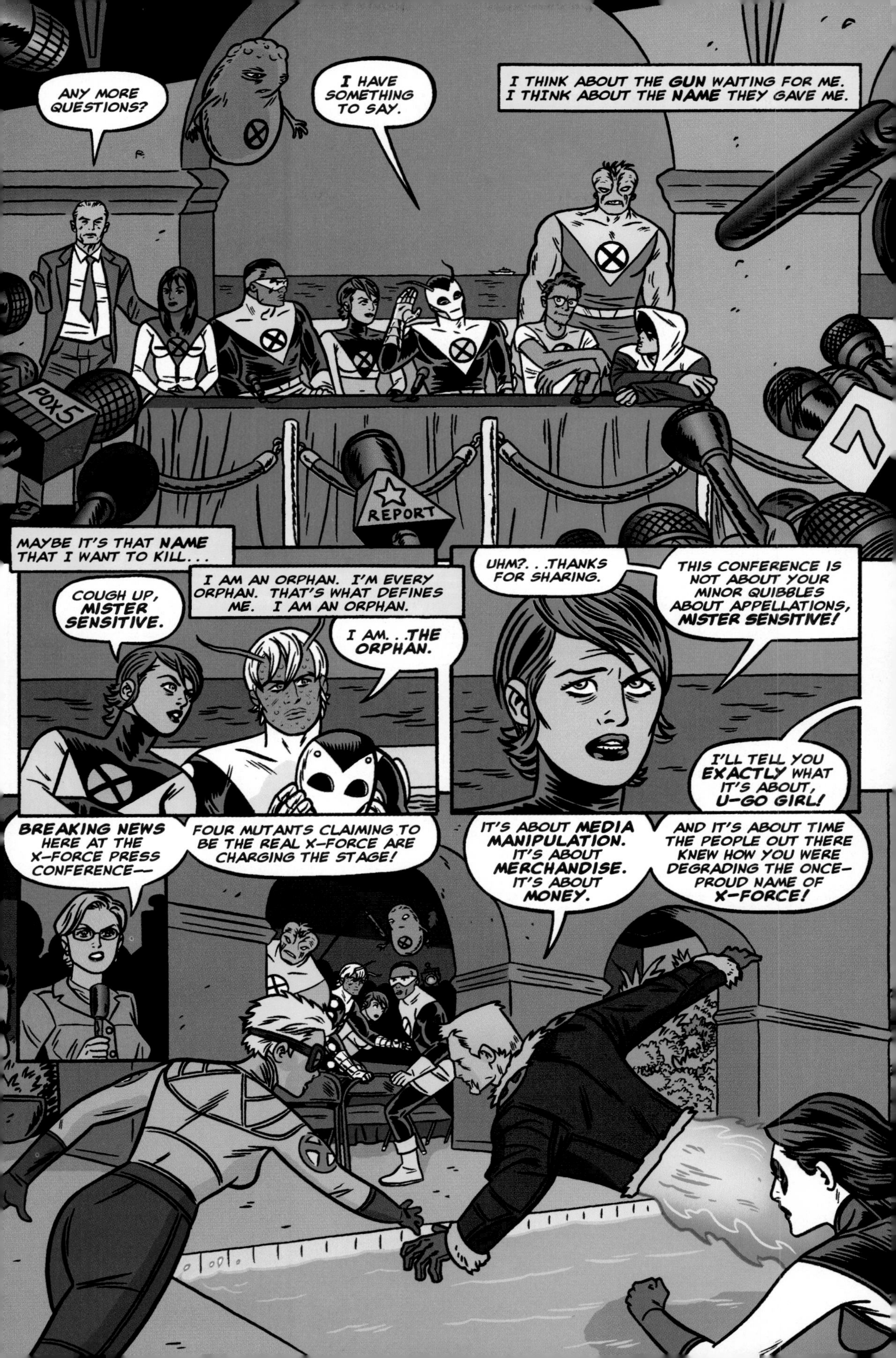
ANY MORE QUESTIONS?
I HAVE SOMETHING TO SAY.
I THINK ABOUT THE GUN WAITING FOR ME. I THINK ABOUT THE NAME THEY GAVE ME.
POX 5
REPORT
MAYBE IT'S THAT NAME THAT I WANT TO KILL...
COUGH UP, MISTER SENSITIVE.
I AM AN ORPHAN. I'M EVERY ORPHAN. THAT'S WHAT DEFINES ME. I AM AN ORPHAN.
I AM...THE ORPHAN.
UHM?...THANKS FOR SHARING.
THIS CONFERENCE IS NOT ABOUT YOUR MINOR QUIBBLES ABOUT APPELLATIONS, MISTER SENSITIVE!
I'LL TELL YOU EXACTLY WHAT IT'S ABOUT, U-GO GIRL!
BREAKING NEWS HERE AT THE X-FORCE PRESS CONFERENCE--
FOUR MUTANTS CLAIMING TO BE THE REAL X-FORCE ARE CHARGING THE STAGE!
IT'S ABOUT MEDIA MANIPULATION. IT'S ABOUT MERCHANDISE. IT'S ABOUT MONEY.
AND IT'S ABOUT TIME THE PEOPLE OUT THERE KNEW HOW YOU WERE DEGRADING THE ONCE-PROUD NAME OF X-FORCE!

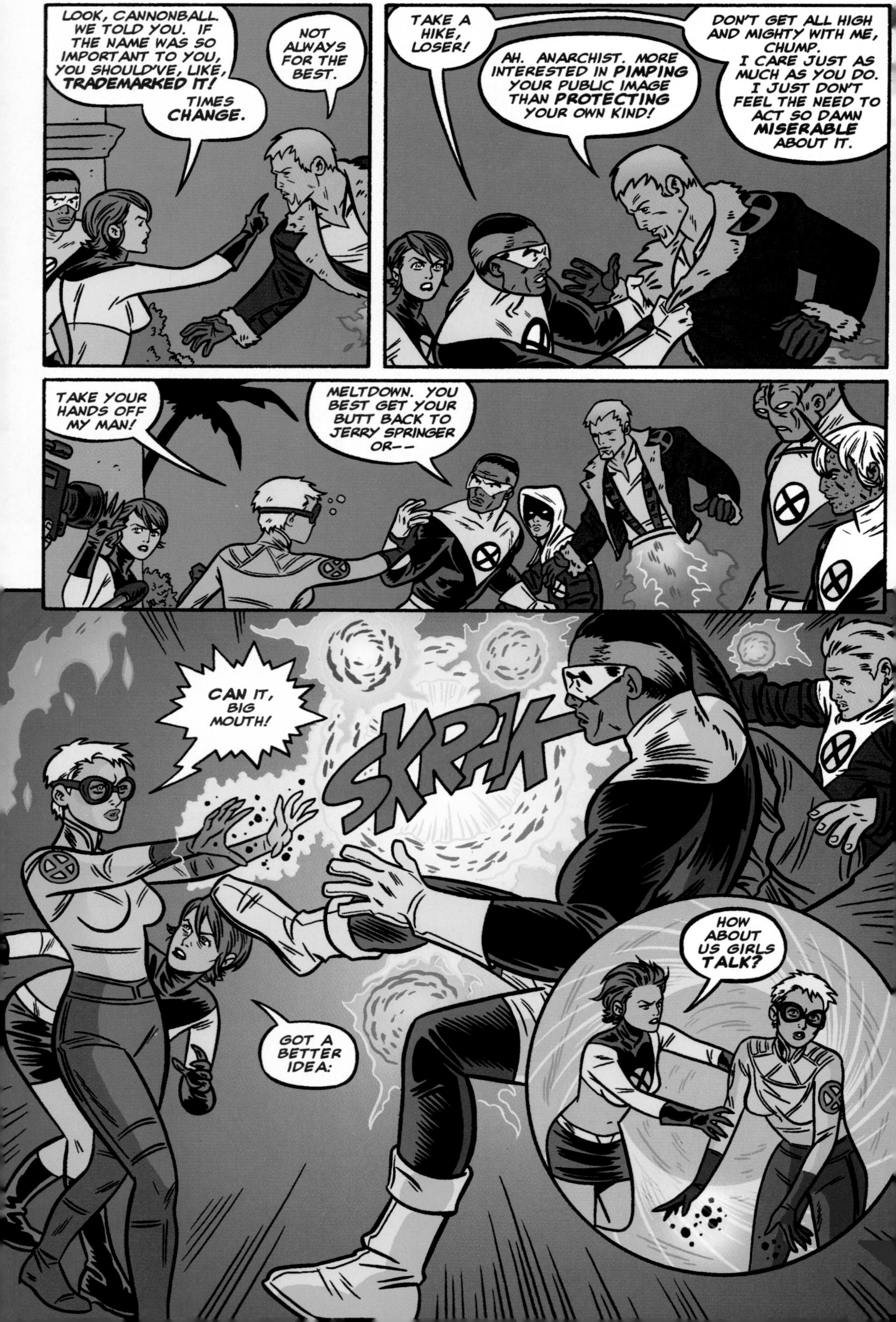
LOOK, CANNONBALL. WE TOLD YOU. IF THE NAME WAS SO IMPORTANT TO YOU, YOU SHOULD'VE, LIKE, TRADEMARKED IT!
TIMES CHANGE.
NOT ALWAYS FOR THE BEST.
TAKE A HIKE, LOSER!
AH. ANARCHIST. MORE INTERESTED IN PIMPING YOUR PUBLIC IMAGE THAN PROTECTING YOUR OWN KIND!
DON'T GET ALL HIGH AND MIGHTY WITH ME, CHUMP. I CARE JUST AS MUCH AS YOU DO. I JUST DON'T FEEL THE NEED TO ACT SO DAMN MISERABLE ABOUT IT.
TAKE YOUR HANDS OFF MY MAN!
MELTDOWN. YOU BEST GET YOUR BUTT BACK TO JERRY SPRINGER OR--
CAN IT, BIG MOUTH!
SKRAK
GOT A BETTER IDEA:
HOW ABOUT US GIRLS TALK?

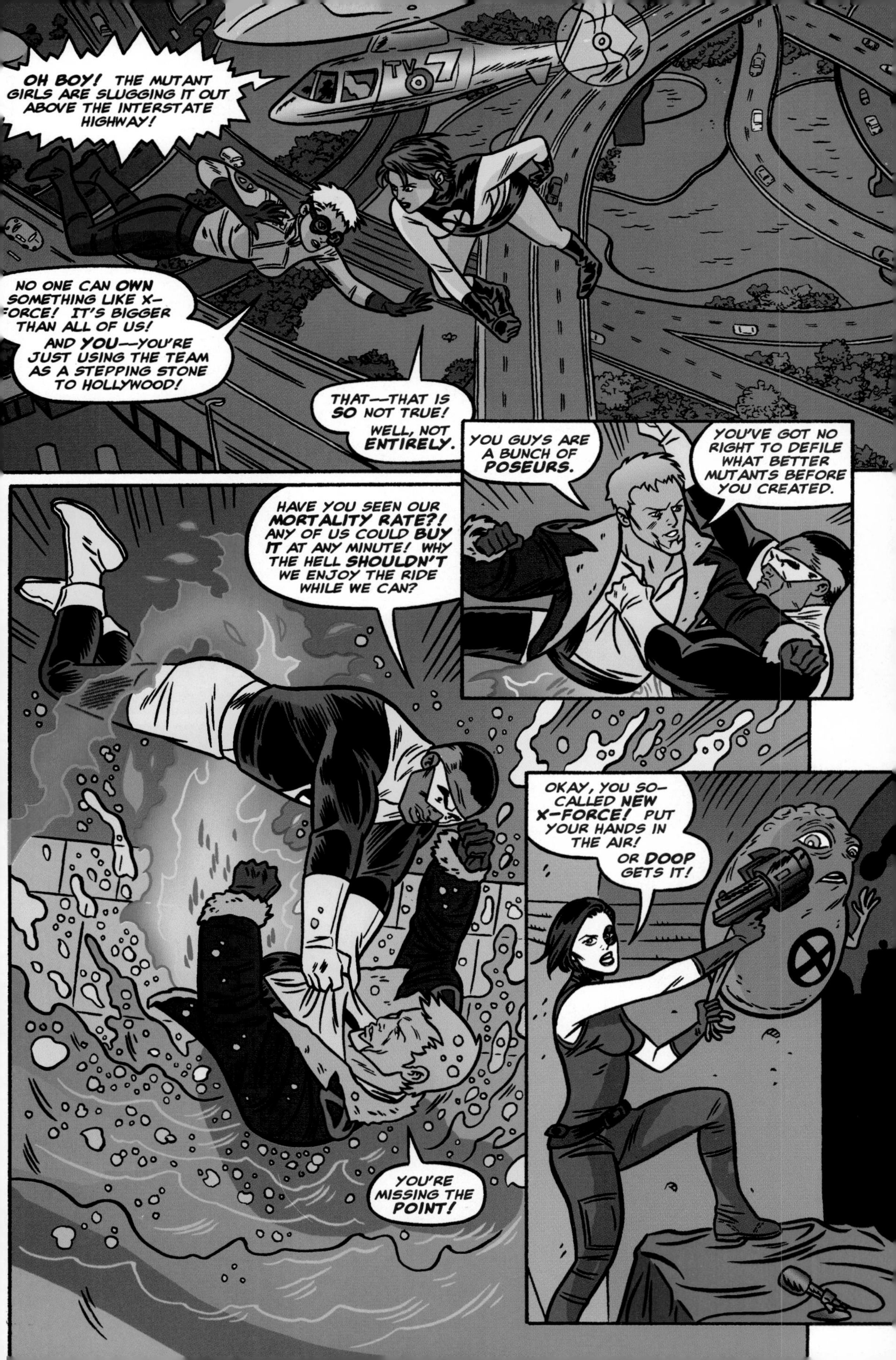
OH BOY! THE MUTANT GIRLS ARE SLUGGING IT OUT ABOVE THE INTERSTATE HIGHWAY!
NO ONE CAN OWN SOMETHING LIKE X-FORCE! IT'S BIGGER THAN ALL OF US!
AND YOU--YOU'RE JUST USING THE TEAM AS A STEPPING STONE TO HOLLYWOOD!
THAT--THAT IS SO NOT TRUE!
WELL, NOT ENTIRELY.
YOU GUYS ARE A BUNCH OF POSEURS.
YOU'VE GOT NO RIGHT TO DEFILE WHAT BETTER MUTANTS BEFORE YOU CREATED.
HAVE YOU SEEN OUR MORTALITY RATE?! ANY OF US COULD BUY IT AT ANY MINUTE! WHY THE HELL SHOULDN'T WE ENJOY THE RIDE WHILE WE CAN?
YOU'RE MISSING THE POINT!
OKAY, YOU SO-CALLED NEW X-FORCE! PUT YOUR HANDS IN THE AIR!
OR DOOP GETS IT!

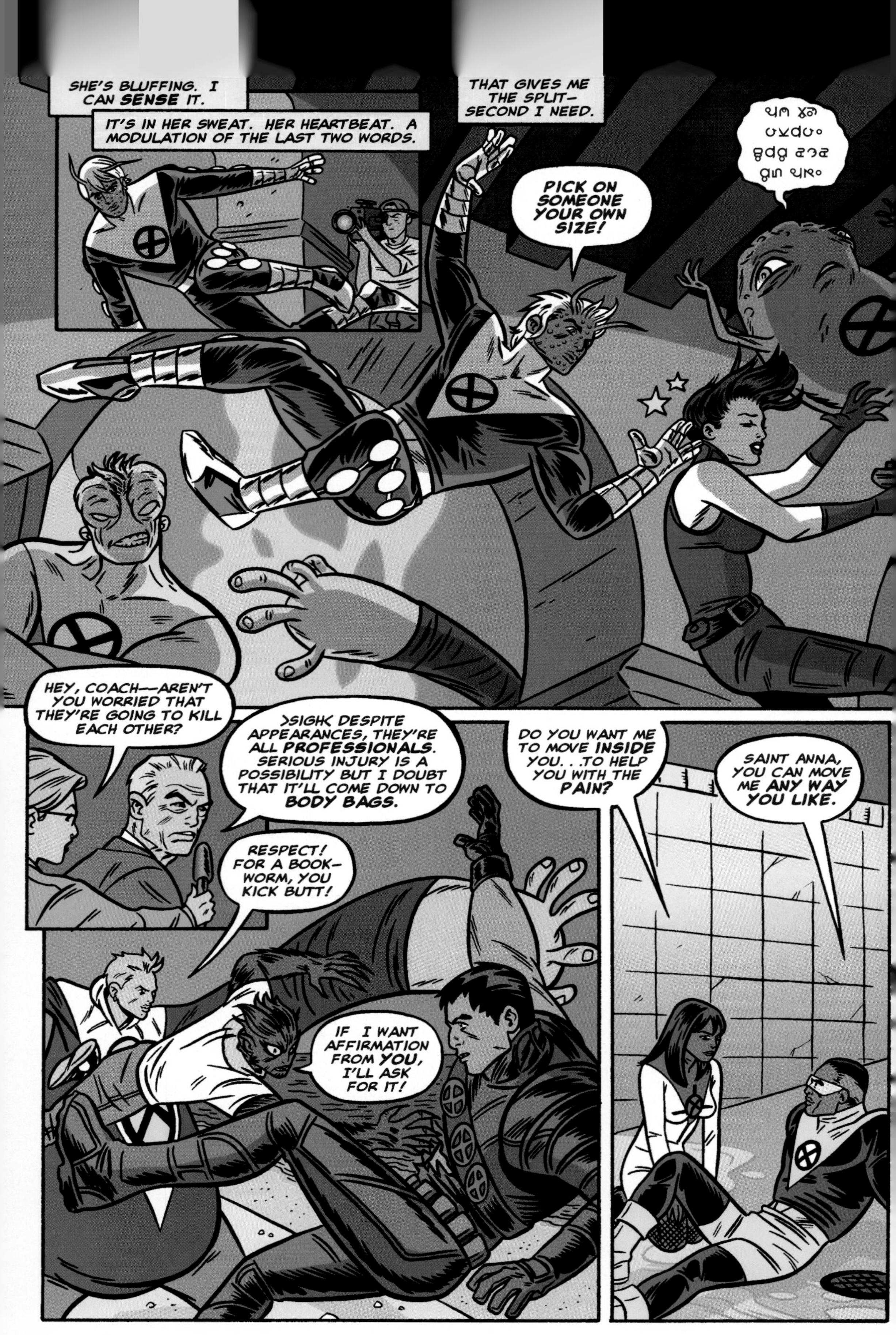
SHE'S BLUFFING. I CAN SENSE IT.
IT'S IN HER SWEAT. HER HEARTBEAT. A MODULATION OF THE LAST TWO WORDS.
THAT GIVES ME THE SPLIT-SECOND I NEED.
PICK ON SOMEONE YOUR OWN SIZE!
HEY, COACH--AREN'T YOU WORRIED THAT THEY'RE GOING TO KILL EACH OTHER?
>SIGH< DESPITE APPEARANCES, THEY'RE ALL PROFESSIONALS. SERIOUS INJURY IS A POSSIBILITY BUT I DOUBT THAT IT'LL COME DOWN TO BODY BAGS.
RESPECT! FOR A BOOK-WORM, YOU KICK BUTT!
IF I WANT AFFIRMATION FROM YOU, I'LL ASK FOR IT!
DO YOU WANT ME TO MOVE INSIDE YOU. . .TO HELP YOU WITH THE PAIN?
SAINT ANNA, YOU CAN MOVE ME ANY WAY YOU LIKE.

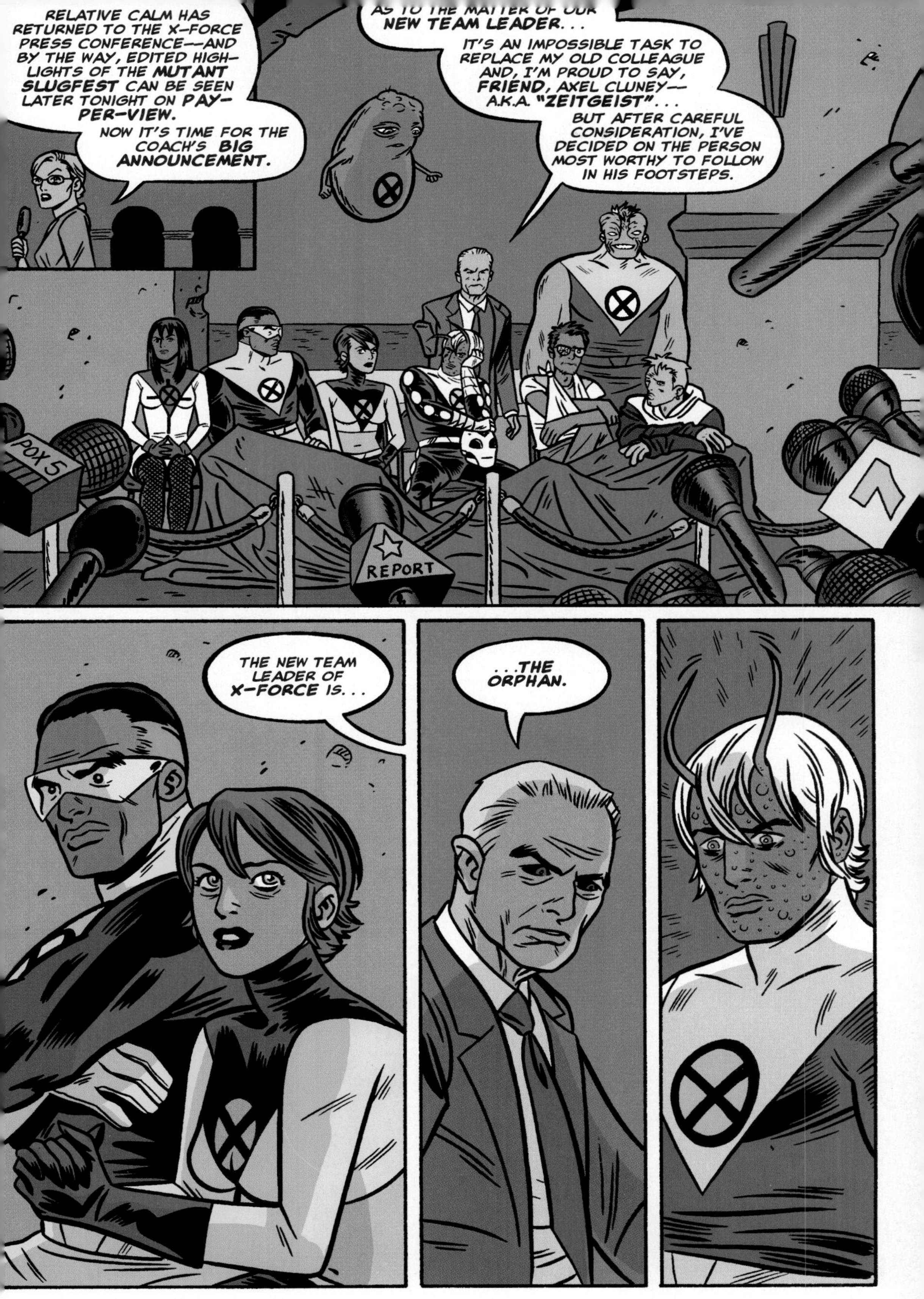

RELATIVE CALM HAS RETURNED TO THE X-FORCE PRESS CONFERENCE--AND BY THE WAY, EDITED HIGHLIGHTS OF THE MUTANT SLUGFEST CAN BE SEEN LATER TONIGHT ON PAY-PER-VIEW.
NOW IT'S TIME FOR THE COACH'S BIG ANNOUNCEMENT.
AS TO THE MATTER OF OUR NEW TEAM LEADER...
IT'S AN IMPOSSIBLE TASK TO REPLACE MY OLD COLLEAGUE AND, I'M PROUD TO SAY, FRIEND, AXEL CLUNEY--A.K.A. "ZEITGEIST"...
BUT AFTER CAREFUL CONSIDERATION, I'VE DECIDED ON THE PERSON MOST WORTHY TO FOLLOW IN HIS FOOTSTEPS.
POX 5
REPORT
THE NEW TEAM LEADER OF X-FORCE IS...
...THE ORPHAN.

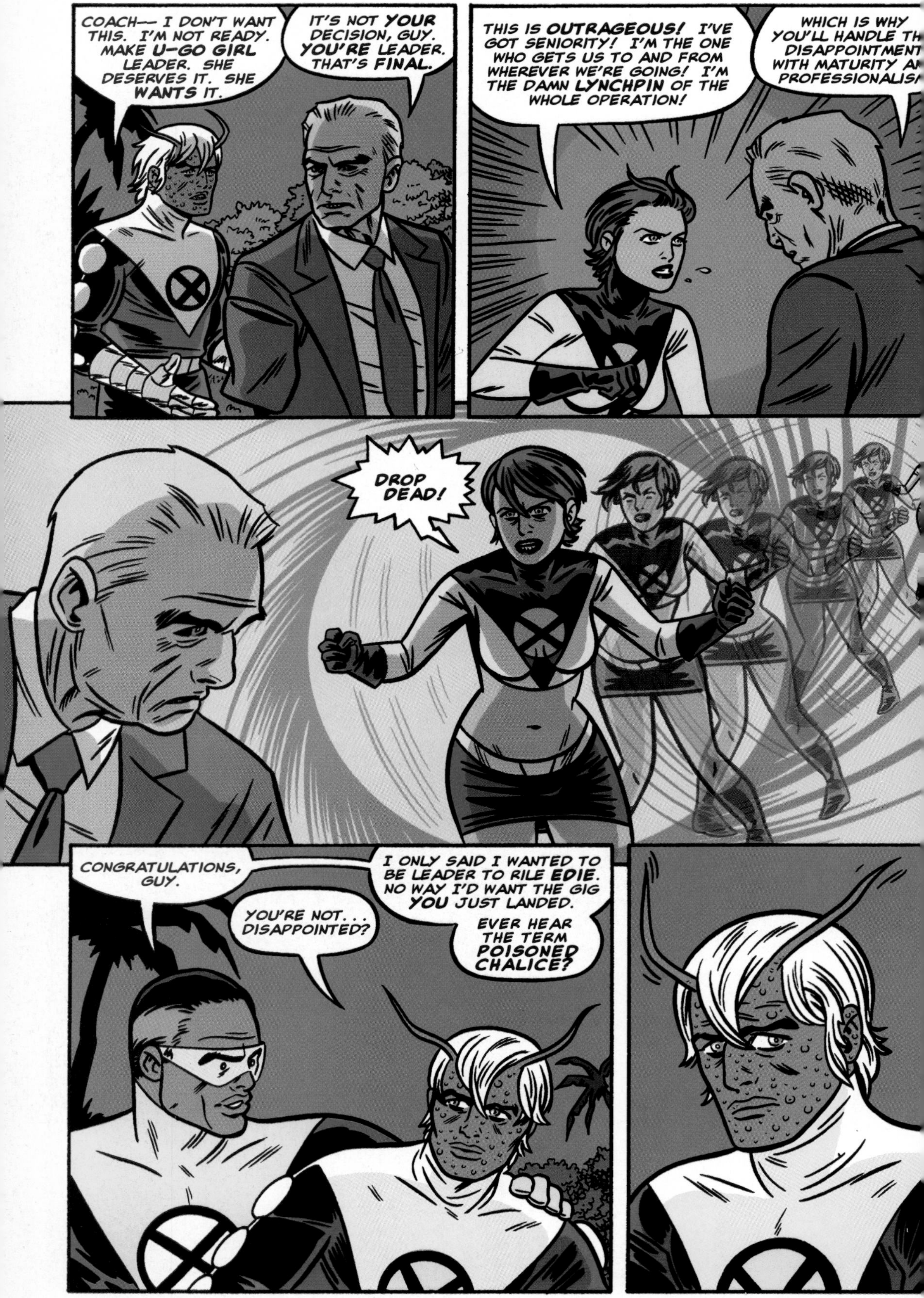
COACH— I DON'T WANT THIS. I'M NOT READY. MAKE U-GO GIRL LEADER. SHE DESERVES IT. SHE WANTS IT.
IT'S NOT YOUR DECISION, GUY. YOU'RE LEADER. THAT'S FINAL.
THIS IS OUTRAGEOUS! I'VE GOT SENIORITY! I'M THE ONE WHO GETS US TO AND FROM WHEREVER WE'RE GOING! I'M THE DAMN LYNCHPIN OF THE WHOLE OPERATION!
WHICH IS WHY YOU'LL HANDLE TH DISAPPOINTMENT WITH MATURITY AN PROFESSIONALIS
DROP DEAD!
CONGRATULATIONS, GUY.
YOU'RE NOT... DISAPPOINTED?
I ONLY SAID I WANTED TO BE LEADER TO RILE EDIE. NO WAY I'D WANT THE GIG YOU JUST LANDED.
EVER HEAR THE TERM POISONED CHALICE?

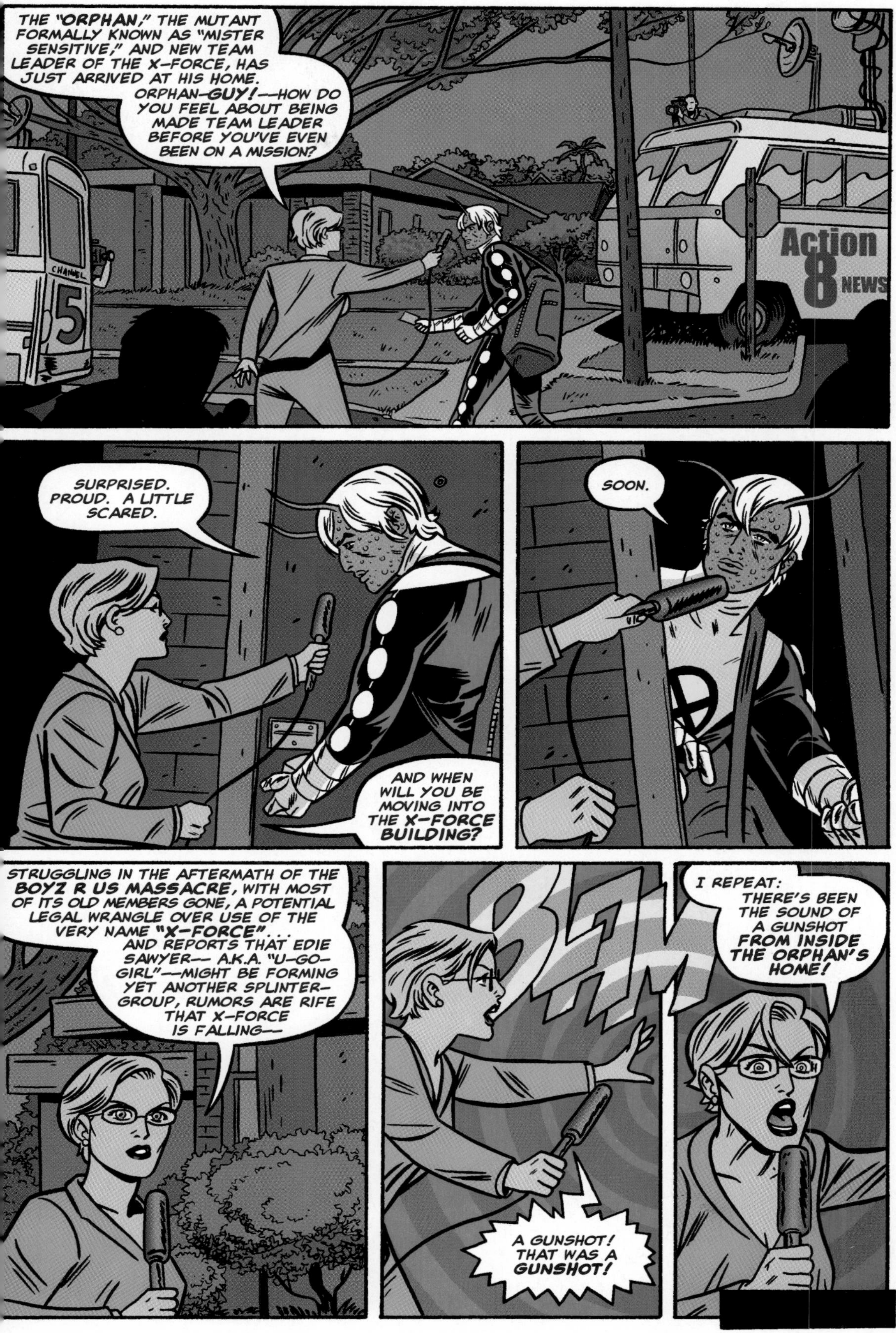

THE "ORPHAN," THE MUTANT FORMALLY KNOWN AS "MISTER SENSITIVE," AND NEW TEAM LEADER OF THE X-FORCE, HAS JUST ARRIVED AT HIS HOME.
ORPHAN-GUY!--HOW DO YOU FEEL ABOUT BEING MADE TEAM LEADER BEFORE YOU'VE EVEN BEEN ON A MISSION?
CHANNEL 5
Action 8 NEWS
SURPRISED. PROUD. A LITTLE SCARED.
AND WHEN WILL YOU BE MOVING INTO THE X-FORCE BUILDING?
SOON.
STRUGGLING IN THE AFTERMATH OF THE BOYZ R US MASSACRE, WITH MOST OF ITS OLD MEMBERS GONE, A POTENTIAL LEGAL WRANGLE OVER USE OF THE VERY NAME "X-FORCE"...
AND REPORTS THAT EDIE SAWYER-- A.K.A. "U-GO-GIRL"--MIGHT BE FORMING YET ANOTHER SPLINTER-GROUP, RUMORS ARE RIFE THAT X-FORCE IS FALLING--
BLAM
A GUNSHOT! THAT WAS A GUNSHOT!
I REPEAT: THERE'S BEEN THE SOUND OF A GUNSHOT FROM INSIDE THE ORPHAN'S HOME!

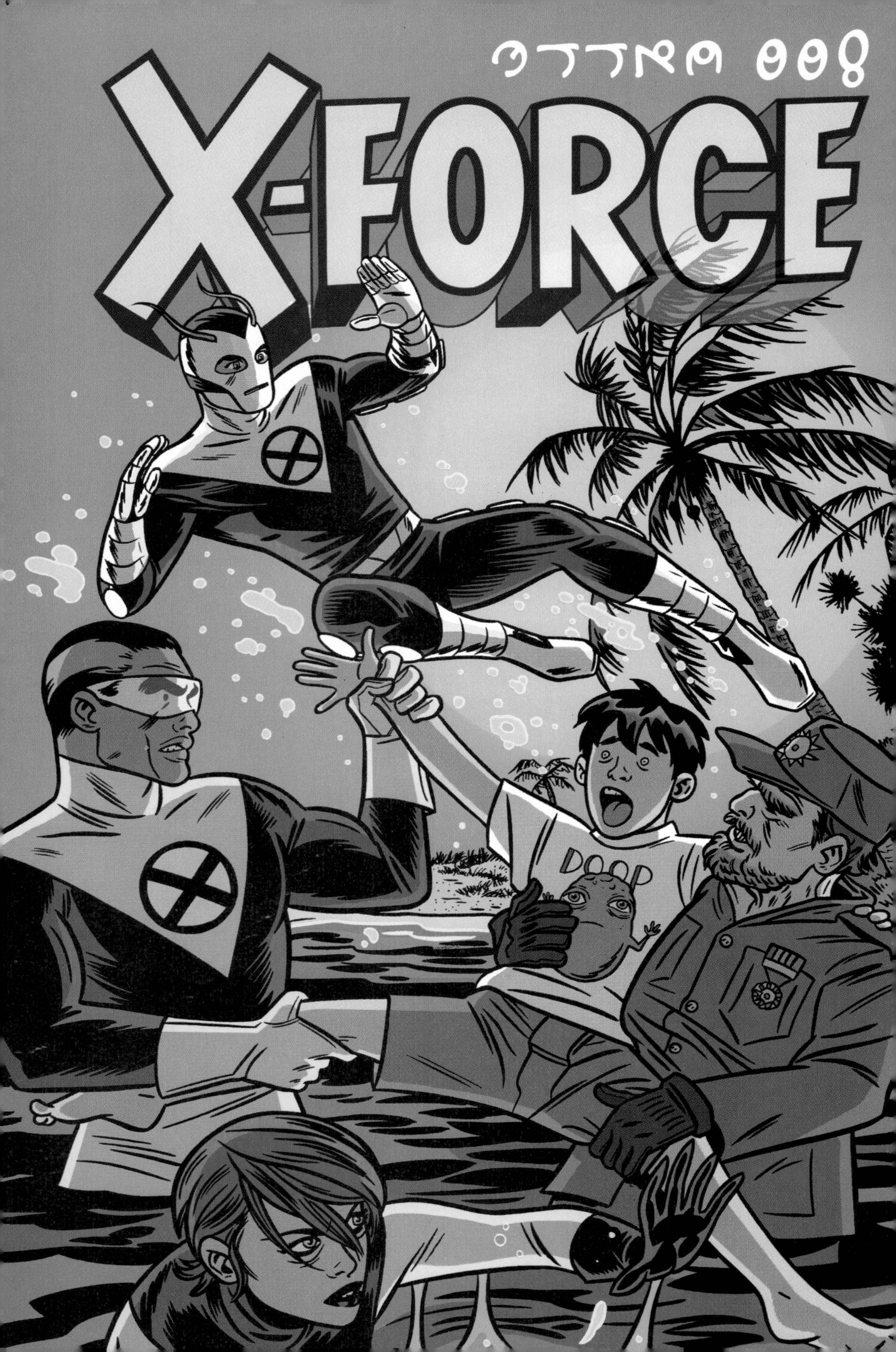
X-FORCE
DOOP

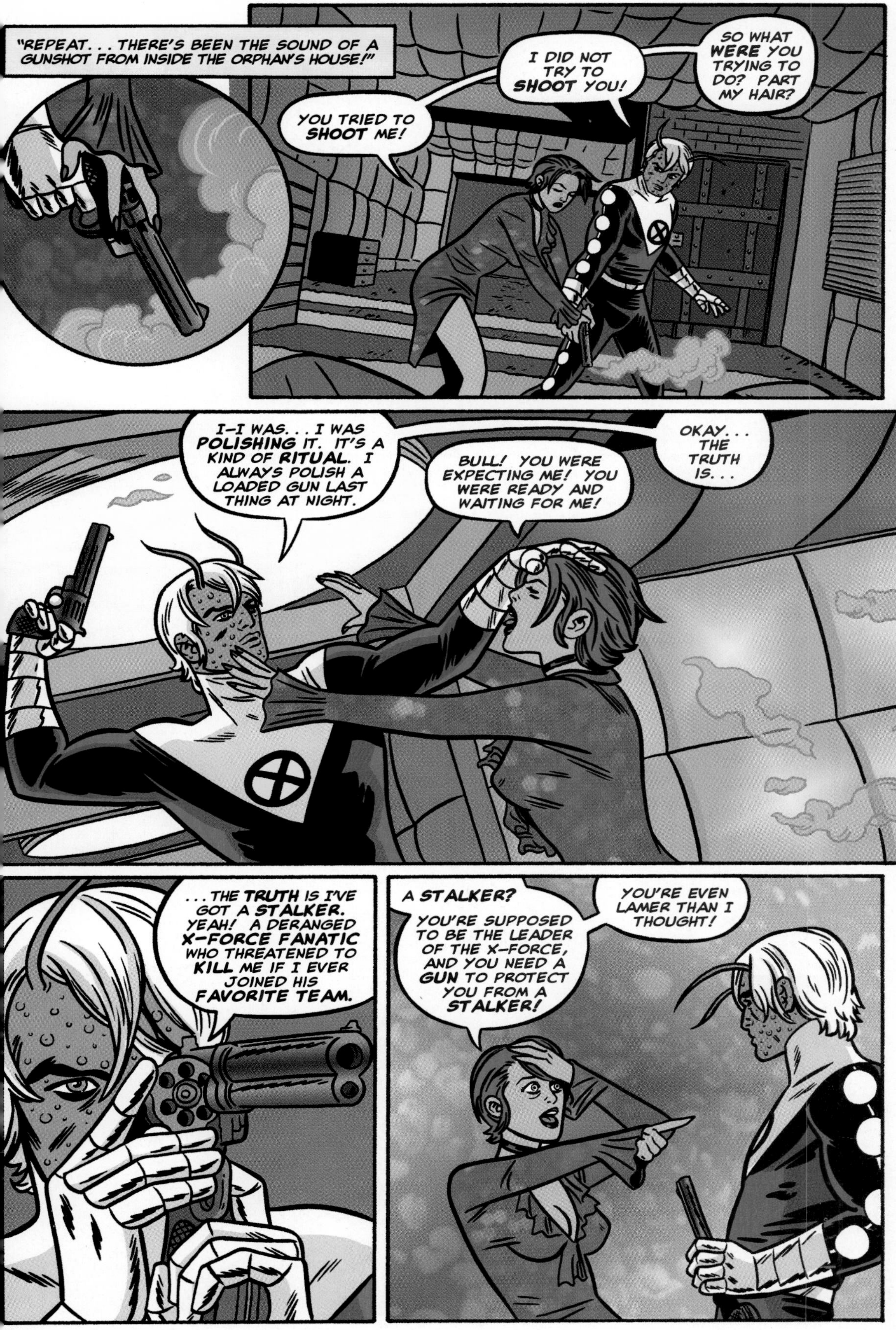
"REPEAT. . . THERE'S BEEN THE SOUND OF A GUNSHOT FROM INSIDE THE ORPHAN'S HOUSE!"
YOU TRIED TO SHOOT ME!
I DID NOT TRY TO SHOOT YOU!
SO WHAT WERE YOU TRYING TO DO? PART MY HAIR?
I–I WAS. . . I WAS POLISHING IT. IT'S A KIND OF RITUAL. I ALWAYS POLISH A LOADED GUN LAST THING AT NIGHT.
BULL! YOU WERE EXPECTING ME! YOU WERE READY AND WAITING FOR ME!
OKAY. . . THE TRUTH IS. . .
. . . THE TRUTH IS I'VE GOT A STALKER. YEAH! A DERANGED X-FORCE FANATIC WHO THREATENED TO KILL ME IF I EVER JOINED HIS FAVORITE TEAM.
A STALKER?
YOU'RE SUPPOSED TO BE THE LEADER OF THE X-FORCE, AND YOU NEED A GUN TO PROTECT YOU FROM A STALKER!
YOU'RE EVEN LAMER THAN I THOUGHT!

WHY DID YOU COME HERE?

I CAME HERE TO **HELP** YOU.

TO MAKE YOU CHANGE YOUR MIND.

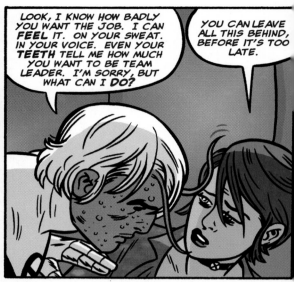

LOOK, I KNOW HOW BADLY YOU WANT THE JOB. I CAN **FEEL** IT. ON YOUR SWEAT. IN YOUR VOICE. EVEN YOUR **TEETH** TELL ME HOW MUCH YOU WANT TO BE TEAM LEADER. I'M SORRY, BUT WHAT CAN I **DO?**

YOU CAN LEAVE ALL THIS BEHIND, BEFORE IT'S TOO LATE.

I CAN **HELP** YOU. I CAN 'PORT YOU SOMEWHERE FAR AWAY. I'VE GOT CASH. I CAN SET YOU UP IN A NEW LIFE, WITH NEW I.D.——

AND I'LL SPEND THE REST OF MY LIFE PRETENDING TO BE SOMEONE I'M NOT?

WE'RE **ALL** PRETENDING TO BE SOMEONE WE'RE NOT, GUY. I MEAN, YOU JUST **REINVENTED** YOURSELF——"MISTER SENSITIVE" BECAME "THE ORPHAN." DO IT AGAIN.

THIS. . .THIS THING I DO. . .IT'S ALL I'M CUT OUT FOR. WITHOUT IT, I'M JUST. . .ANOTHER MUTANT.

WHAT ARE YOU DOING?

SHUT UP AND **THINK,** WHILE YOU STILL CAN.

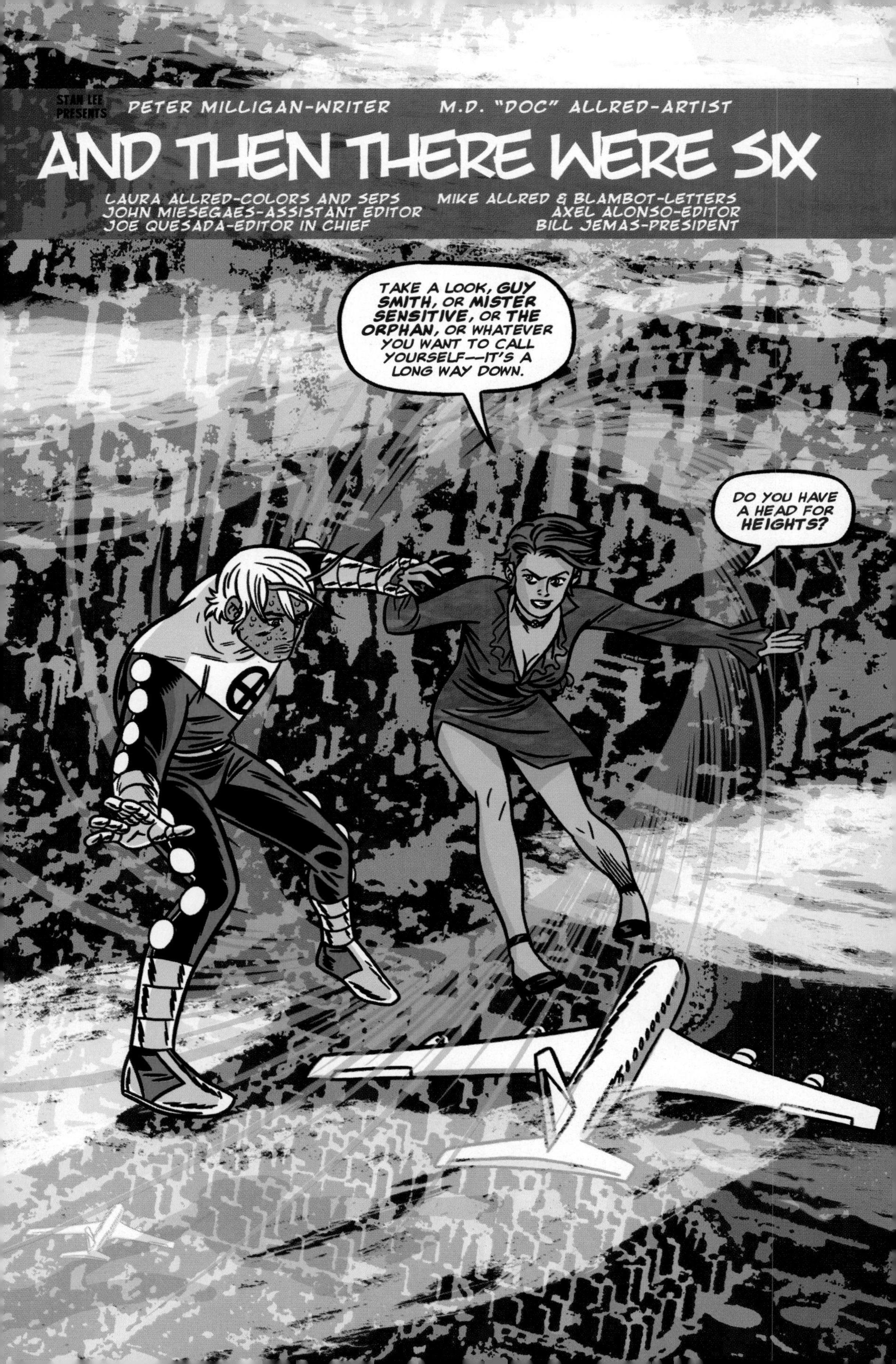
STAN LEE PRESENTS
PETER MILLIGAN-WRITER
M.D. "DOC" ALLRED-ARTIST
AND THEN THERE WERE SIX
LAURA ALLRED-COLORS AND SEPS
JOHN MIESEGAES-ASSISTANT EDITOR
JOE QUESADA-EDITOR IN CHIEF
MIKE ALLRED & BLAMBOT-LETTERS
AXEL ALONSO-EDITOR
BILL JEMAS-PRESIDENT
TAKE A LOOK, GUY SMITH, OR MISTER SENSITIVE, OR THE ORPHAN, OR WHATEVER YOU WANT TO CALL YOURSELF--IT'S A LONG WAY DOWN.
DO YOU HAVE A HEAD FOR HEIGHTS?

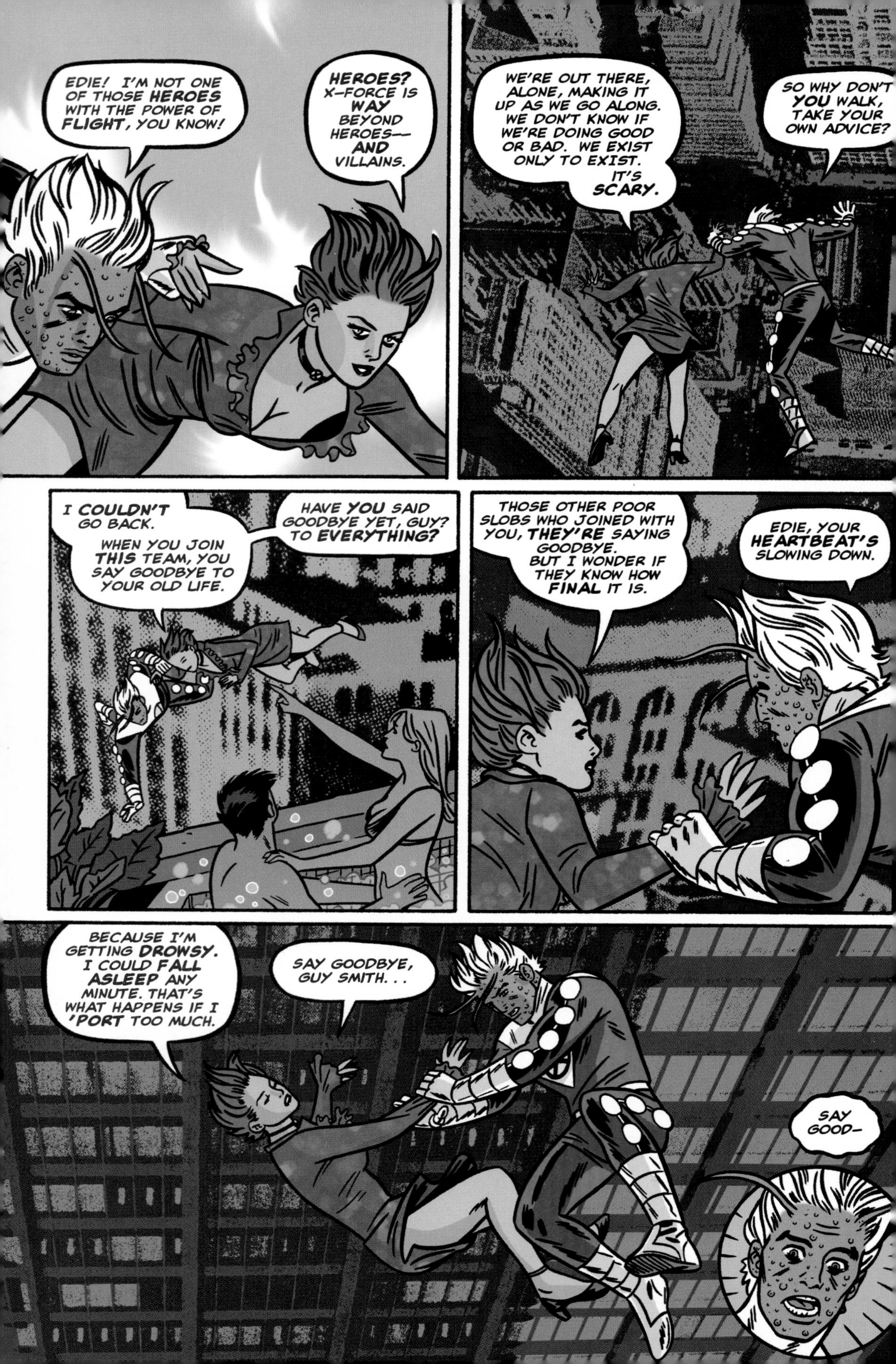

EDIE! I'M NOT ONE OF THOSE HEROES WITH THE POWER OF FLIGHT, YOU KNOW!
HEROES? X-FORCE IS WAY BEYOND HEROES-- AND VILLAINS.
WE'RE OUT THERE, ALONE, MAKING IT UP AS WE GO ALONG. WE DON'T KNOW IF WE'RE DOING GOOD OR BAD. WE EXIST ONLY TO EXIST. IT'S SCARY.
SO WHY DON'T YOU WALK, TAKE YOUR OWN ADVICE?
I COULDN'T GO BACK.
WHEN YOU JOIN THIS TEAM, YOU SAY GOODBYE TO YOUR OLD LIFE.
HAVE YOU SAID GOODBYE YET, GUY? TO EVERYTHING?
THOSE OTHER POOR SLOBS WHO JOINED WITH YOU, THEY'RE SAYING GOODBYE.
BUT I WONDER IF THEY KNOW HOW FINAL IT IS.
EDIE, YOUR HEARTBEAT'S SLOWING DOWN.
BECAUSE I'M GETTING DROWSY. I COULD FALL ASLEEP ANY MINUTE. THAT'S WHAT HAPPENS IF I 'PORT TOO MUCH.
SAY GOODBYE, GUY SMITH. . .
SAY GOOD-

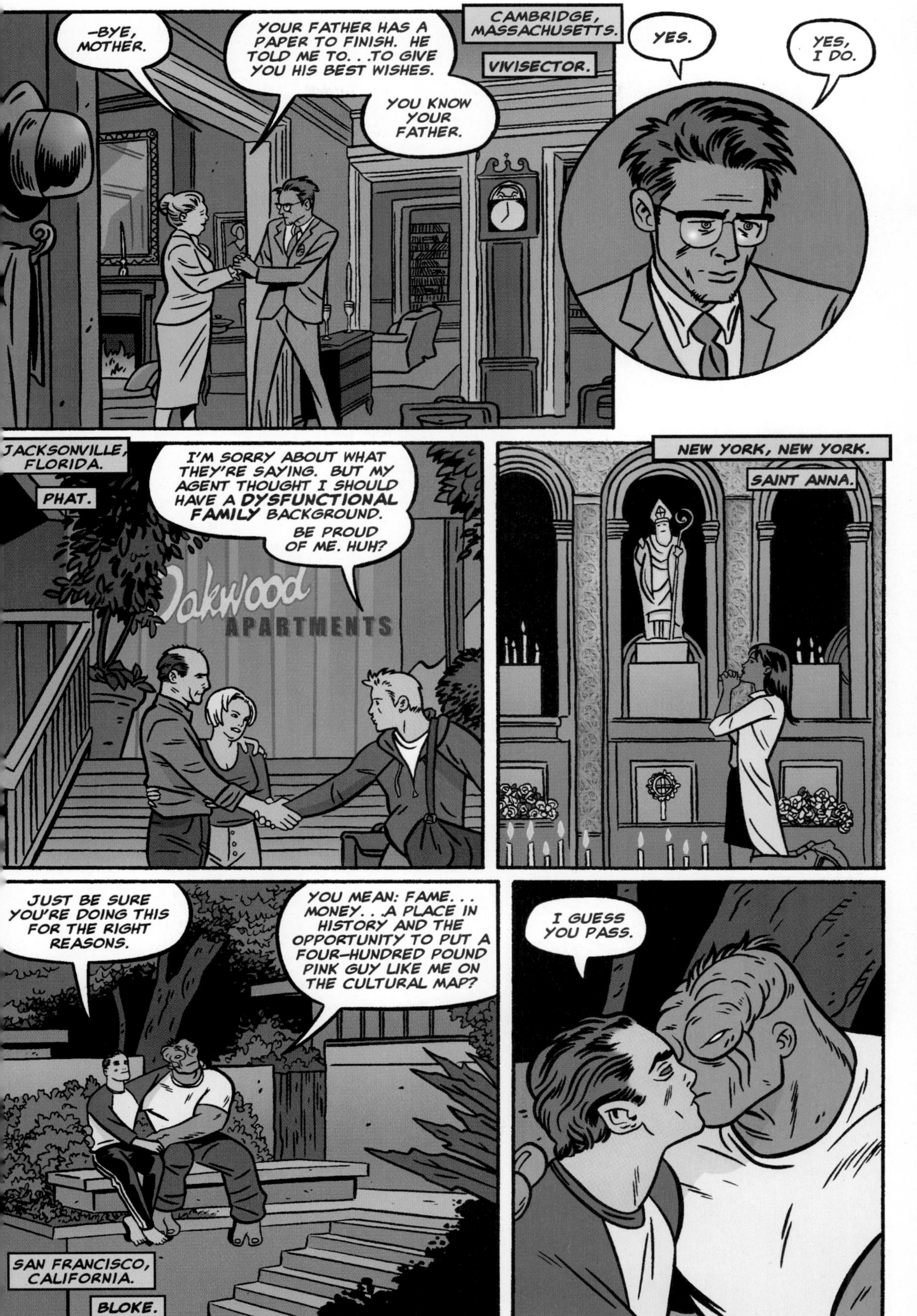

CAMBRIDGE, MASSACHUSETTS.
VIVISECTOR.
–BYE, MOTHER.
YOUR FATHER HAS A PAPER TO FINISH. HE TOLD ME TO. . .TO GIVE YOU HIS BEST WISHES.
YOU KNOW YOUR FATHER.
YES.
YES, I DO.
JACKSONVILLE, FLORIDA.
PHAT.
I'M SORRY ABOUT WHAT THEY'RE SAYING. BUT MY AGENT THOUGHT I SHOULD HAVE A DYSFUNCTIONAL FAMILY BACKGROUND.
BE PROUD OF ME. HUH?
Oakwood
APARTMENTS
NEW YORK, NEW YORK.
SAINT ANNA.
SAN FRANCISCO, CALIFORNIA.
BLOKE.
JUST BE SURE YOU'RE DOING THIS FOR THE RIGHT REASONS.
YOU MEAN: FAME. . . MONEY. . .A PLACE IN HISTORY AND THE OPPORTUNITY TO PUT A FOUR–HUNDRED POUND PINK GUY LIKE ME ON THE CULTURAL MAP?
I GUESS YOU PASS.

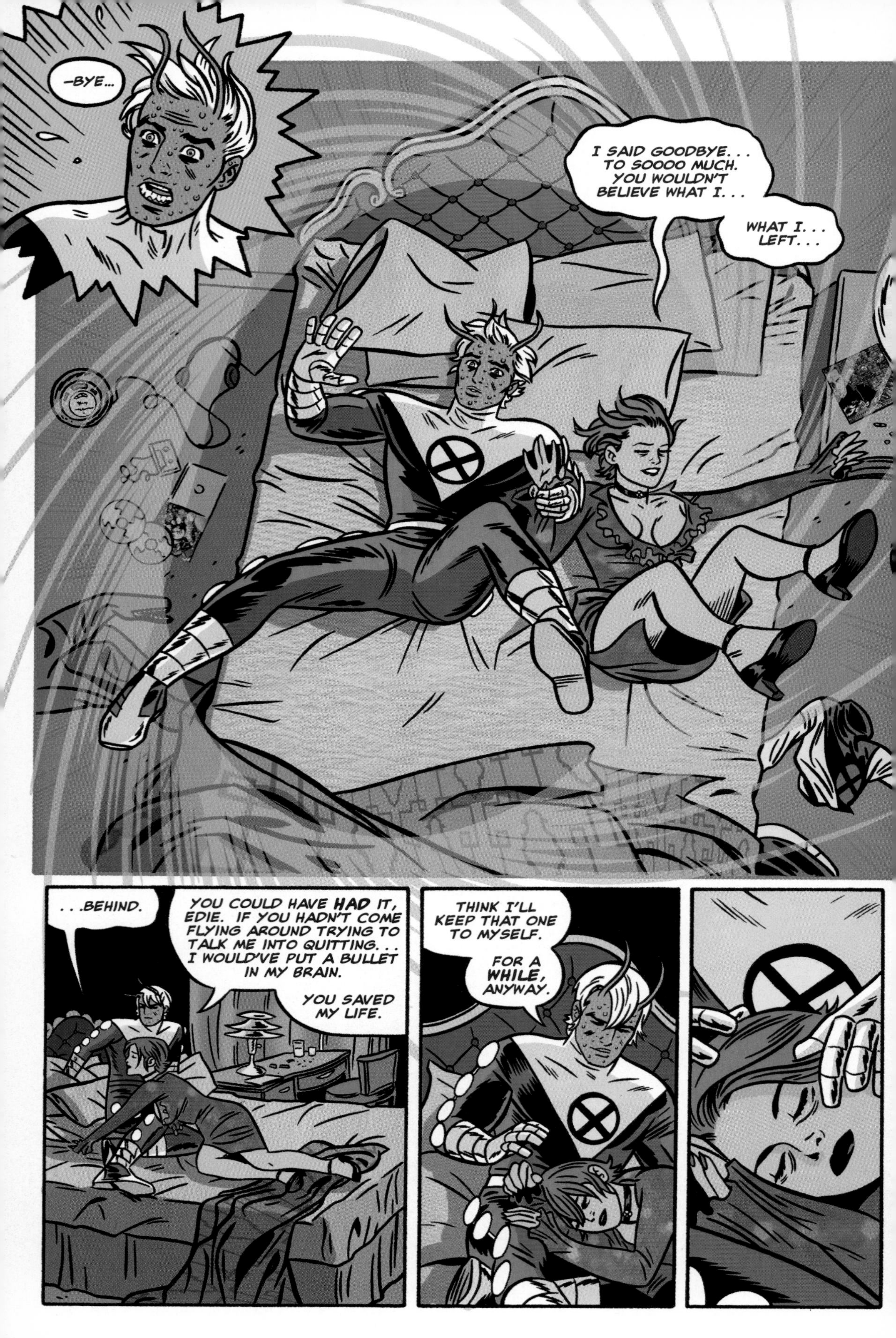
–BYE...
I SAID GOODBYE. . . TO SOOOO MUCH. YOU WOULDN'T BELIEVE WHAT I. . .
WHAT I. . . LEFT. . .
. . .BEHIND.
YOU COULD HAVE HAD IT, EDIE. IF YOU HADN'T COME FLYING AROUND TRYING TO TALK ME INTO QUITTING. . . I WOULD'VE PUT A BULLET IN MY BRAIN.
YOU SAVED MY LIFE.
THINK I'LL KEEP THAT ONE TO MYSELF.
FOR A WHILE, ANYWAY.

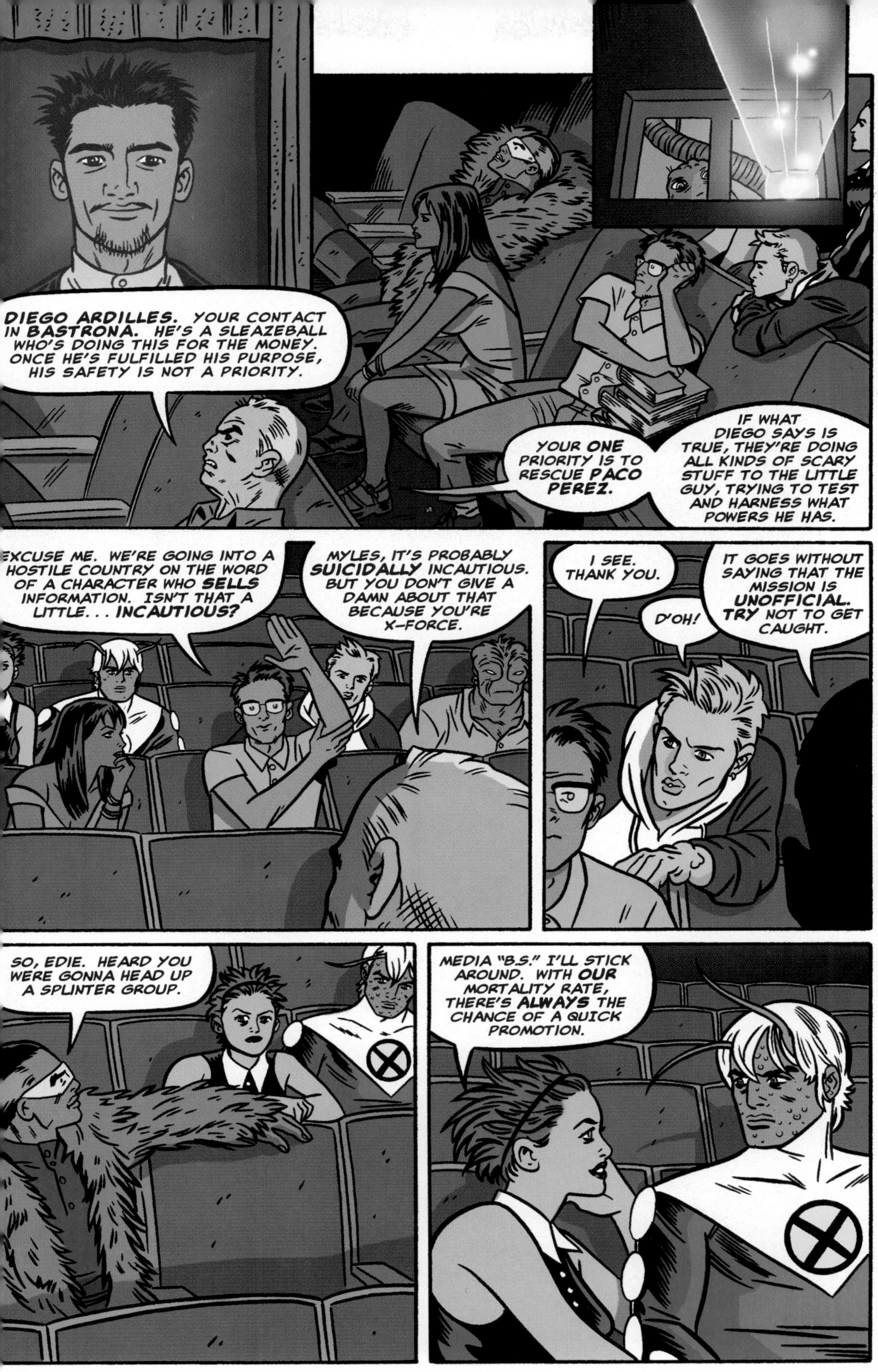
DIEGO ARDILLES. YOUR CONTACT IN BASTRONA. HE'S A SLEAZEBALL WHO'S DOING THIS FOR THE MONEY. ONCE HE'S FULFILLED HIS PURPOSE, HIS SAFETY IS NOT A PRIORITY.
YOUR ONE PRIORITY IS TO RESCUE PACO PEREZ.
IF WHAT DIEGO SAYS IS TRUE, THEY'RE DOING ALL KINDS OF SCARY STUFF TO THE LITTLE GUY, TRYING TO TEST AND HARNESS WHAT POWERS HE HAS.
EXCUSE ME. WE'RE GOING INTO A HOSTILE COUNTRY ON THE WORD OF A CHARACTER WHO SELLS INFORMATION. ISN'T THAT A LITTLE... INCAUTIOUS?
MYLES, IT'S PROBABLY SUICIDALLY INCAUTIOUS. BUT YOU DON'T GIVE A DAMN ABOUT THAT BECAUSE YOU'RE X-FORCE.
I SEE. THANK YOU.
D'OH!
IT GOES WITHOUT SAYING THAT THE MISSION IS UNOFFICIAL. TRY NOT TO GET CAUGHT.
SO, EDIE. HEARD YOU WERE GONNA HEAD UP A SPLINTER GROUP.
MEDIA "B.S." I'LL STICK AROUND. WITH OUR MORTALITY RATE, THERE'S ALWAYS THE CHANCE OF A QUICK PROMOTION.

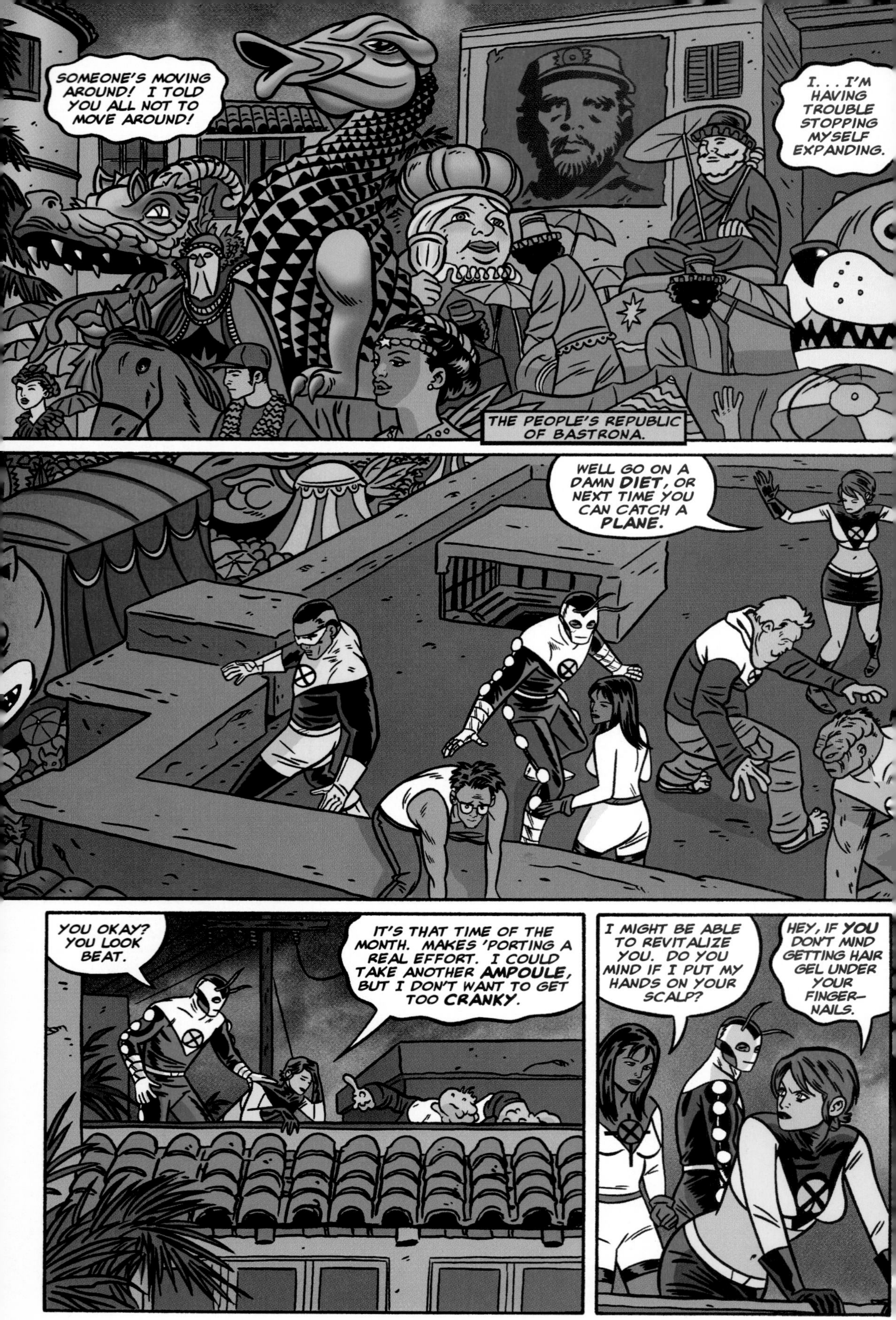
SOMEONE'S MOVING AROUND! I TOLD YOU ALL NOT TO MOVE AROUND!
I . . . I'M HAVING TROUBLE STOPPING MYSELF EXPANDING.
THE PEOPLE'S REPUBLIC OF BASTRONA.
WELL GO ON A DAMN DIET, OR NEXT TIME YOU CAN CATCH A PLANE.
YOU OKAY? YOU LOOK BEAT.
IT'S THAT TIME OF THE MONTH. MAKES 'PORTING A REAL EFFORT. I COULD TAKE ANOTHER AMPOULE, BUT I DON'T WANT TO GET TOO CRANKY.
I MIGHT BE ABLE TO REVITALIZE YOU. DO YOU MIND IF I PUT MY HANDS ON YOUR SCALP?
HEY, IF YOU DON'T MIND GETTING HAIR GEL UNDER YOUR FINGER-NAILS.

QUITE FASCINATING IMAGERY. INDIGENOUS SPIRIT WORSHIP... UNRECONSTRUCTED SOCIALISM... HALF-REMEMBERED CATHOLICISM.

AND SOME A DEM CHICKENS CAN REALLY SHAKE IT.

NOT TO MENTION THE ROOSTERS.

WAIT FOR ME HERE.

YOU'RE NOT GOING DOWN THERE ON YOUR OWN?

I THOUGHT THAT WAS THE KIND OF THING TEAM LEADERS DID.

MAYBE IF I ACT LIKE ONE, I'LL START TO FEEL LIKE ONE.

DOOP, GET SOME SHOTS OF THE PARADE. IT'LL GIVE THE FILM SOME- THING INTERESTING TO CUT AWAY TO.

LISTEN TO YOU, MR. SODERBERGH!

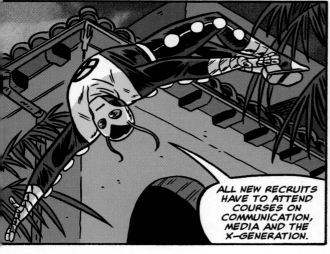

ALL NEW RECRUITS HAVE TO ATTEND COURSES ON COMMUNICATION, MEDIA AND THE X-GENERATION.

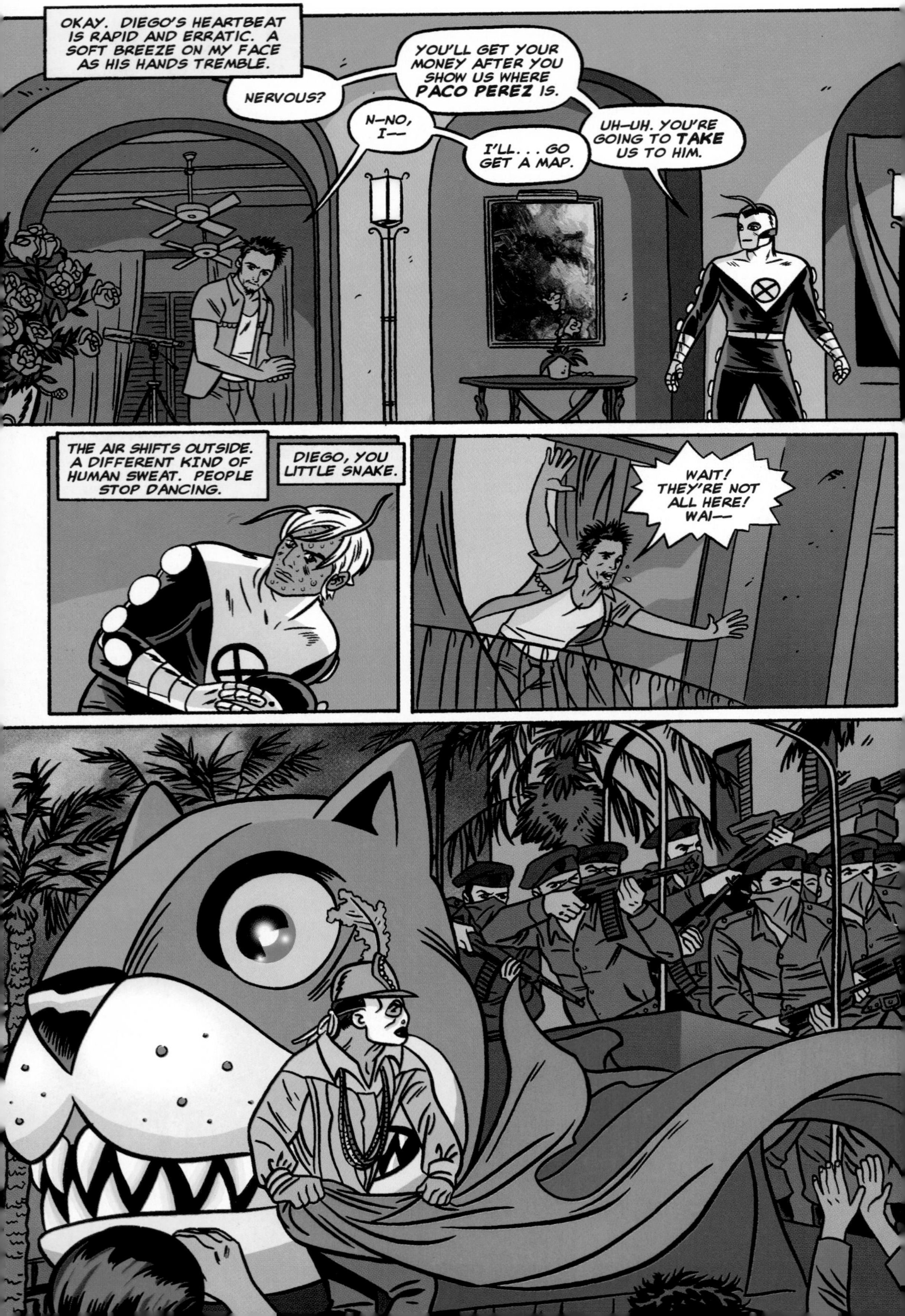
OKAY. DIEGO'S HEARTBEAT IS RAPID AND ERRATIC. A SOFT BREEZE ON MY FACE AS HIS HANDS TREMBLE.
NERVOUS?
YOU'LL GET YOUR MONEY AFTER YOU SHOW US WHERE PACO PEREZ IS.
N—NO, I—
I'LL. . . GO GET A MAP.
UH—UH. YOU'RE GOING TO TAKE US TO HIM.
THE AIR SHIFTS OUTSIDE. A DIFFERENT KIND OF HUMAN SWEAT. PEOPLE STOP DANCING.
DIEGO, YOU LITTLE SNAKE.
WAIT! THEY'RE NOT ALL HERE! WAI—

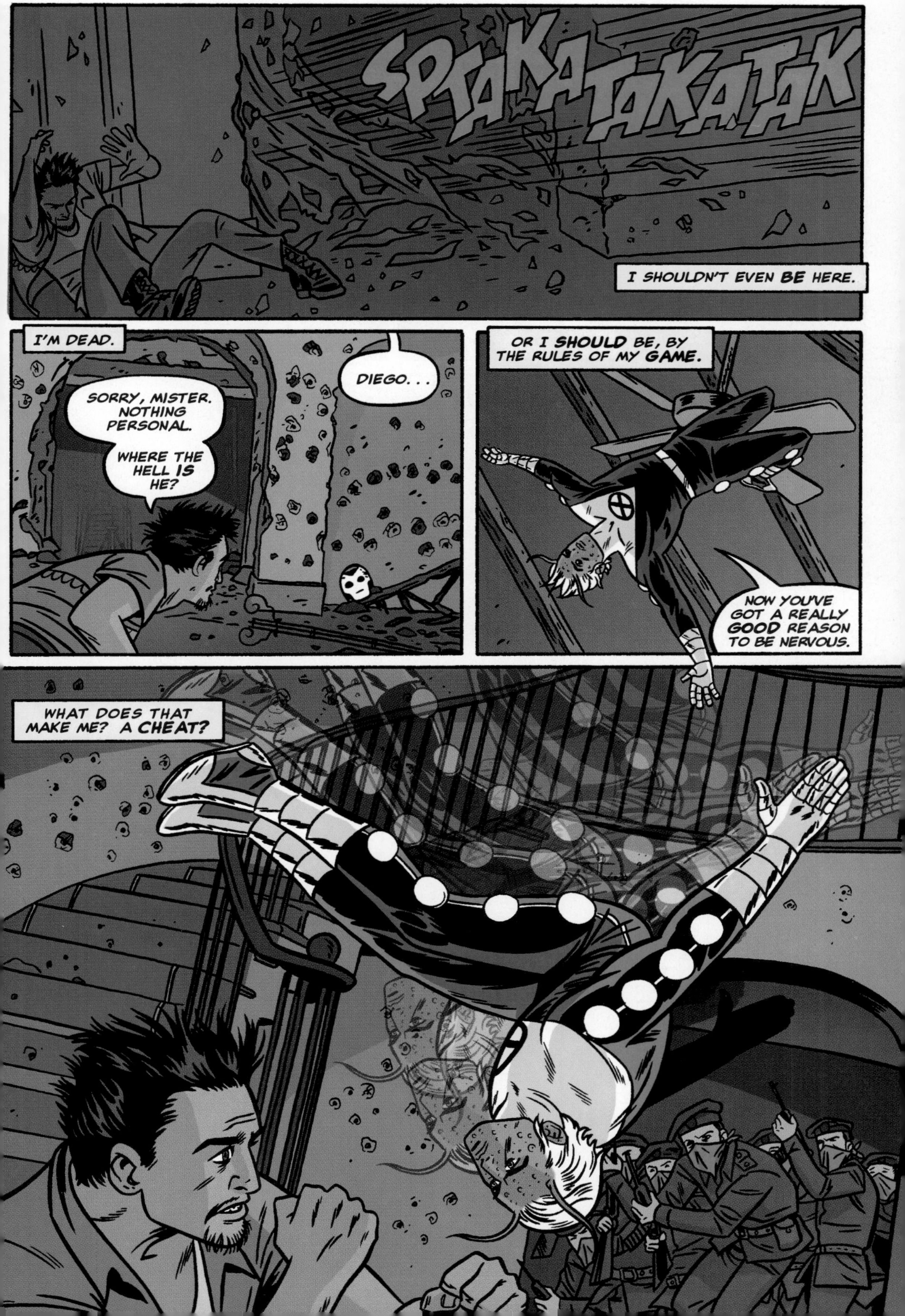
SPTAKATAKATAK
I SHOULDN'T EVEN BE HERE.
I'M DEAD.
SORRY, MISTER. NOTHING PERSONAL.
WHERE THE HELL IS HE?
DIEGO. . .
OR I SHOULD BE, BY THE RULES OF MY GAME.
NOW YOU'VE GOT A REALLY GOOD REASON TO BE NERVOUS.
WHAT DOES THAT MAKE ME? A CHEAT?

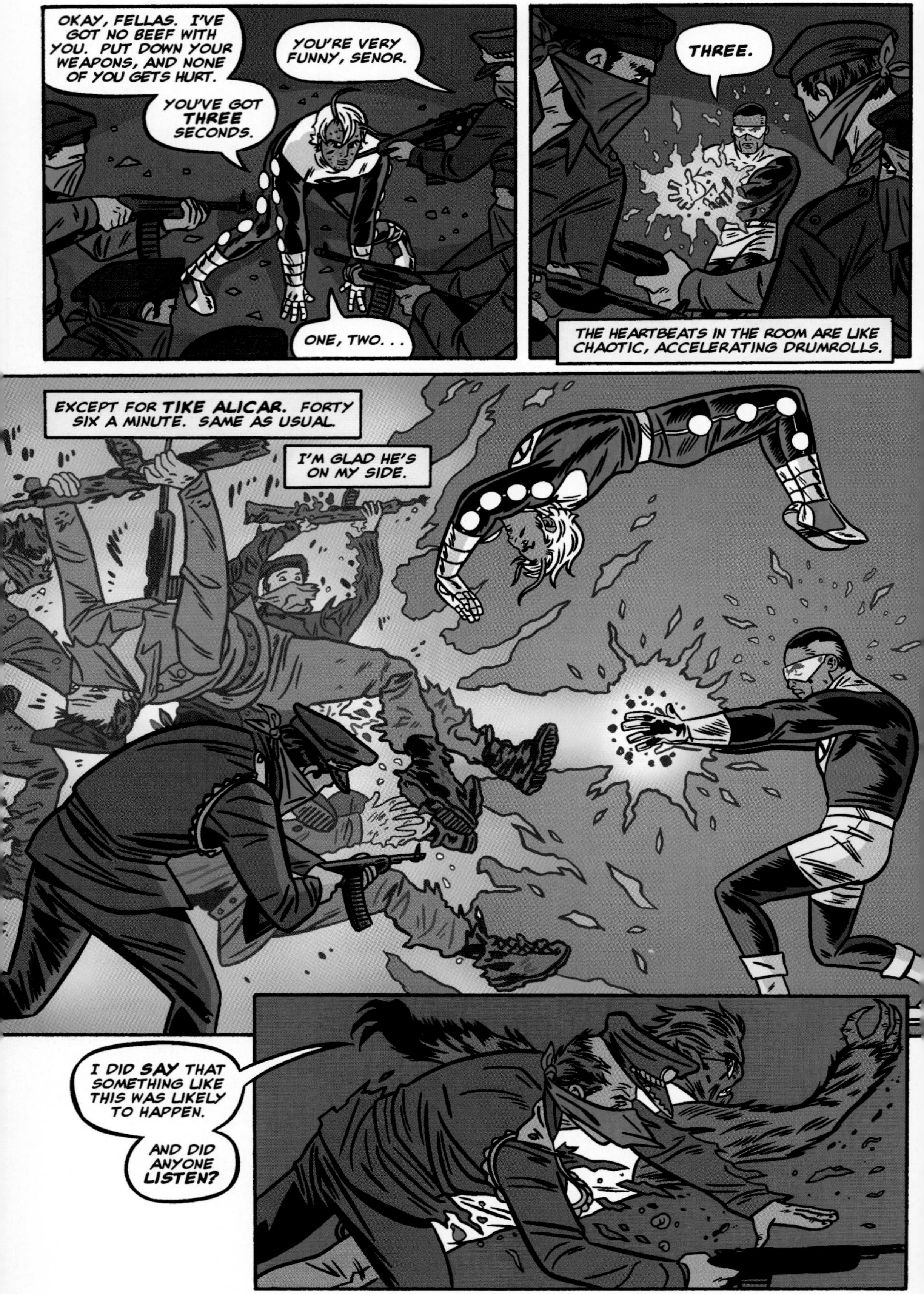
OKAY, FELLAS. I'VE GOT NO BEEF WITH YOU. PUT DOWN YOUR WEAPONS, AND NONE OF YOU GETS HURT.
YOU'VE GOT THREE SECONDS.
YOU'RE VERY FUNNY, SENOR.
ONE, TWO. . .
THREE.
THE HEARTBEATS IN THE ROOM ARE LIKE CHAOTIC, ACCELERATING DRUMROLLS.
EXCEPT FOR TIKE ALICAR. FORTY SIX A MINUTE. SAME AS USUAL.
I'M GLAD HE'S ON MY SIDE.
I DID SAY THAT SOMETHING LIKE THIS WAS LIKELY TO HAPPEN.
AND DID ANYONE LISTEN?

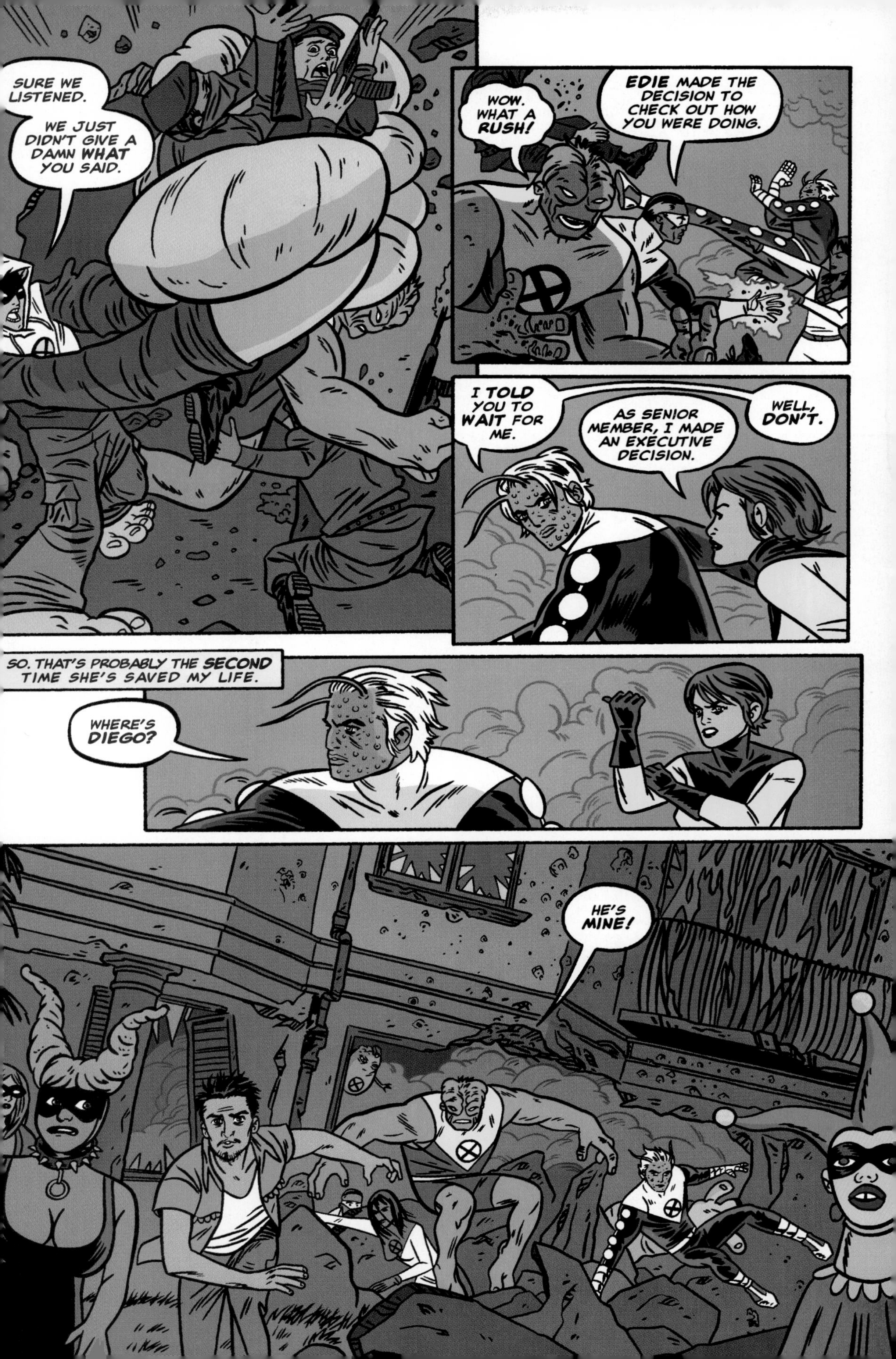
SURE WE LISTENED.
WE JUST DIDN'T GIVE A DAMN WHAT YOU SAID.
WOW. WHAT A RUSH!
EDIE MADE THE DECISION TO CHECK OUT HOW YOU WERE DOING.
I TOLD YOU TO WAIT FOR ME.
AS SENIOR MEMBER, I MADE AN EXECUTIVE DECISION.
WELL, DON'T.
SO. THAT'S PROBABLY THE SECOND TIME SHE'S SAVED MY LIFE.
WHERE'S DIEGO?
HE'S MINE!

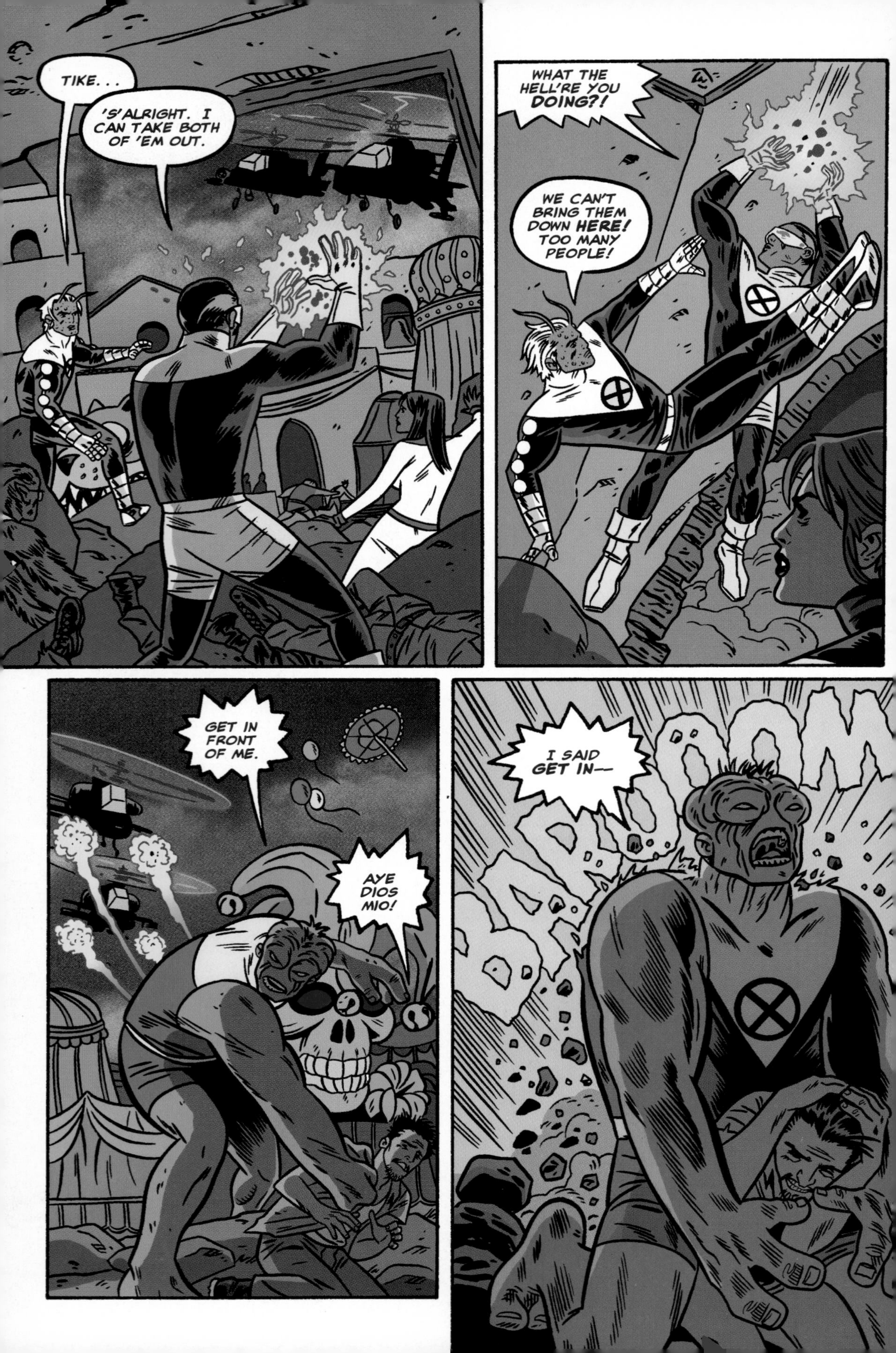
TIKE...
'S' ALRIGHT. I CAN TAKE BOTH OF 'EM OUT.
WHAT THE HELL'RE YOU DOING?!
WE CAN'T BRING THEM DOWN HERE! TOO MANY PEOPLE!
GET IN FRONT OF ME.
AYE DIOS MIO!
I SAID GET IN--

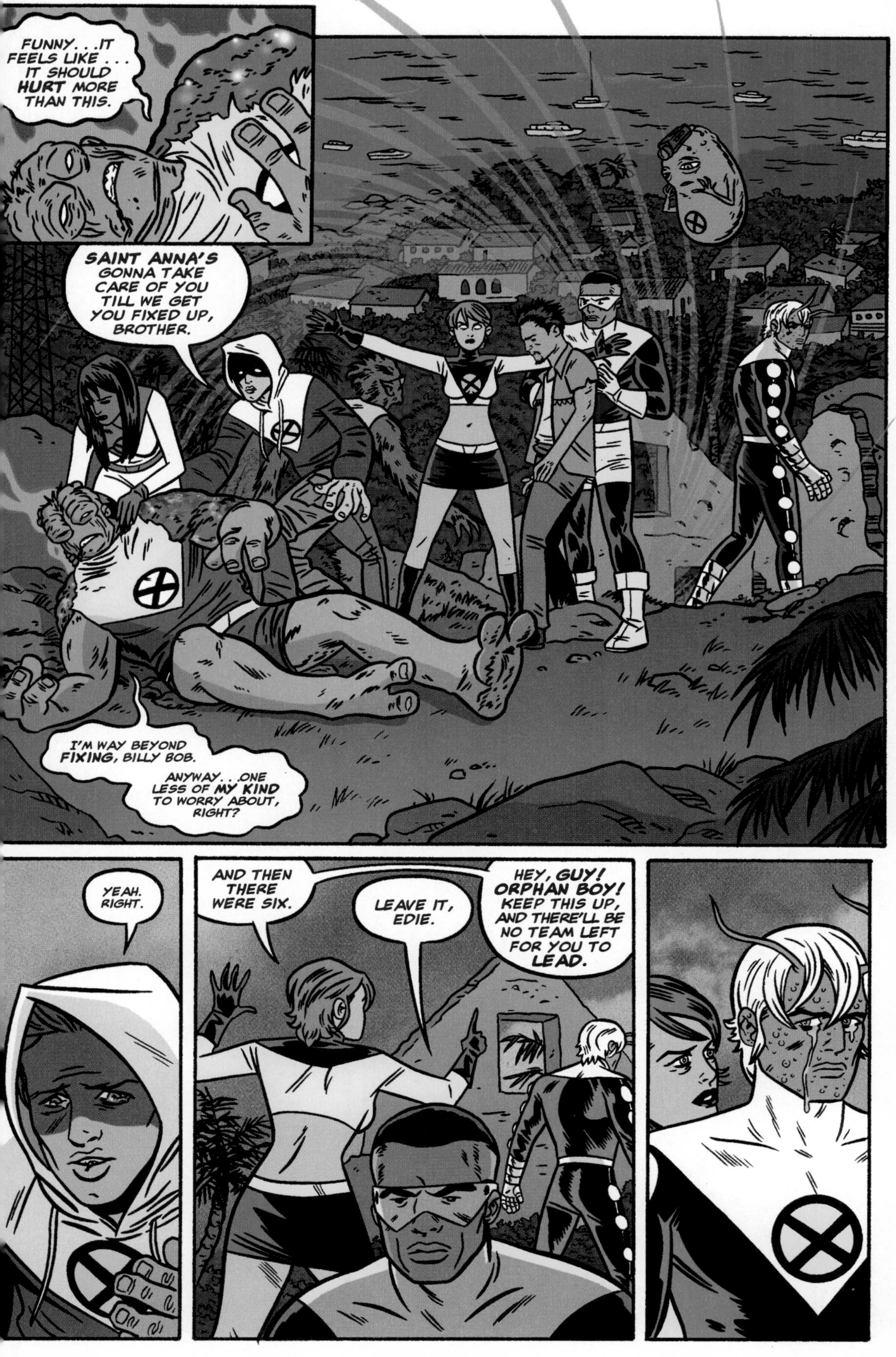
FUNNY. . .IT FEELS LIKE . . . IT SHOULD HURT MORE THAN THIS.
SAINT ANNA'S GONNA TAKE CARE OF YOU TILL WE GET YOU FIXED UP, BROTHER.
I'M WAY BEYOND FIXING, BILLY BOB.
ANYWAY. . .ONE LESS OF MY KIND TO WORRY ABOUT, RIGHT?
YEAH. RIGHT.
AND THEN THERE WERE SIX.
LEAVE IT, EDIE.
HEY, GUY! ORPHAN BOY! KEEP THIS UP, AND THERE'LL BE NO TEAM LEFT FOR YOU TO LEAD.

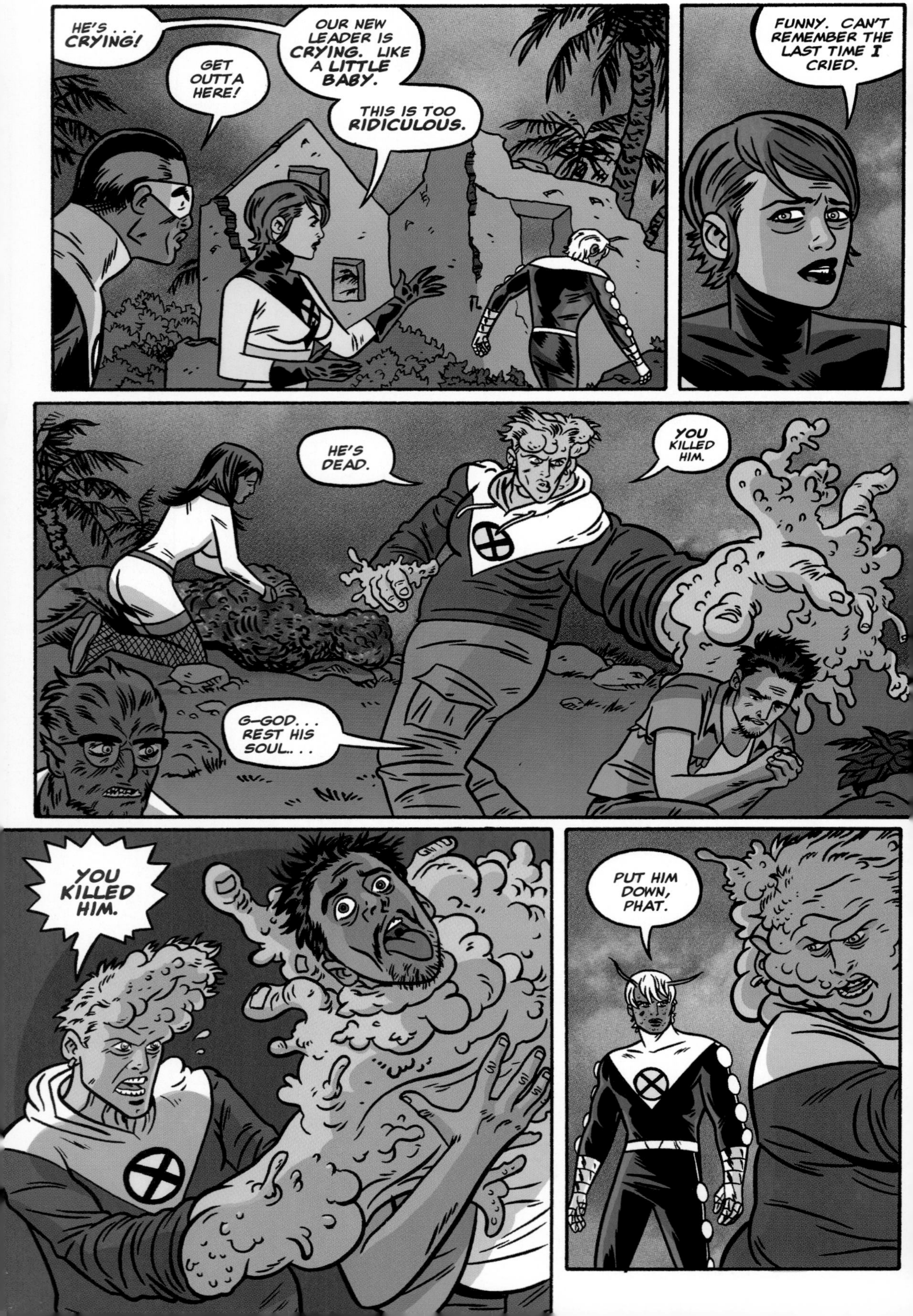

HE'S . . . CRYING!
GET OUTTA HERE!
OUR NEW LEADER IS CRYING. LIKE A LITTLE BABY.
THIS IS TOO RIDICULOUS.
FUNNY. CAN'T REMEMBER THE LAST TIME I CRIED.
HE'S DEAD.
YOU KILLED HIM.
G-GOD. . . REST HIS SOUL. . .
YOU KILLED HIM.
PUT HIM DOWN, PHAT.

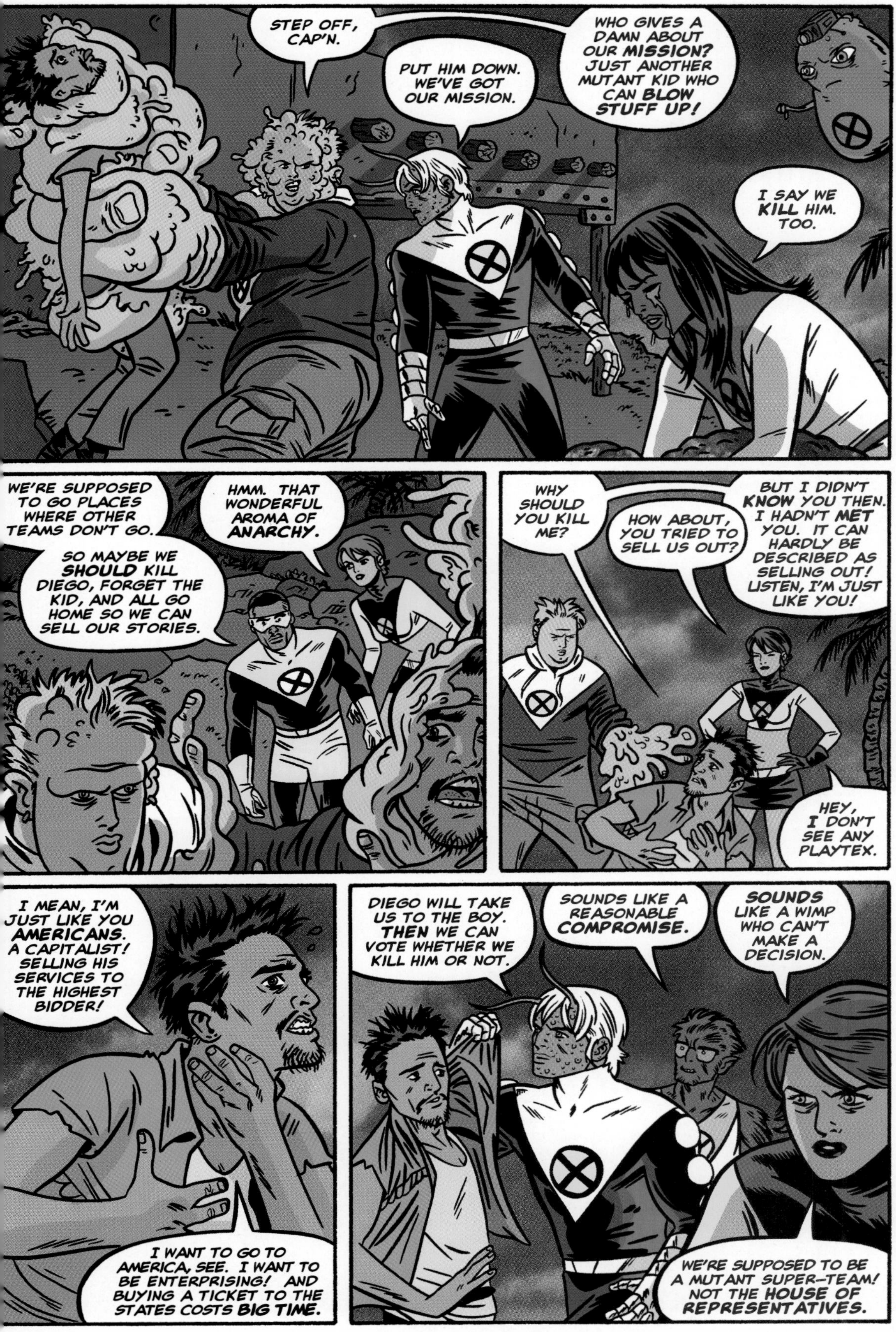
STEP OFF, CAP'N.
PUT HIM DOWN. WE'VE GOT OUR MISSION.
WHO GIVES A DAMN ABOUT OUR MISSION? JUST ANOTHER MUTANT KID WHO CAN BLOW STUFF UP!
I SAY WE KILL HIM. TOO.
WE'RE SUPPOSED TO GO PLACES WHERE OTHER TEAMS DON'T GO.
HMM. THAT WONDERFUL AROMA OF ANARCHY.
SO MAYBE WE SHOULD KILL DIEGO, FORGET THE KID, AND ALL GO HOME SO WE CAN SELL OUR STORIES.
WHY SHOULD YOU KILL ME?
HOW ABOUT, YOU TRIED TO SELL US OUT?
BUT I DIDN'T KNOW YOU THEN. I HADN'T MET YOU. IT CAN HARDLY BE DESCRIBED AS SELLING OUT! LISTEN, I'M JUST LIKE YOU!
HEY, I DON'T SEE ANY PLAYTEX.
I MEAN, I'M JUST LIKE YOU AMERICANS. A CAPITALIST! SELLING HIS SERVICES TO THE HIGHEST BIDDER!
I WANT TO GO TO AMERICA, SEE. I WANT TO BE ENTERPRISING! AND BUYING A TICKET TO THE STATES COSTS BIG TIME.
DIEGO WILL TAKE US TO THE BOY. THEN WE CAN VOTE WHETHER WE KILL HIM OR NOT.
SOUNDS LIKE A REASONABLE COMPROMISE.
SOUNDS LIKE A WIMP WHO CAN'T MAKE A DECISION.
WE'RE SUPPOSED TO BE A MUTANT SUPER-TEAM! NOT THE HOUSE OF REPRESENTATIVES.

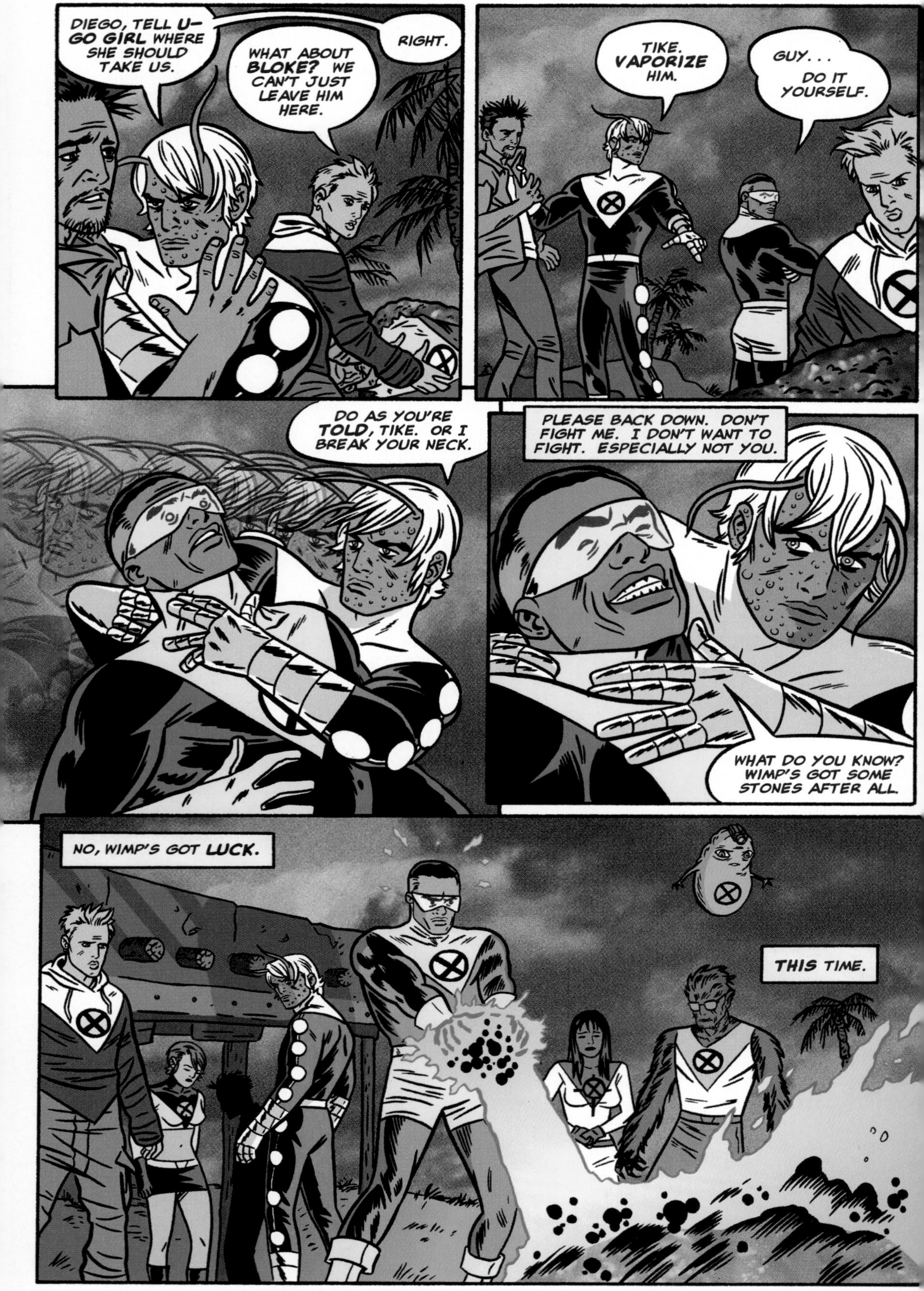
DIEGO, TELL U-GO GIRL WHERE SHE SHOULD TAKE US.
WHAT ABOUT BLOKE? WE CAN'T JUST LEAVE HIM HERE.
RIGHT.
TIKE. VAPORIZE HIM.
GUY... DO IT YOURSELF.
DO AS YOU'RE TOLD, TIKE. OR I BREAK YOUR NECK.
PLEASE BACK DOWN. DON'T FIGHT ME. I DON'T WANT TO FIGHT. ESPECIALLY NOT YOU.
WHAT DO YOU KNOW? WIMP'S GOT SOME STONES AFTER ALL.
NO, WIMP'S GOT LUCK.
THIS TIME.

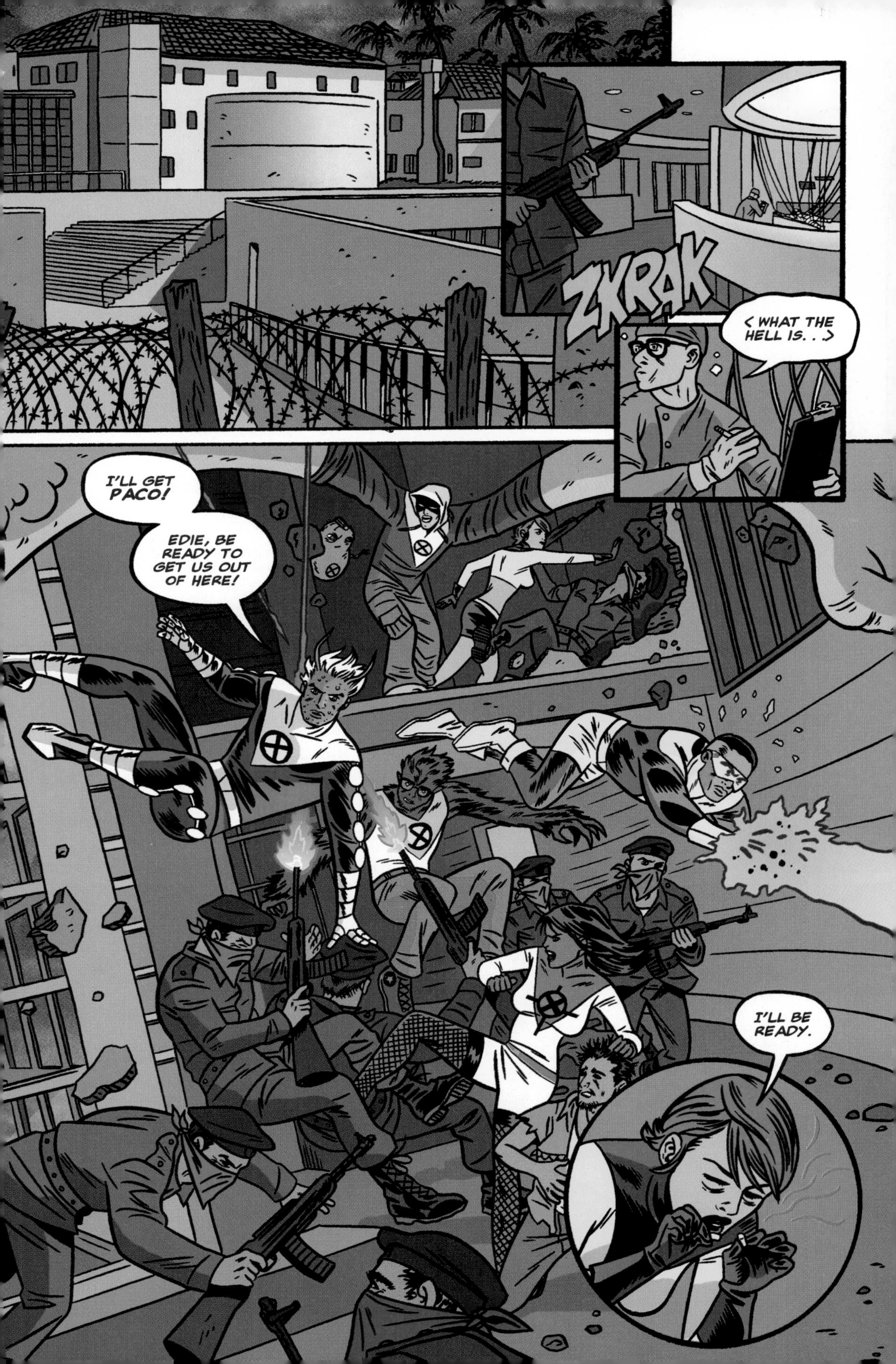
ZKRAK
< WHAT THE HELL IS. . . >
I'LL GET PACO!
EDIE, BE READY TO GET US OUT OF HERE!
I'LL BE READY.

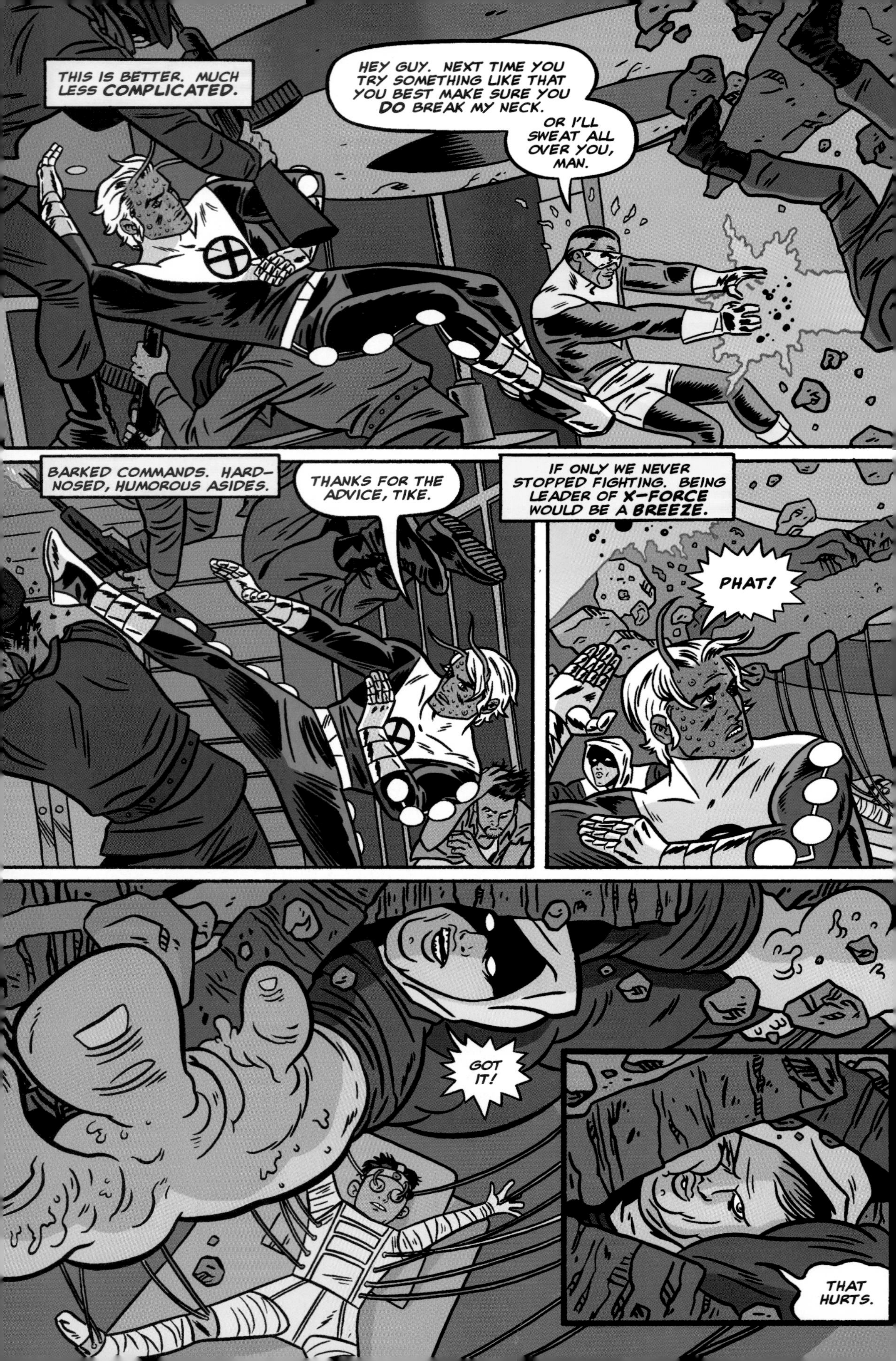
THIS IS BETTER. MUCH LESS COMPLICATED.
HEY GUY. NEXT TIME YOU TRY SOMETHING LIKE THAT YOU BEST MAKE SURE YOU DO BREAK MY NECK.
OR I'LL SWEAT ALL OVER YOU, MAN.
BARKED COMMANDS. HARD-NOSED, HUMOROUS ASIDES.
THANKS FOR THE ADVICE, TIKE.
IF ONLY WE NEVER STOPPED FIGHTING. BEING LEADER OF X-FORCE WOULD BE A BREEZE.
PHAT!
GOT IT!
THAT HURTS.

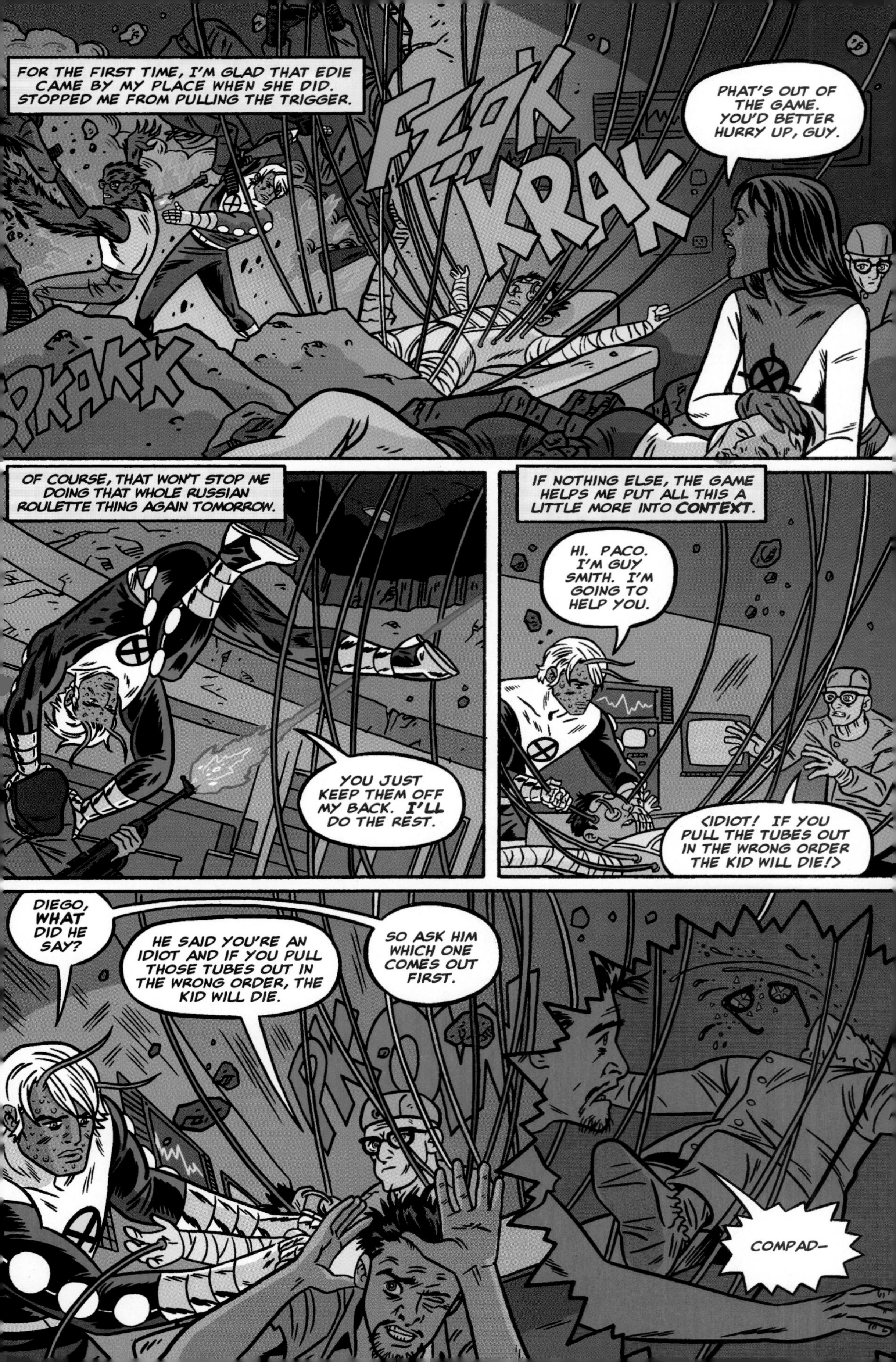
FOR THE FIRST TIME, I'M GLAD THAT EDIE CAME BY MY PLACE WHEN SHE DID. STOPPED ME FROM PULLING THE TRIGGER.
FZAK
KRAK
PHAT'S OUT OF THE GAME. YOU'D BETTER HURRY UP, GUY.
PKAKK
OF COURSE, THAT WON'T STOP ME DOING THAT WHOLE RUSSIAN ROULETTE THING AGAIN TOMORROW.
YOU JUST KEEP THEM OFF MY BACK. I'LL DO THE REST.
IF NOTHING ELSE, THE GAME HELPS ME PUT ALL THIS A LITTLE MORE INTO CONTEXT.
HI. PACO. I'M GUY SMITH. I'M GOING TO HELP YOU.
<IDIOT! IF YOU PULL THE TUBES OUT IN THE WRONG ORDER THE KID WILL DIE!>
DIEGO, WHAT DID HE SAY?
HE SAID YOU'RE AN IDIOT AND IF YOU PULL THOSE TUBES OUT IN THE WRONG ORDER, THE KID WILL DIE.
SO ASK HIM WHICH ONE COMES OUT FIRST.
COMPAD–

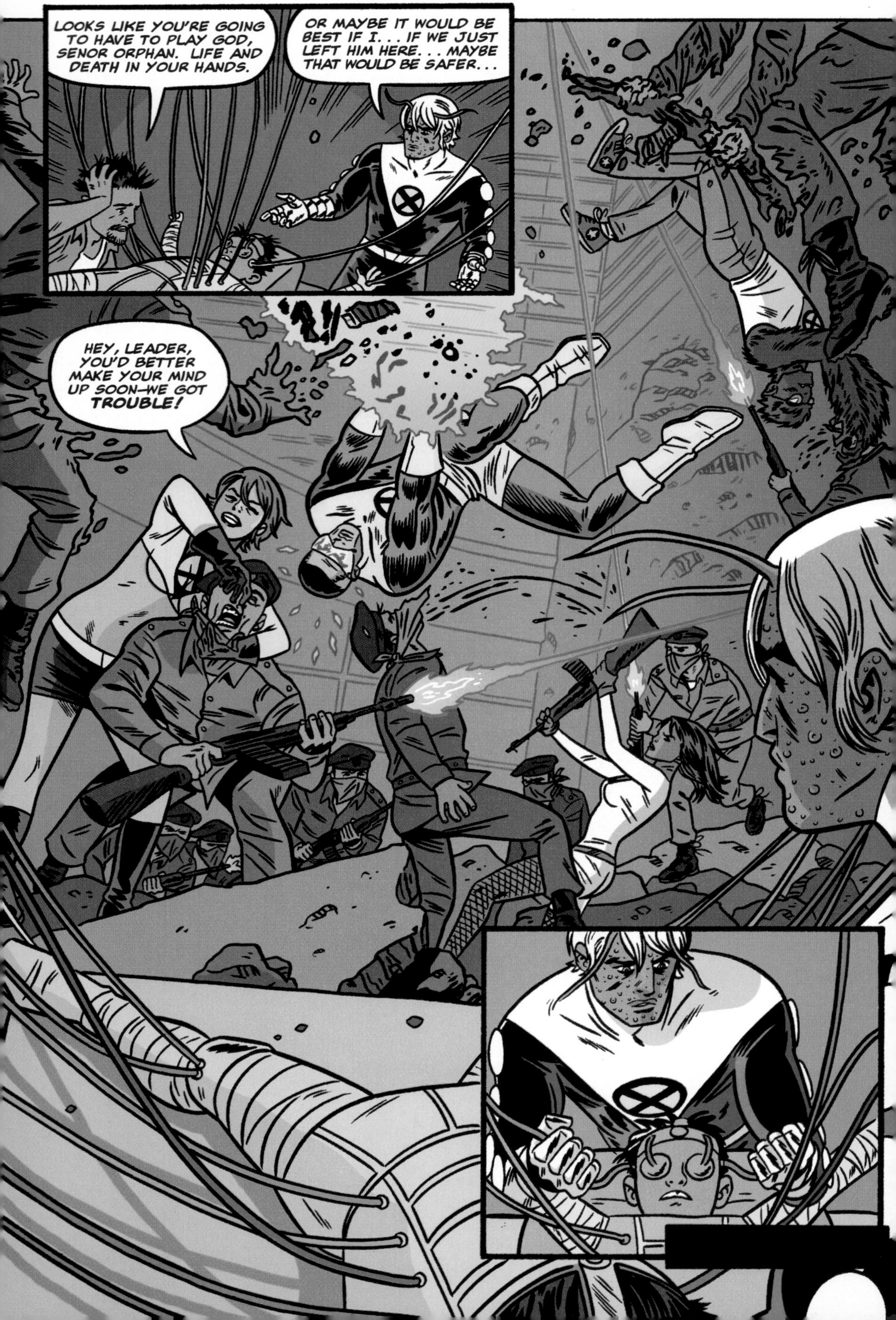
LOOKS LIKE YOU'RE GOING TO HAVE TO PLAY GOD, SENOR ORPHAN. LIFE AND DEATH IN YOUR HANDS.
OR MAYBE IT WOULD BE BEST IF I. . . IF WE JUST LEFT HIM HERE. . . MAYBE THAT WOULD BE SAFER. . .
'Z!
HEY, LEADER, YOU'D BETTER MAKE YOUR MIND UP SOON—WE GOT TROUBLE!

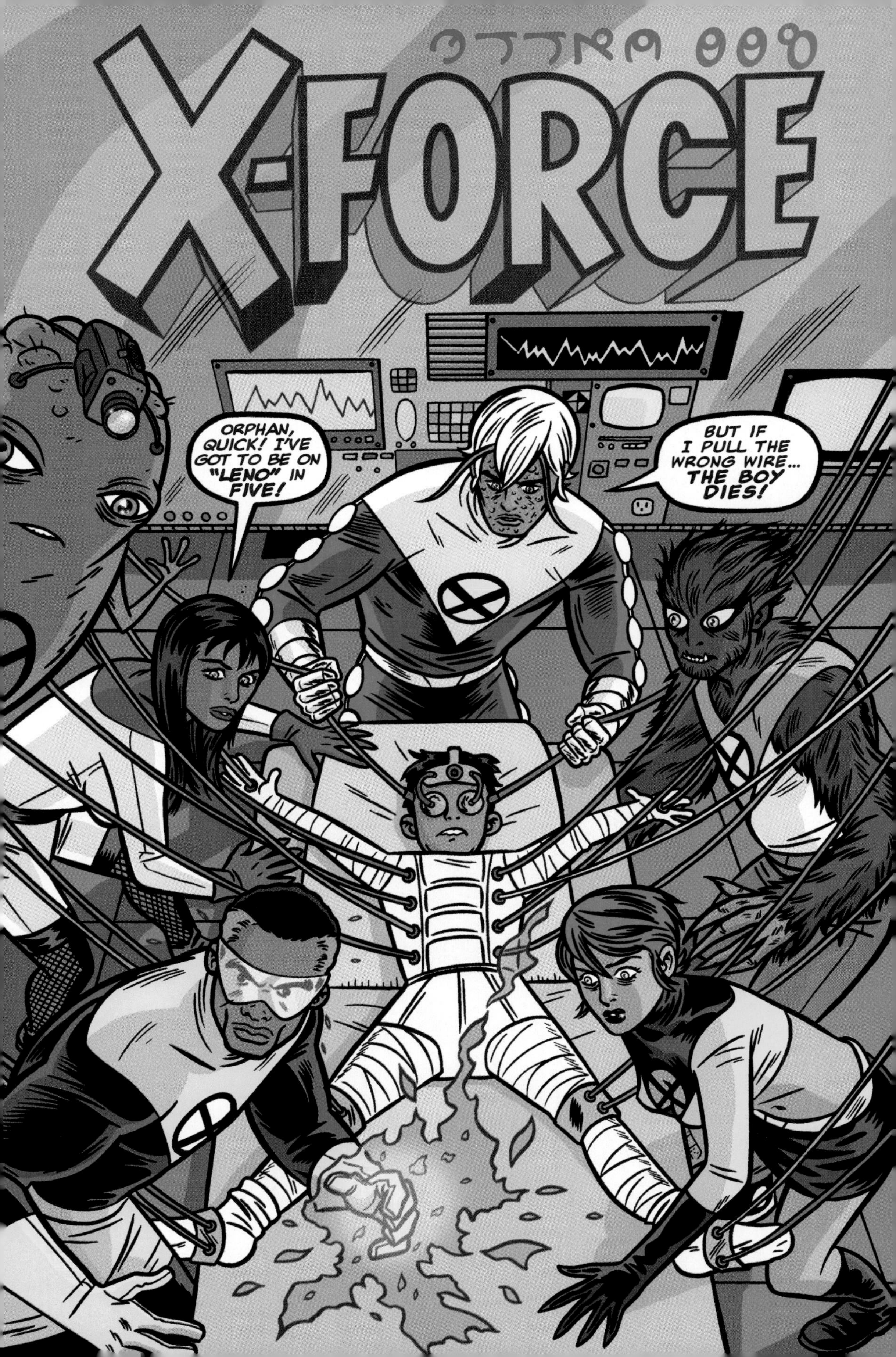
X-FORCE
ORPHAN, QUICK! I'VE GOT TO BE ON "LENO" IN FIVE!
BUT IF I PULL THE WRONG WIRE... THE BOY DIES!

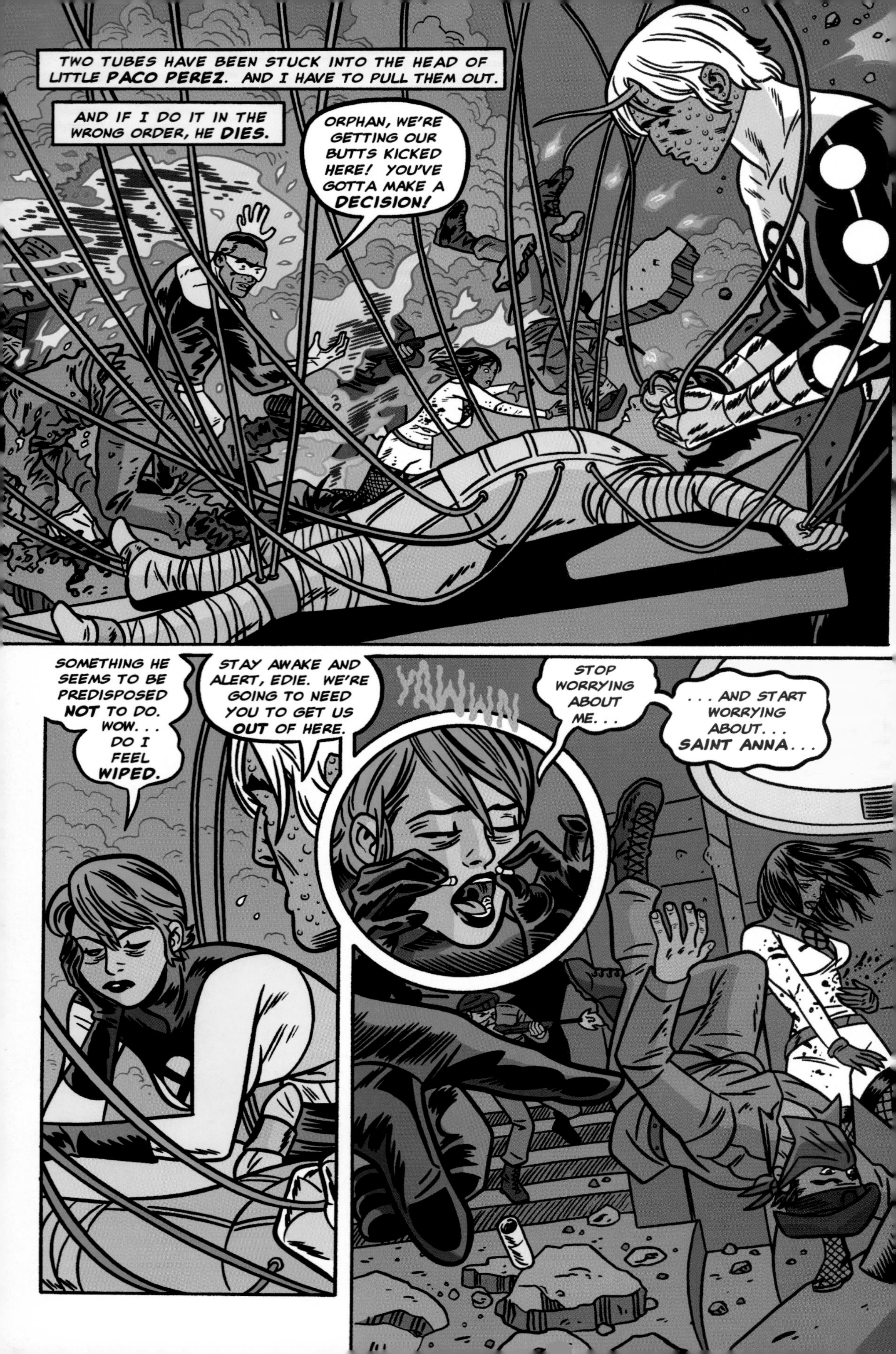
TWO TUBES HAVE BEEN STUCK INTO THE HEAD OF LITTLE PACO PEREZ. AND I HAVE TO PULL THEM OUT.
AND IF I DO IT IN THE WRONG ORDER, HE DIES.
ORPHAN, WE'RE GETTING OUR BUTTS KICKED HERE! YOU'VE GOTTA MAKE A DECISION!
SOMETHING HE SEEMS TO BE PREDISPOSED NOT TO DO. WOW... DO I FEEL WIPED.
STAY AWAKE AND ALERT, EDIE. WE'RE GOING TO NEED YOU TO GET US OUT OF HERE.
YAWWN
STOP WORRYING ABOUT ME...
...AND START WORRYING ABOUT... SAINT ANNA...

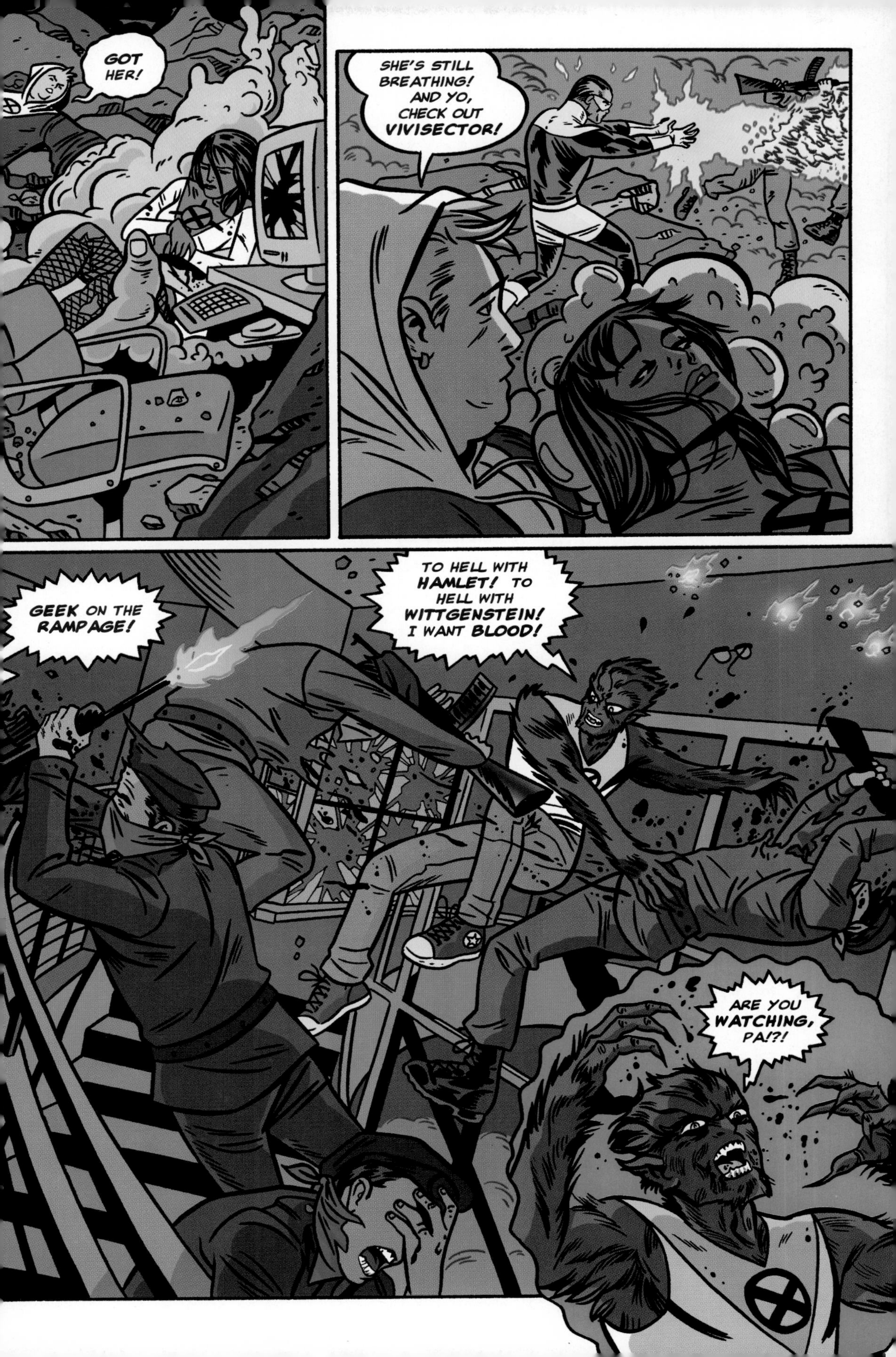
GOT HER!
SHE'S STILL BREATHING! AND YO, CHECK OUT VIVISECTOR!
GEEK ON THE RAMPAGE!
TO HELL WITH HAMLET! TO HELL WITH WITTGENSTEIN! I WANT BLOOD!
ARE YOU WATCHING, PA!?!

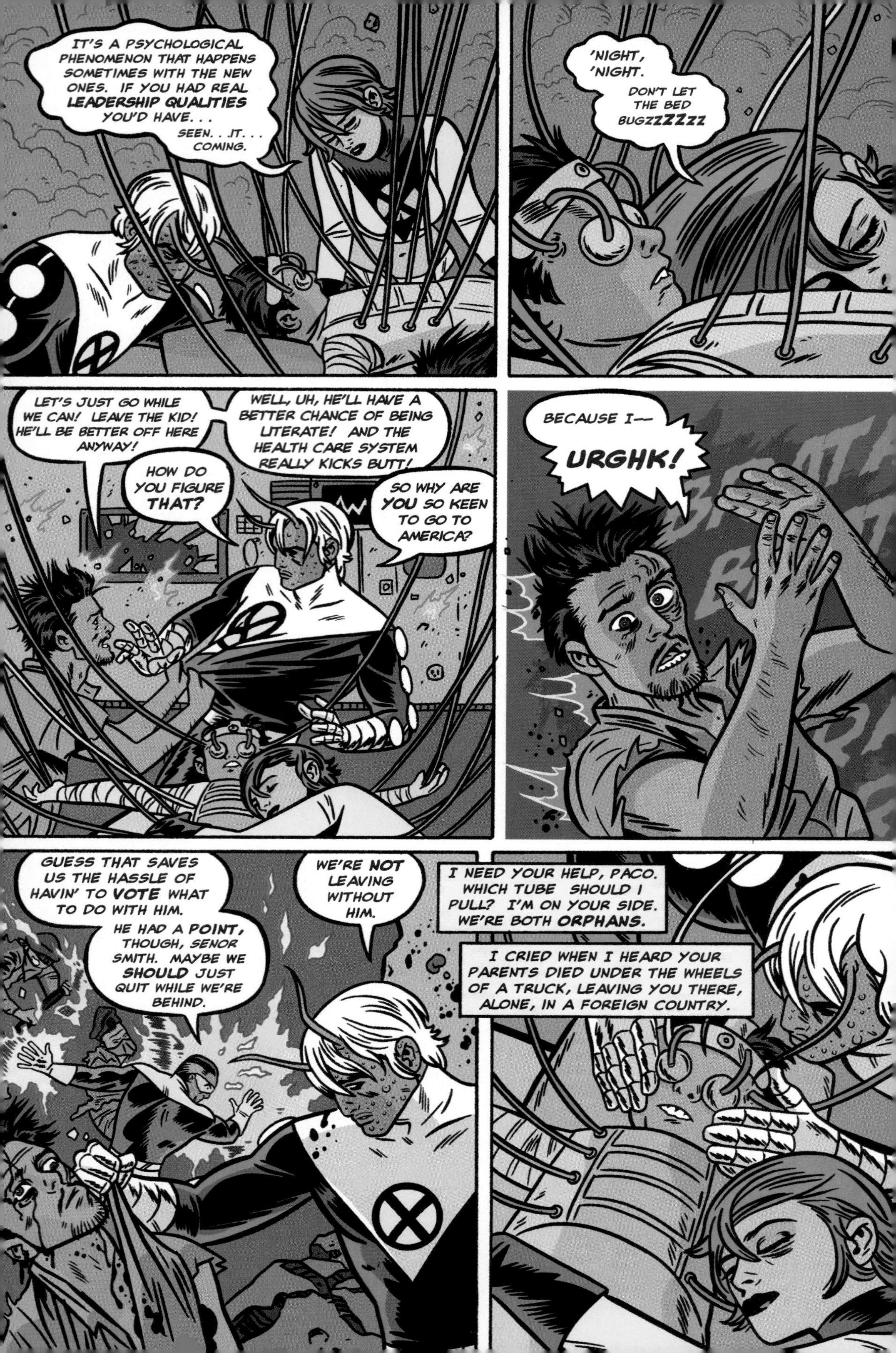
IT'S A PSYCHOLOGICAL PHENOMENON THAT HAPPENS SOMETIMES WITH THE NEW ONES. IF YOU HAD REAL LEADERSHIP QUALITIES YOU'D HAVE. . .
SEEN. . .IT. . . COMING.
'NIGHT, 'NIGHT.
DON'T LET THE BED BUGZZZZZz
LET'S JUST GO WHILE WE CAN! LEAVE THE KID! HE'LL BE BETTER OFF HERE ANYWAY!
HOW DO YOU FIGURE THAT?
WELL, UH, HE'LL HAVE A BETTER CHANCE OF BEING LITERATE! AND THE HEALTH CARE SYSTEM REALLY KICKS BUTT!
SO WHY ARE YOU SO KEEN TO GO TO AMERICA?
BECAUSE I--
URGHK!
GUESS THAT SAVES US THE HASSLE OF HAVIN' TO VOTE WHAT TO DO WITH HIM.
HE HAD A POINT, THOUGH, SENOR SMITH. MAYBE WE SHOULD JUST QUIT WHILE WE'RE BEHIND.
WE'RE NOT LEAVING WITHOUT HIM.
I NEED YOUR HELP, PACO. WHICH TUBE SHOULD I PULL? I'M ON YOUR SIDE. WE'RE BOTH ORPHANS.
I CRIED WHEN I HEARD YOUR PARENTS DIED UNDER THE WHEELS OF A TRUCK, LEAVING YOU THERE, ALONE, IN A FOREIGN COUNTRY.

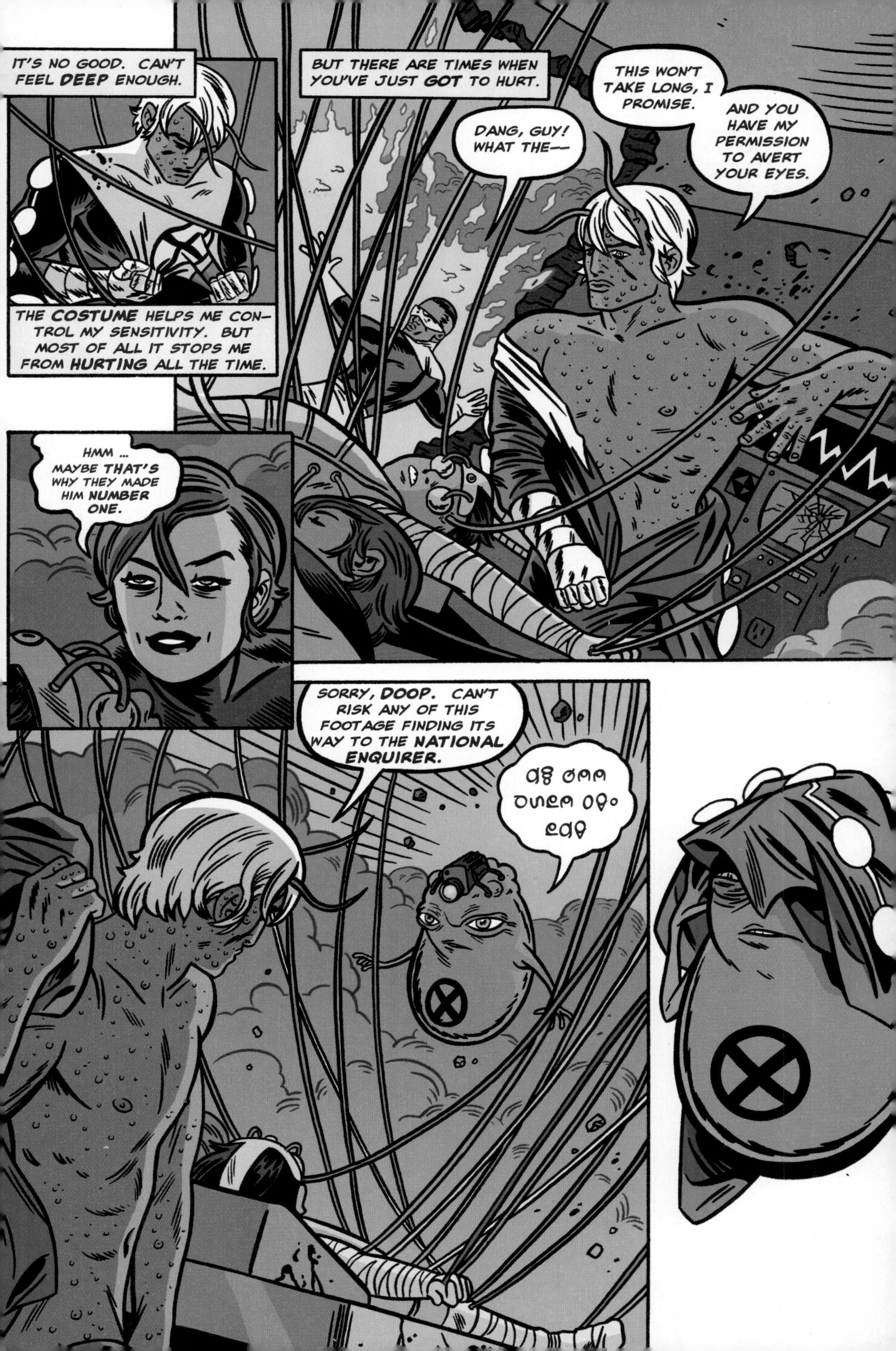
IT'S NO GOOD. CAN'T FEEL DEEP ENOUGH.
THE COSTUME HELPS ME CONTROL MY SENSITIVITY. BUT MOST OF ALL IT STOPS ME FROM HURTING ALL THE TIME.
BUT THERE ARE TIMES WHEN YOU'VE JUST GOT TO HURT.
DANG, GUY! WHAT THE--
THIS WON'T TAKE LONG, I PROMISE.
AND YOU HAVE MY PERMISSION TO AVERT YOUR EYES.
HMM ... MAYBE THAT'S WHY THEY MADE HIM NUMBER ONE.
SORRY, DOOP. CAN'T RISK ANY OF THIS FOOTAGE FINDING ITS WAY TO THE NATIONAL ENQUIRER.

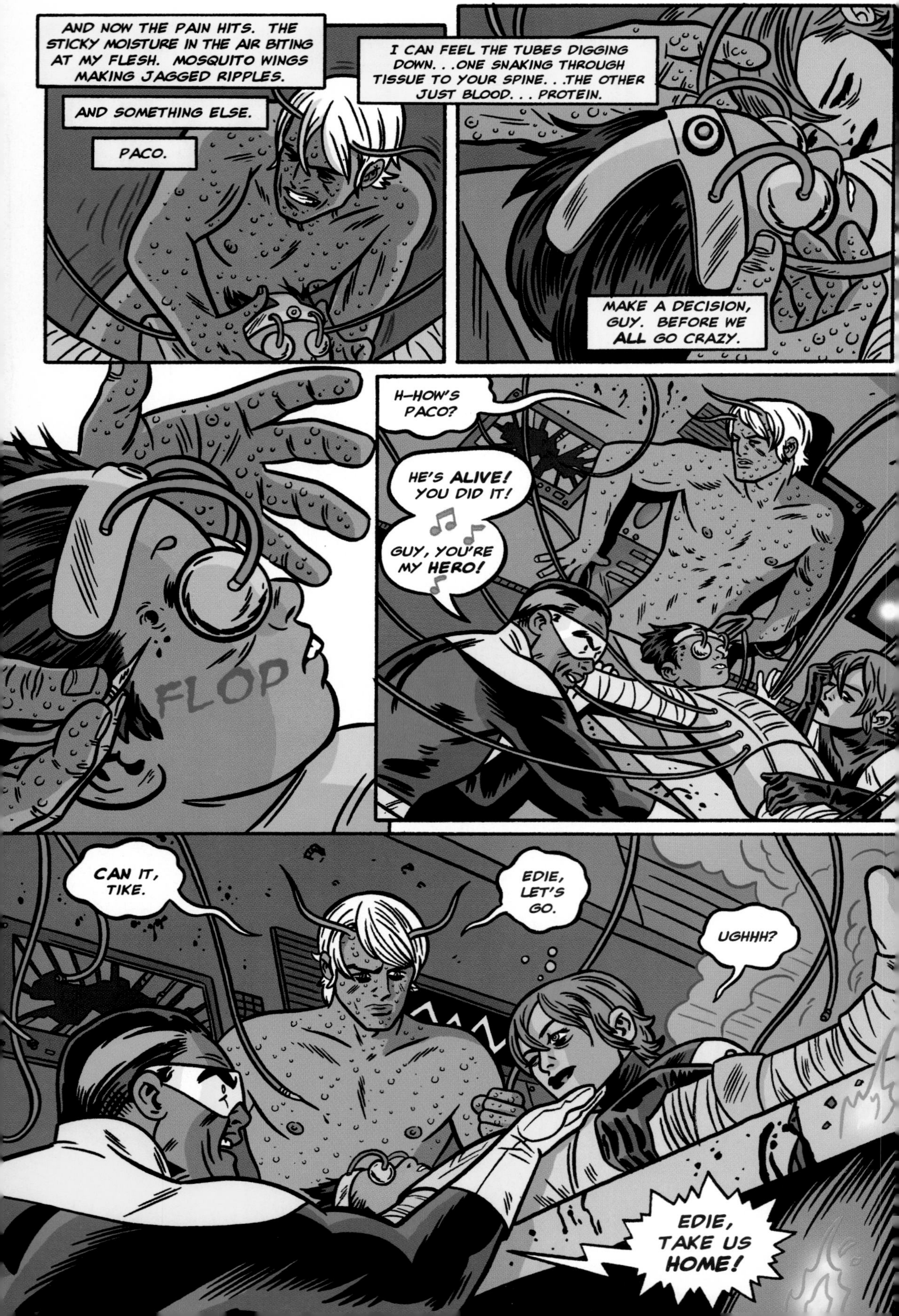
AND NOW THE PAIN HITS. THE STICKY MOISTURE IN THE AIR BITING AT MY FLESH. MOSQUITO WINGS MAKING JAGGED RIPPLES.
AND SOMETHING ELSE.
PACO.
I CAN FEEL THE TUBES DIGGING DOWN. . .ONE SNAKING THROUGH TISSUE TO YOUR SPINE. . .THE OTHER JUST BLOOD. . . PROTEIN.
MAKE A DECISION, GUY. BEFORE WE ALL GO CRAZY.
FLOP
H-HOW'S PACO?
HE'S ALIVE! YOU DID IT!
GUY, YOU'RE MY HERO!
CAN IT, TIKE.
EDIE, LET'S GO.
UGHHH?
EDIE, TAKE US HOME!

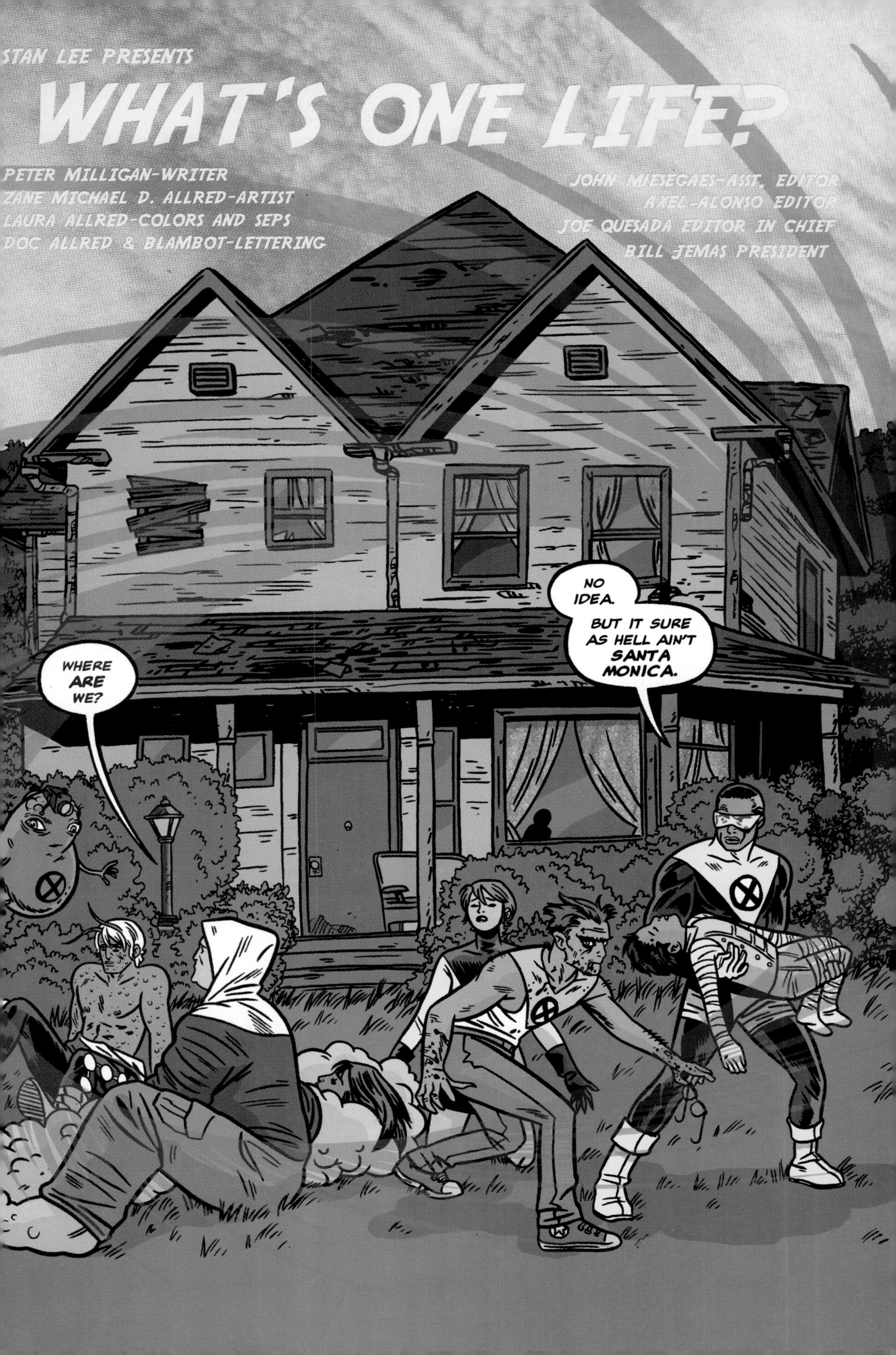
STAN LEE PRESENTS
WHAT'S ONE LIFE?
PETER MILLIGAN-WRITER
ZANE MICHAEL D. ALLRED-ARTIST
LAURA ALLRED-COLORS AND SEPS
DOC ALLRED & BLAMBOT-LETTERING
JOHN MIESEGAES-ASST. EDITOR
AXEL ALONSO EDITOR
JOE QUESADA EDITOR IN CHIEF
BILL JEMAS PRESIDENT
WHERE ARE WE?
NO IDEA. BUT IT SURE AS HELL AIN'T SANTA MONICA.

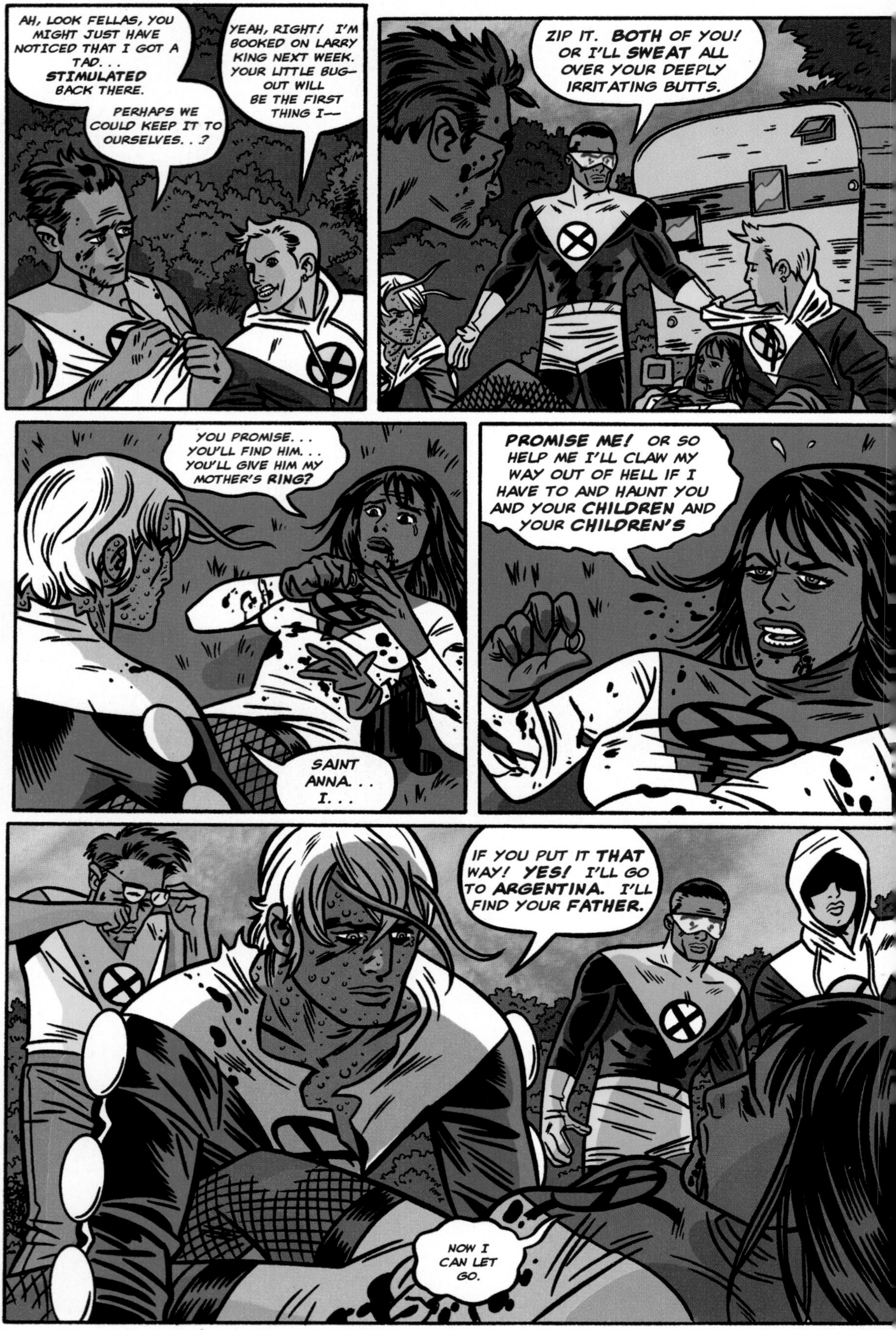
AH, LOOK FELLAS, YOU MIGHT JUST HAVE NOTICED THAT I GOT A TAD... STIMULATED BACK THERE.
PERHAPS WE COULD KEEP IT TO OURSELVES...?
YEAH, RIGHT! I'M BOOKED ON LARRY KING NEXT WEEK. YOUR LITTLE BUG-OUT WILL BE THE FIRST THING I--
ZIP IT. BOTH OF YOU! OR I'LL SWEAT ALL OVER YOUR DEEPLY IRRITATING BUTTS.
YOU PROMISE... YOU'LL FIND HIM... YOU'LL GIVE HIM MY MOTHER'S RING?
SAINT ANNA... I...
PROMISE ME! OR SO HELP ME I'LL CLAW MY WAY OUT OF HELL IF I HAVE TO AND HAUNT YOU AND YOUR CHILDREN AND YOUR CHILDREN'S
IF YOU PUT IT THAT WAY! YES! I'LL GO TO ARGENTINA. I'LL FIND YOUR FATHER.
NOW I CAN LET GO.

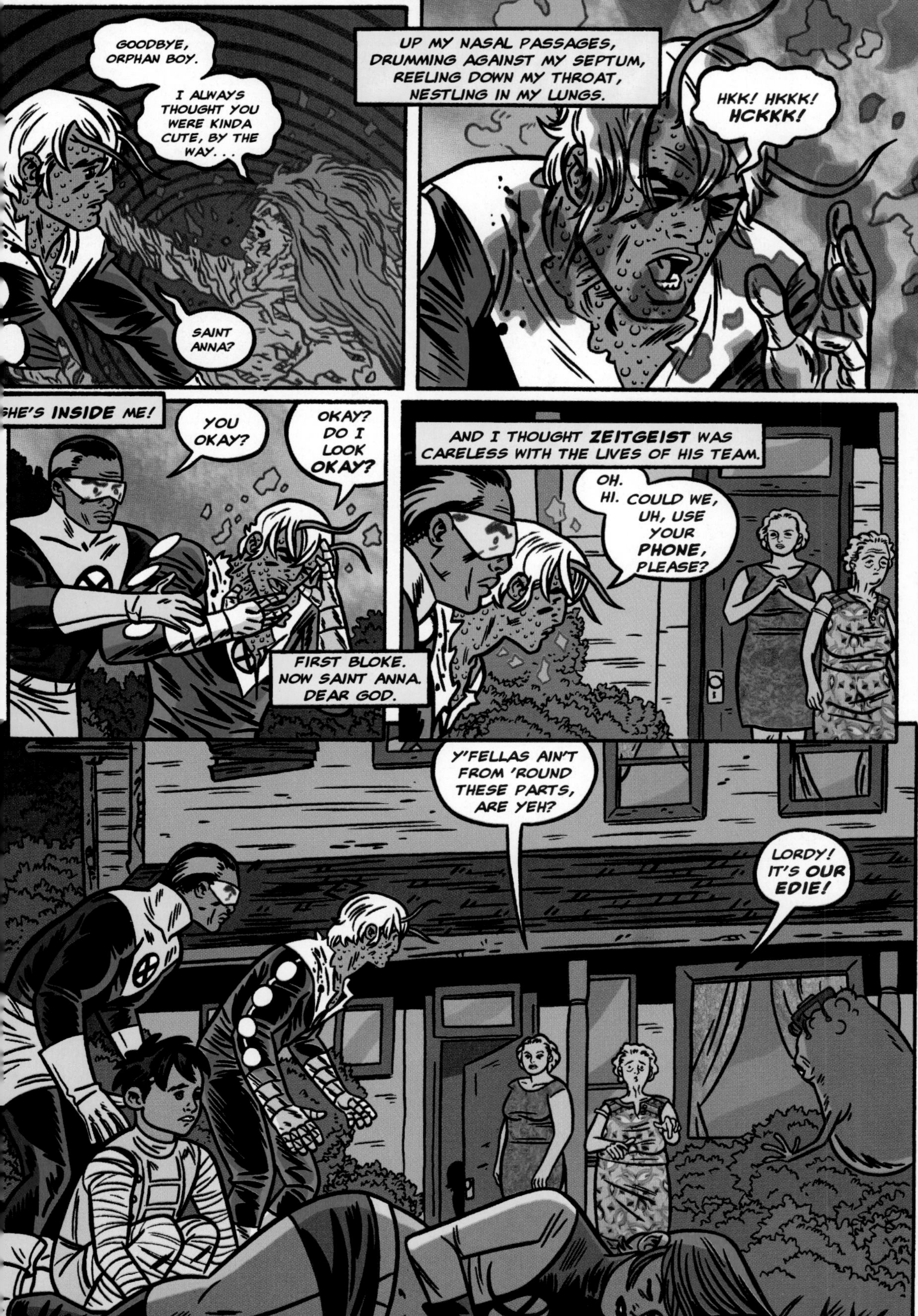
GOODBYE, ORPHAN BOY.
I ALWAYS THOUGHT YOU WERE KINDA CUTE, BY THE WAY. . .
SAINT ANNA?
UP MY NASAL PASSAGES, DRUMMING AGAINST MY SEPTUM, REELING DOWN MY THROAT, NESTLING IN MY LUNGS.
HKK! HKKK! HCKKK!
SHE'S INSIDE ME!
YOU OKAY?
OKAY? DO I LOOK OKAY?
FIRST BLOKE. NOW SAINT ANNA. DEAR GOD.
AND I THOUGHT ZEITGEIST WAS CARELESS WITH THE LIVES OF HIS TEAM.
OH. HI. COULD WE, UH, USE YOUR PHONE, PLEASE?
Y'FELLAS AIN'T FROM 'ROUND THESE PARTS, ARE YEH?
LORDY! IT'S OUR EDIE!

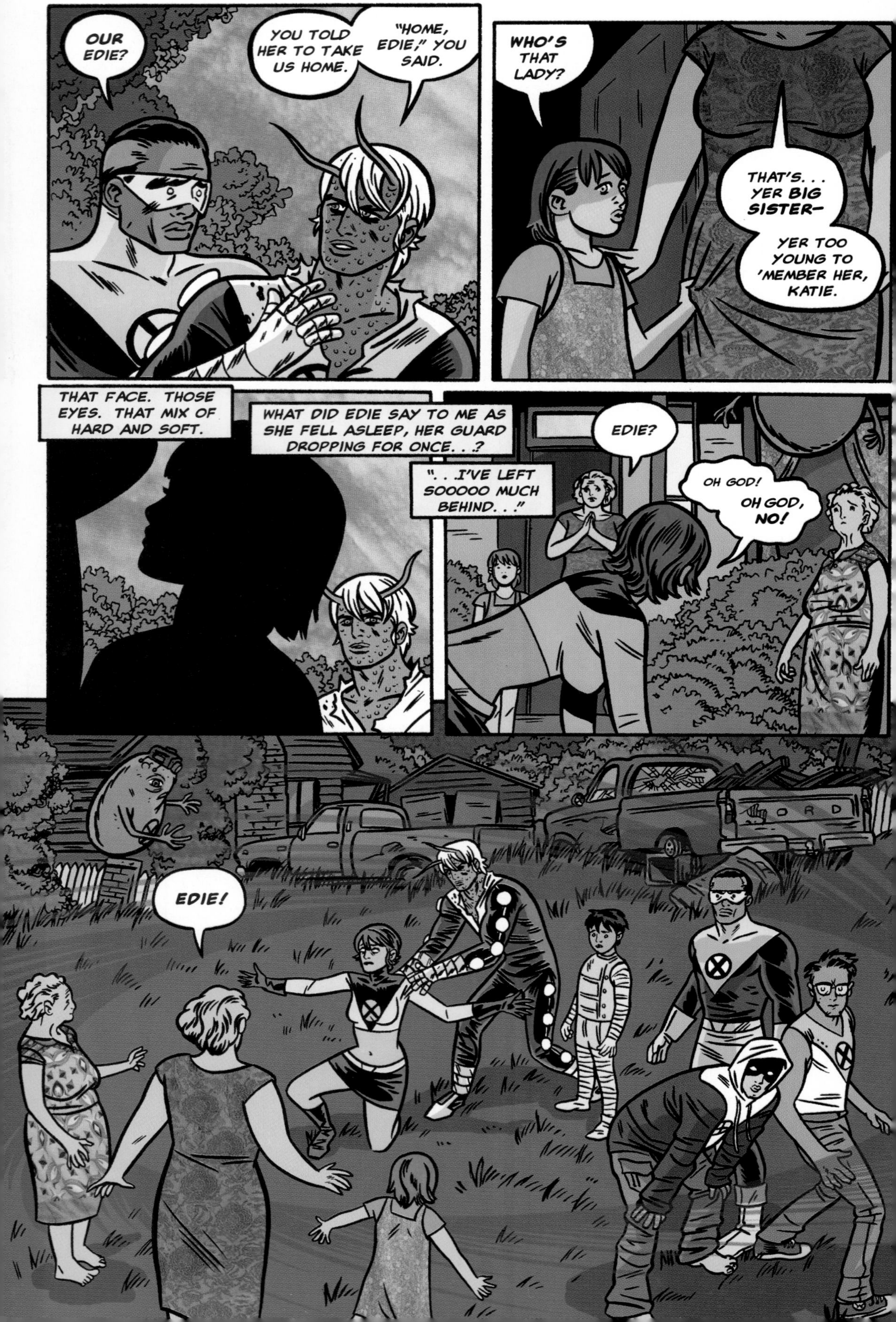
OUR EDIE?
YOU TOLD HER TO TAKE US HOME.
"HOME, EDIE," YOU SAID.
WHO'S THAT LADY?
THAT'S. . . YER BIG SISTER—
YER TOO YOUNG TO 'MEMBER HER, KATIE.
THAT FACE. THOSE EYES. THAT MIX OF HARD AND SOFT.
WHAT DID EDIE SAY TO ME AS SHE FELL ASLEEP, HER GUARD DROPPING FOR ONCE. . .?
". . .I'VE LEFT SOOOOO MUCH BEHIND. . ."
EDIE?
OH GOD!
OH GOD, NO!
FORD
EDIE!

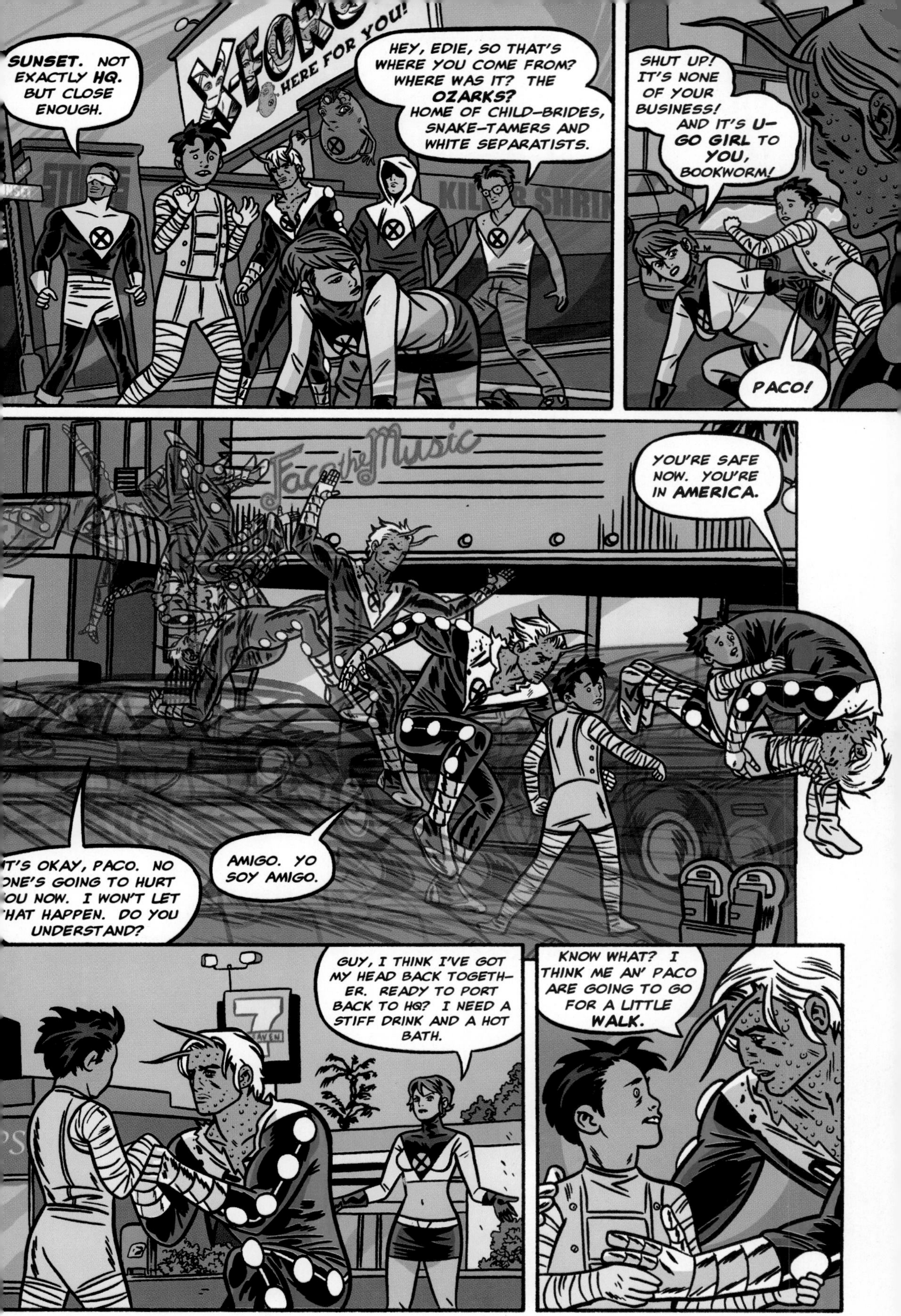

HERE FOR YOU!
SUNSET. NOT EXACTLY HQ. BUT CLOSE ENOUGH.
HEY, EDIE, SO THAT'S WHERE YOU COME FROM? WHERE WAS IT? THE OZARKS? HOME OF CHILD-BRIDES, SNAKE-TAMERS AND WHITE SEPARATISTS.
SHUT UP! IT'S NONE OF YOUR BUSINESS! AND IT'S U-GO GIRL TO YOU, BOOKWORM!
PACO!
Face the Music
YOU'RE SAFE NOW. YOU'RE IN AMERICA.
T'S OKAY, PACO. NO ONE'S GOING TO HURT OU NOW. I WON'T LET HAT HAPPEN. DO YOU UNDERSTAND?
AMIGO. YO SOY AMIGO.
GUY, I THINK I'VE GOT MY HEAD BACK TOGETHER. READY TO PORT BACK TO HQ? I NEED A STIFF DRINK AND A HOT BATH.
KNOW WHAT? I THINK ME AN' PACO ARE GOING TO GO FOR A LITTLE WALK.

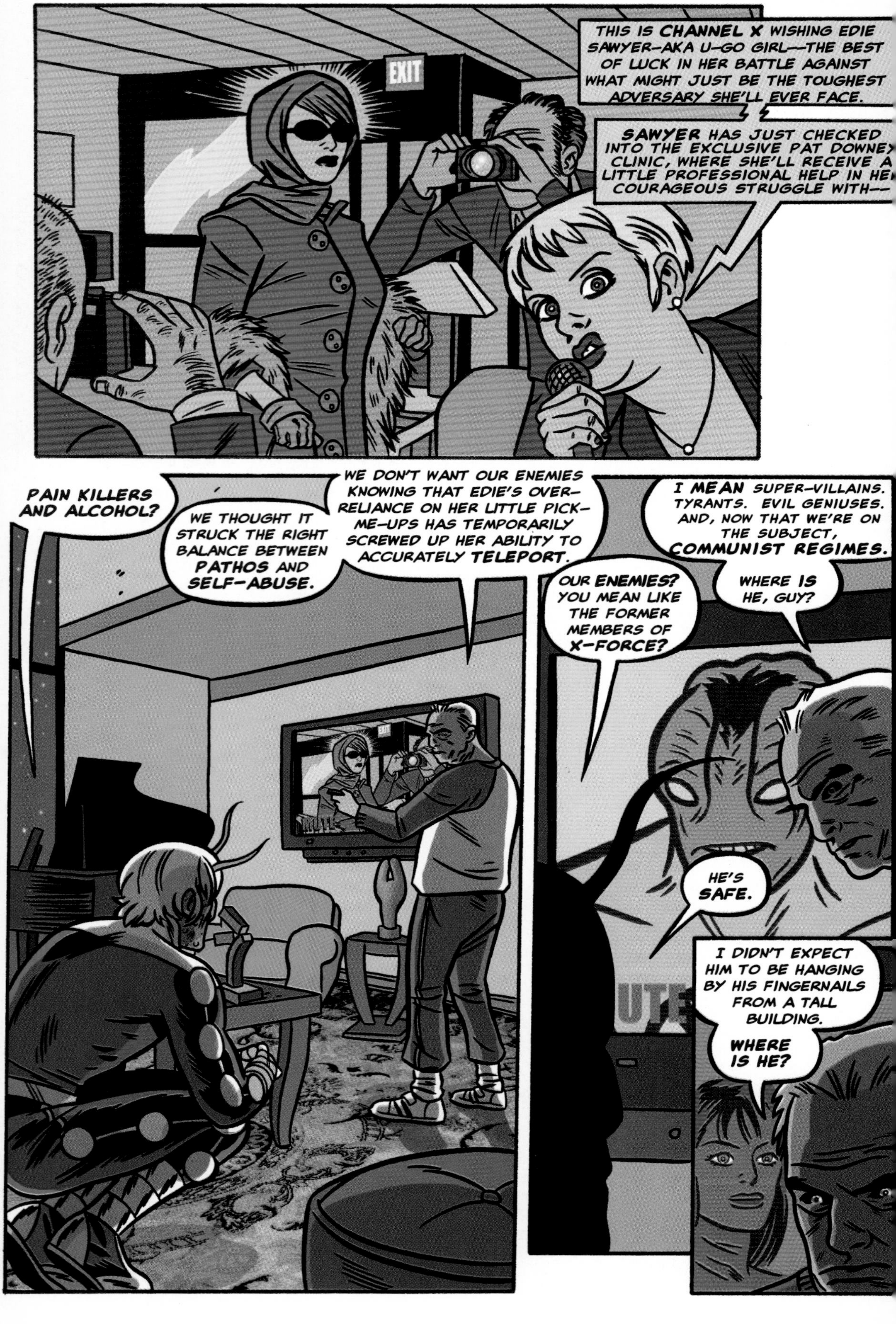

EXIT
THIS IS CHANNEL X WISHING EDIE SAWYER—AKA U-GO GIRL—THE BEST OF LUCK IN HER BATTLE AGAINST WHAT MIGHT JUST BE THE TOUGHEST ADVERSARY SHE'LL EVER FACE.
SAWYER HAS JUST CHECKED INTO THE EXCLUSIVE PAT DOWNE CLINIC, WHERE SHE'LL RECEIVE A LITTLE PROFESSIONAL HELP IN HE COURAGEOUS STRUGGLE WITH—
PAIN KILLERS AND ALCOHOL?
WE THOUGHT IT STRUCK THE RIGHT BALANCE BETWEEN PATHOS AND SELF-ABUSE.
WE DON'T WANT OUR ENEMIES KNOWING THAT EDIE'S OVER-RELIANCE ON HER LITTLE PICK-ME-UPS HAS TEMPORARILY SCREWED UP HER ABILITY TO ACCURATELY TELEPORT.
OUR ENEMIES? YOU MEAN LIKE THE FORMER MEMBERS OF X-FORCE?
I MEAN SUPER-VILLAINS. TYRANTS. EVIL GENIUSES. AND, NOW THAT WE'RE ON THE SUBJECT, COMMUNIST REGIMES.
WHERE IS HE, GUY?
HE'S SAFE.
I DIDN'T EXPECT HIM TO BE HANGING BY HIS FINGERNAILS FROM A TALL BUILDING.
WHERE IS HE?

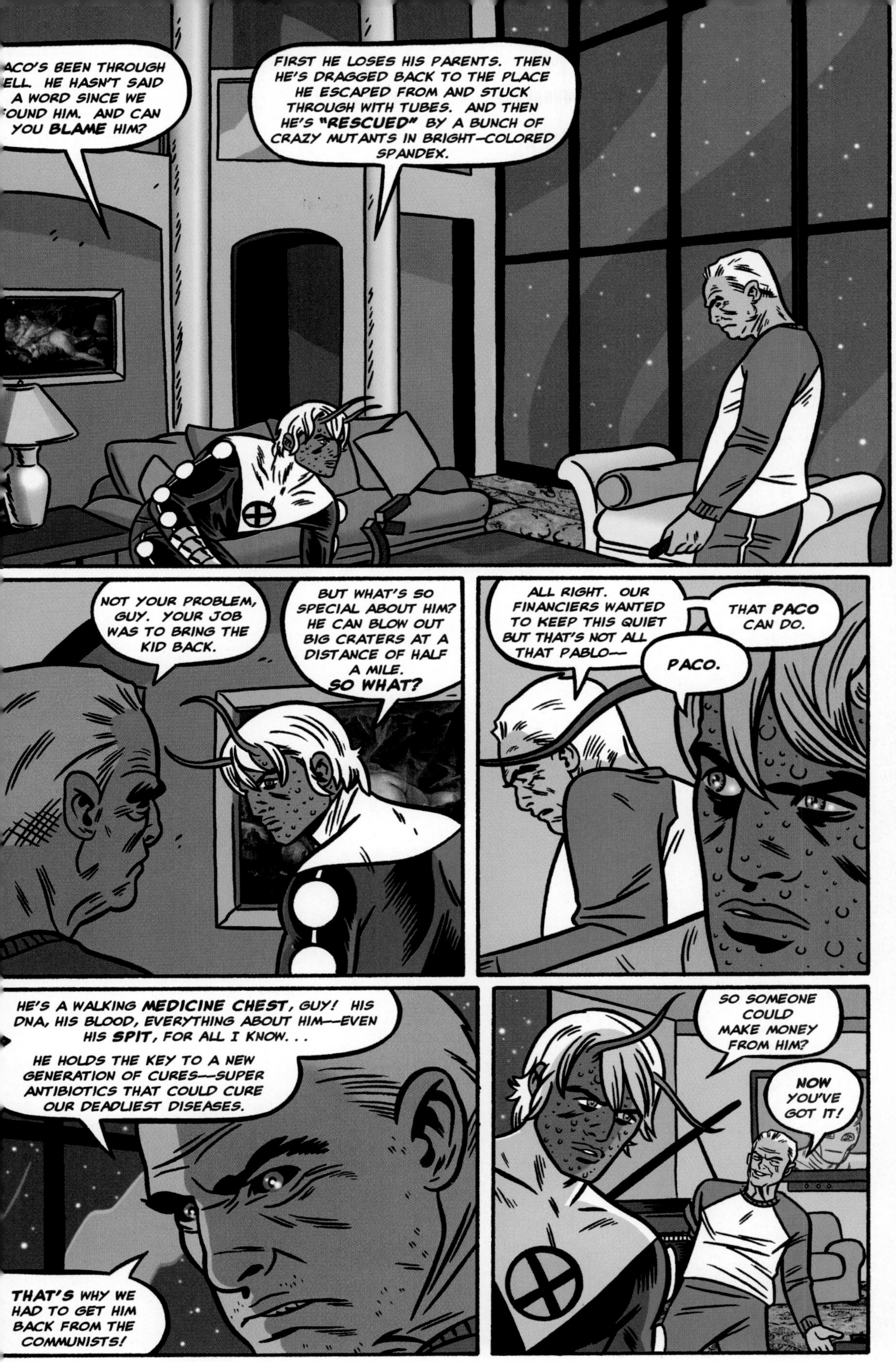
ACO'S BEEN THROUGH ELL. HE HASN'T SAID A WORD SINCE WE FOUND HIM. AND CAN YOU BLAME HIM?
FIRST HE LOSES HIS PARENTS. THEN HE'S DRAGGED BACK TO THE PLACE HE ESCAPED FROM AND STUCK THROUGH WITH TUBES. AND THEN HE'S "RESCUED" BY A BUNCH OF CRAZY MUTANTS IN BRIGHT-COLORED SPANDEX.
NOT YOUR PROBLEM, GUY. YOUR JOB WAS TO BRING THE KID BACK.
BUT WHAT'S SO SPECIAL ABOUT HIM? HE CAN BLOW OUT BIG CRATERS AT A DISTANCE OF HALF A MILE. SO WHAT?
ALL RIGHT. OUR FINANCIERS WANTED TO KEEP THIS QUIET BUT THAT'S NOT ALL THAT PABLO--
PACO.
THAT PACO CAN DO.
HE'S A WALKING MEDICINE CHEST, GUY! HIS DNA, HIS BLOOD, EVERYTHING ABOUT HIM--EVEN HIS SPIT, FOR ALL I KNOW. . .
HE HOLDS THE KEY TO A NEW GENERATION OF CURES--SUPER ANTIBIOTICS THAT COULD CURE OUR DEADLIEST DISEASES.
THAT'S WHY WE HAD TO GET HIM BACK FROM THE COMMUNISTS!
SO SOMEONE COULD MAKE MONEY FROM HIM?
NOW YOU'VE GOT IT!

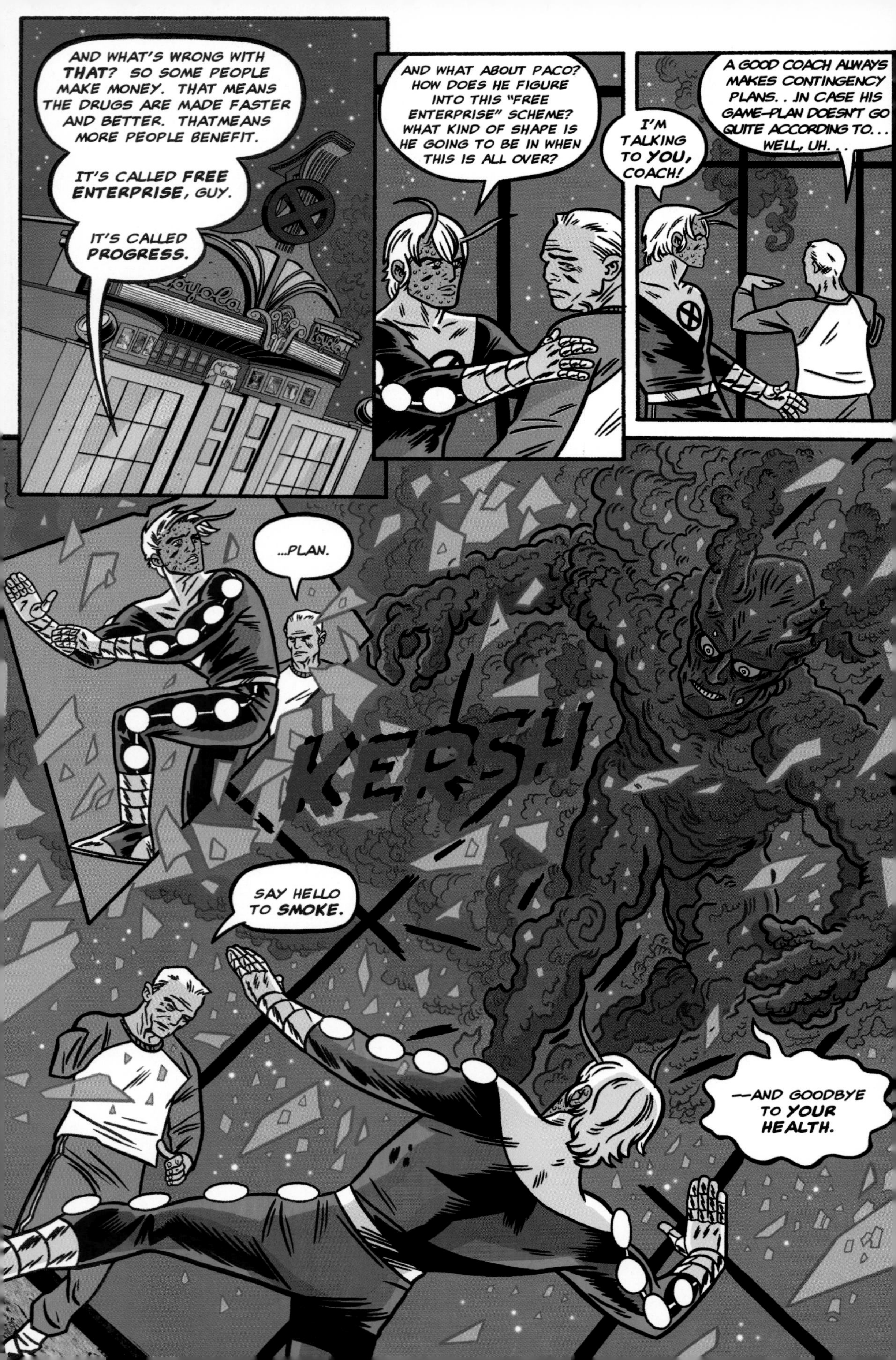
AND WHAT'S WRONG WITH THAT? SO SOME PEOPLE MAKE MONEY. THAT MEANS THE DRUGS ARE MADE FASTER AND BETTER. THATMEANS MORE PEOPLE BENEFIT.
IT'S CALLED FREE ENTERPRISE, GUY.
IT'S CALLED PROGRESS.
AND WHAT ABOUT PACO? HOW DOES HE FIGURE INTO THIS "FREE ENTERPRISE" SCHEME? WHAT KIND OF SHAPE IS HE GOING TO BE IN WHEN THIS IS ALL OVER?
I'M TALKING TO YOU, COACH!
A GOOD COACH ALWAYS MAKES CONTINGENCY PLANS. . IN CASE HIS GAME-PLAN DOESN'T GO QUITE ACCORDING TO. . . WELL, UH. . .
...PLAN.
KERSH
SAY HELLO TO SMOKE.
--AND GOODBYE TO YOUR HEALTH.

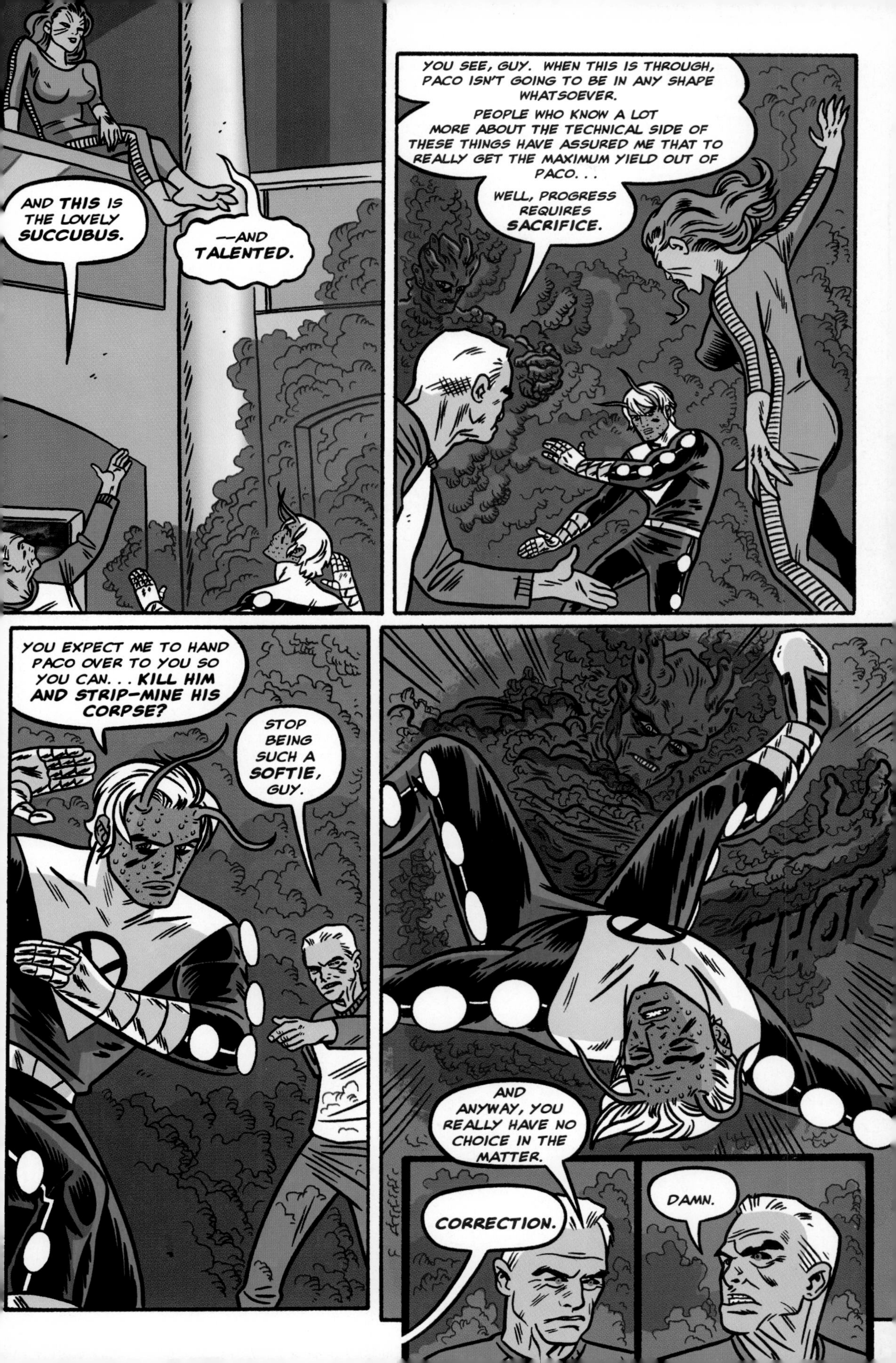

AND THIS IS THE LOVELY SUCCUBUS.
--AND TALENTED.
YOU SEE, GUY. WHEN THIS IS THROUGH, PACO ISN'T GOING TO BE IN ANY SHAPE WHATSOEVER.
PEOPLE WHO KNOW A LOT MORE ABOUT THE TECHNICAL SIDE OF THESE THINGS HAVE ASSURED ME THAT TO REALLY GET THE MAXIMUM YIELD OUT OF PACO. . .
WELL, PROGRESS REQUIRES SACRIFICE.
YOU EXPECT ME TO HAND PACO OVER TO YOU SO YOU CAN. . . KILL HIM AND STRIP-MINE HIS CORPSE?
STOP BEING SUCH A SOFTIE, GUY.
THOK
AND ANYWAY, YOU REALLY HAVE NO CHOICE IN THE MATTER.
CORRECTION.
DAMN.

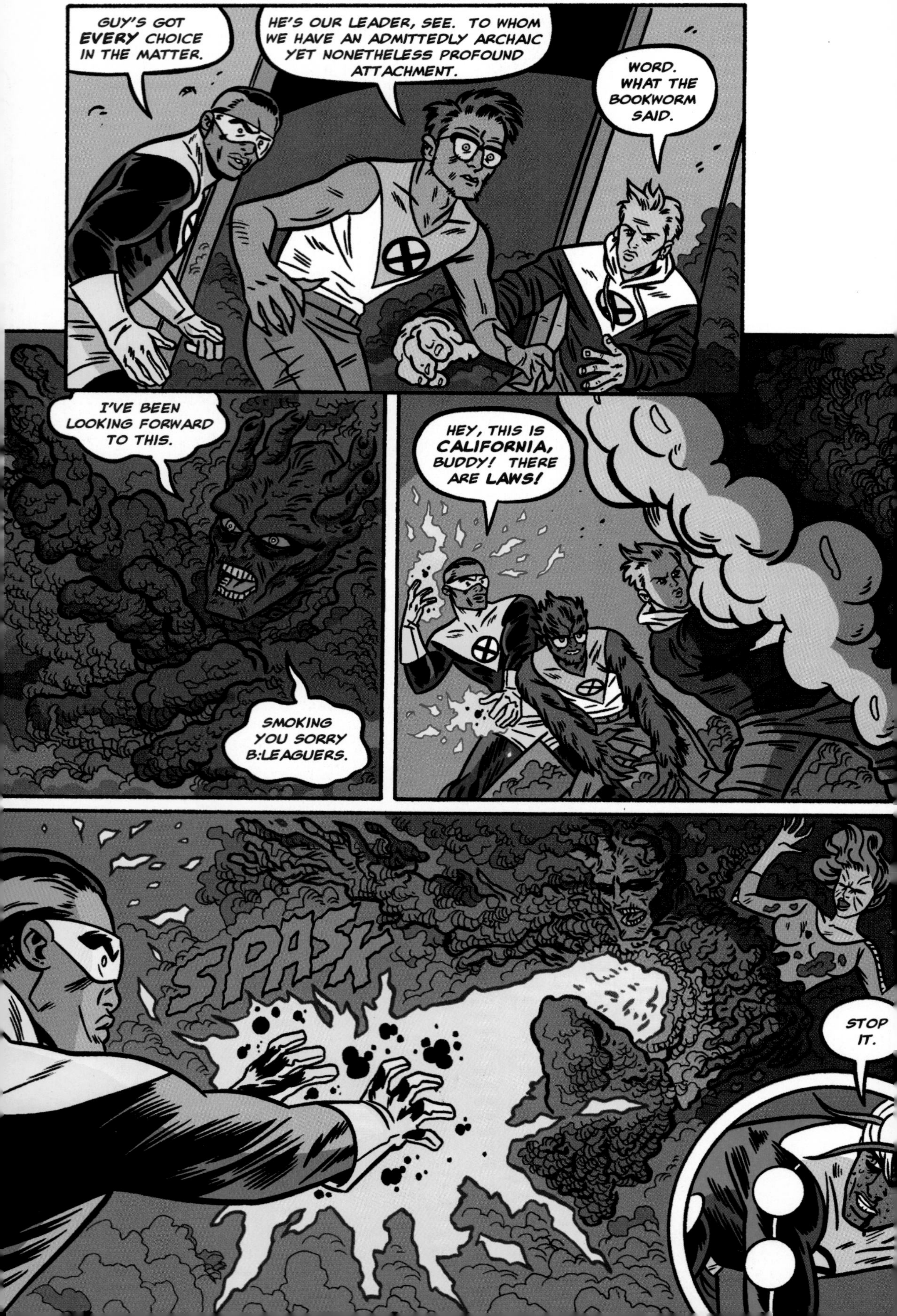

GUY'S GOT EVERY CHOICE IN THE MATTER.
HE'S OUR LEADER, SEE. TO WHOM WE HAVE AN ADMITTEDLY ARCHAIC YET NONETHELESS PROFOUND ATTACHMENT.
WORD. WHAT THE BOOKWORM SAID.
I'VE BEEN LOOKING FORWARD TO THIS.
SMOKING YOU SORRY B:LEAGUERS.
HEY, THIS IS CALIFORNIA, BUDDY! THERE ARE LAWS!
SPAK
STOP IT.

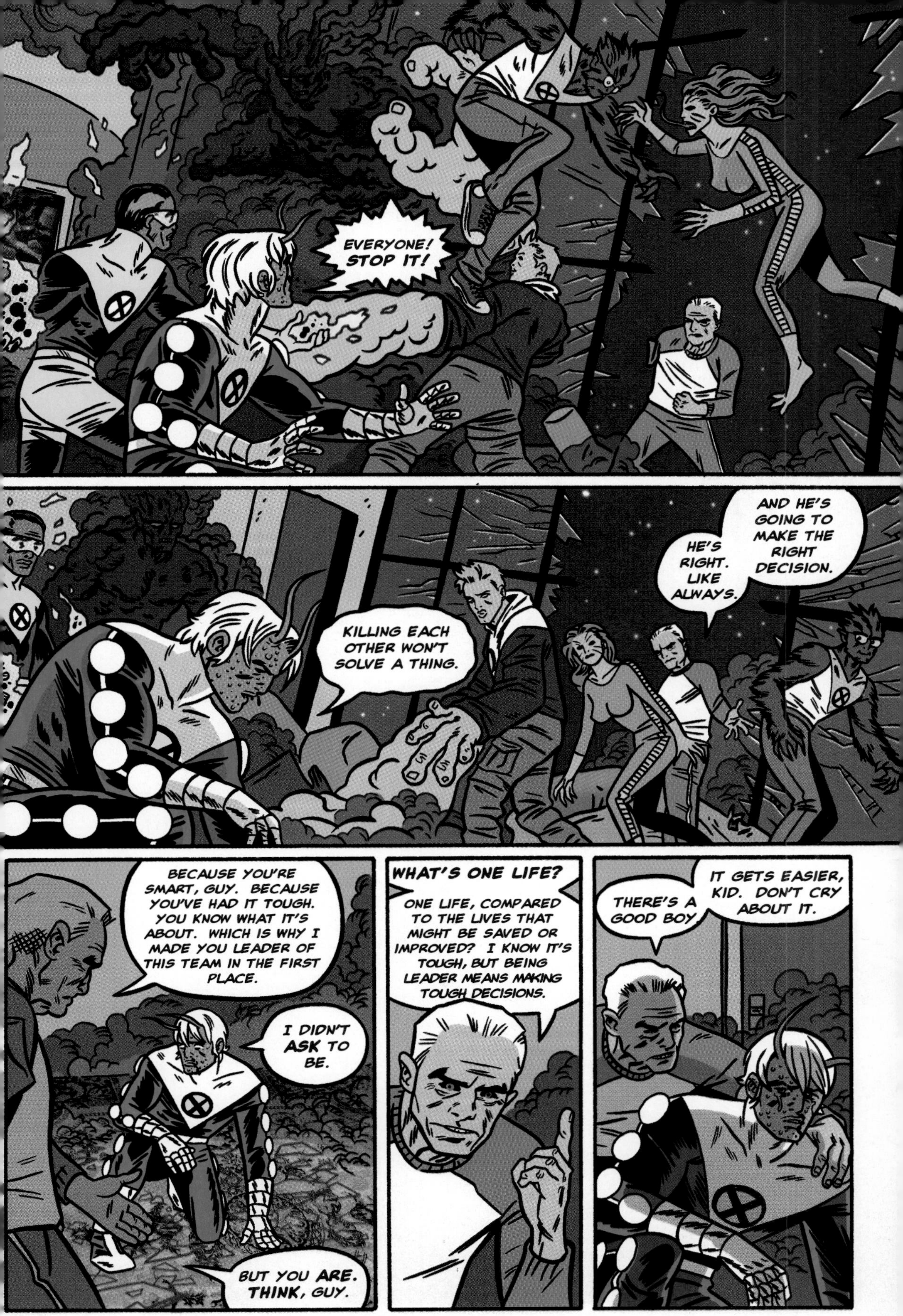

EVERYONE! STOP IT!
KILLING EACH OTHER WON'T SOLVE A THING.
HE'S RIGHT. LIKE ALWAYS.
AND HE'S GOING TO MAKE THE RIGHT DECISION.
BECAUSE YOU'RE SMART, GUY. BECAUSE YOU'VE HAD IT TOUGH. YOU KNOW WHAT IT'S ABOUT. WHICH IS WHY I MADE YOU LEADER OF THIS TEAM IN THE FIRST PLACE.
I DIDN'T ASK TO BE.
BUT YOU ARE. THINK, GUY.
WHAT'S ONE LIFE?
ONE LIFE, COMPARED TO THE LIVES THAT MIGHT BE SAVED OR IMPROVED? I KNOW IT'S TOUGH, BUT BEING LEADER MEANS MAKING TOUGH DECISIONS.
THERE'S A GOOD BOY.
IT GETS EASIER, KID. DON'T CRY ABOUT IT.

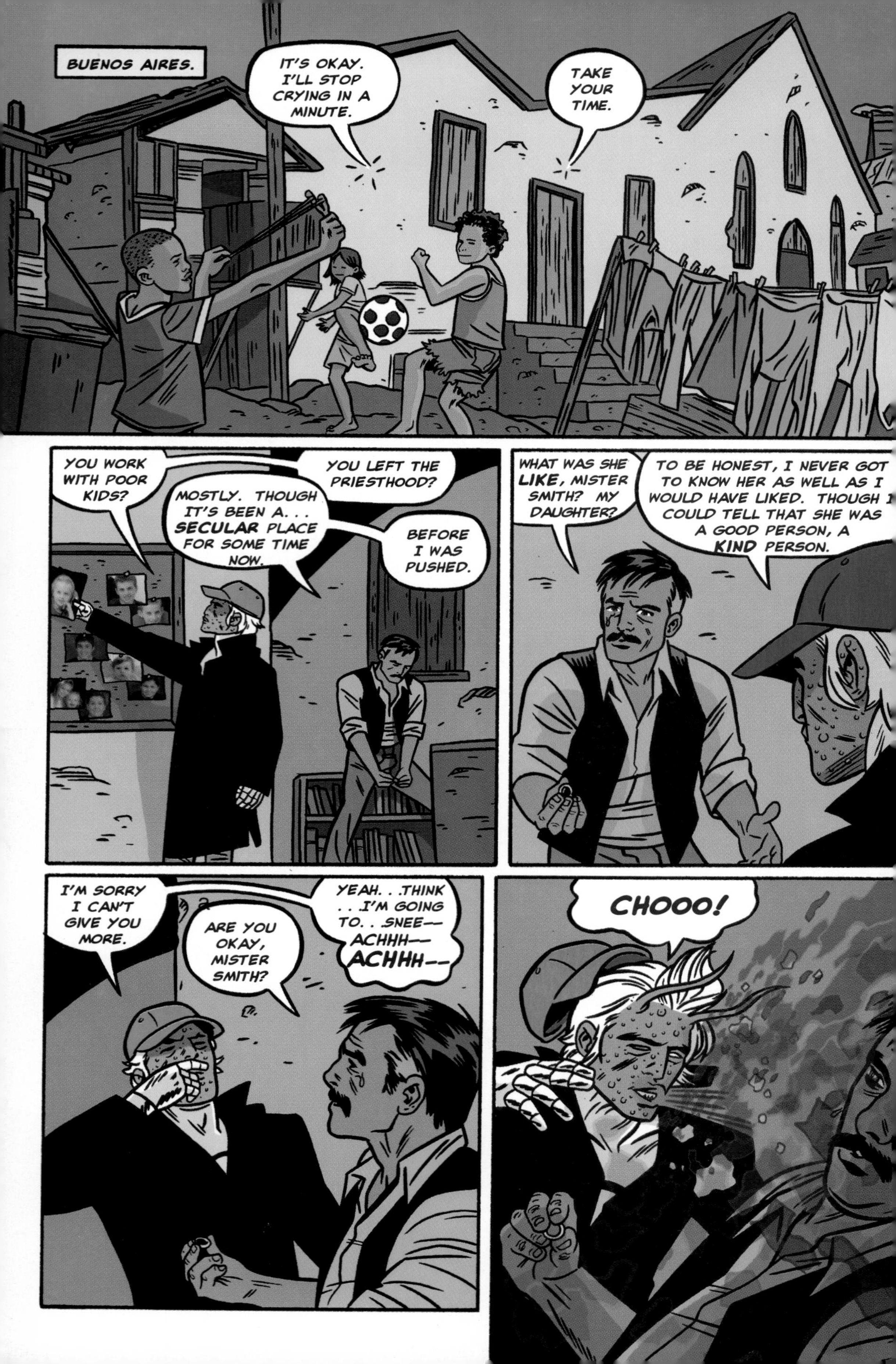
BUENOS AIRES.
IT'S OKAY. I'LL STOP CRYING IN A MINUTE.
TAKE YOUR TIME.
YOU WORK WITH POOR KIDS?
YOU LEFT THE PRIESTHOOD?
MOSTLY. THOUGH IT'S BEEN A. . . SECULAR PLACE FOR SOME TIME NOW.
BEFORE I WAS PUSHED.
WHAT WAS SHE LIKE, MISTER SMITH? MY DAUGHTER?
TO BE HONEST, I NEVER GOT TO KNOW HER AS WELL AS I WOULD HAVE LIKED. THOUGH I COULD TELL THAT SHE WAS A GOOD PERSON, A KIND PERSON.
I'M SORRY I CAN'T GIVE YOU MORE.
YEAH. . .THINK . . .I'M GOING TO. . .SNEE-- ACHHH-- ACHHH--
ARE YOU OKAY, MISTER SMITH?
CHOOO!

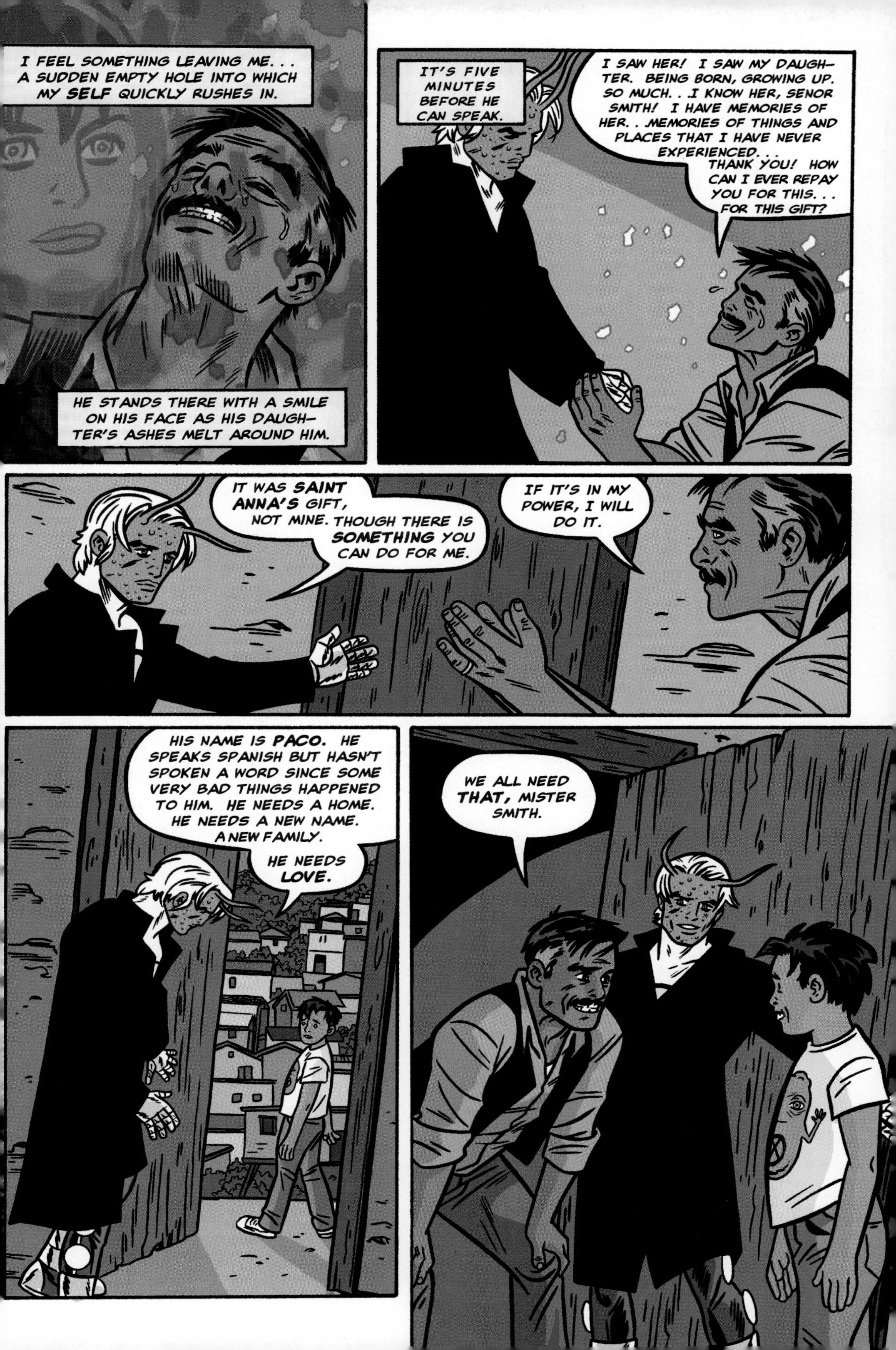
I FEEL SOMETHING LEAVING ME. . . A SUDDEN EMPTY HOLE INTO WHICH MY **SELF** QUICKLY RUSHES IN.
HE STANDS THERE WITH A SMILE ON HIS FACE AS HIS DAUGHTER'S ASHES MELT AROUND HIM.
IT'S FIVE MINUTES BEFORE HE CAN SPEAK.
I SAW HER! I SAW MY DAUGHTER. BEING BORN, GROWING UP. SO MUCH. . .I KNOW HER, SENOR SMITH! I HAVE MEMORIES OF HER. . .MEMORIES OF THINGS AND PLACES THAT I HAVE NEVER EXPERIENCED. . .
THANK YOU! HOW CAN I EVER REPAY YOU FOR THIS. . . FOR THIS GIFT?
IT WAS **SAINT ANNA'S** GIFT, NOT MINE.
THOUGH THERE IS **SOMETHING** YOU CAN DO FOR ME.
IF IT'S IN MY POWER, I WILL DO IT.
HIS NAME IS **PACO.** HE SPEAKS SPANISH BUT HASN'T SPOKEN A WORD SINCE SOME VERY BAD THINGS HAPPENED TO HIM. HE NEEDS A HOME. HE NEEDS A NEW NAME. A NEW FAMILY.
HE NEEDS **LOVE.**
WE ALL NEED **THAT,** MISTER SMITH.

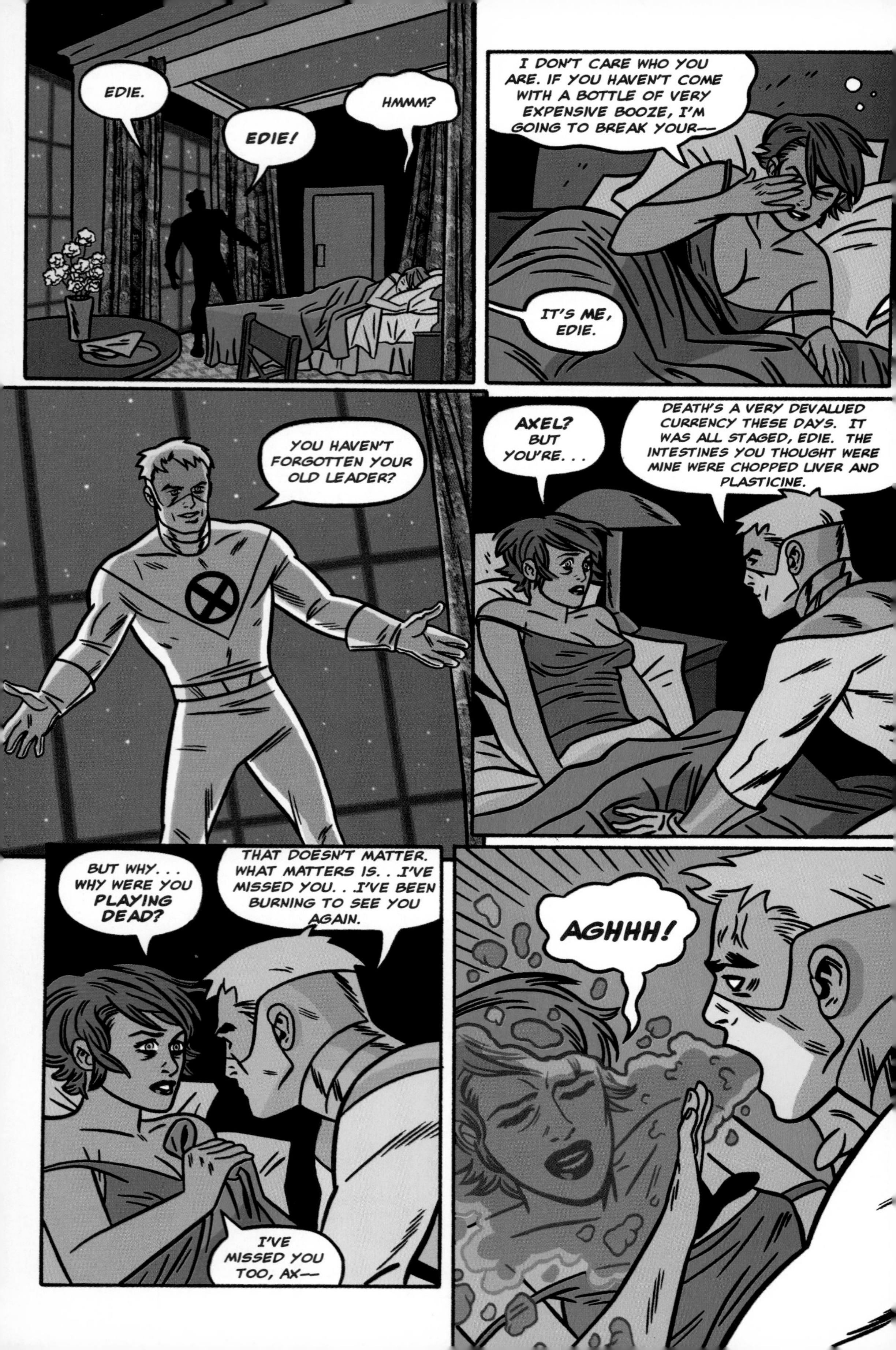
EDIE.
EDIE!
HMMM?
I DON'T CARE WHO YOU ARE. IF YOU HAVEN'T COME WITH A BOTTLE OF VERY EXPENSIVE BOOZE, I'M GOING TO BREAK YOUR--
IT'S ME, EDIE.
YOU HAVEN'T FORGOTTEN YOUR OLD LEADER?
AXEL? BUT YOU'RE. . .
DEATH'S A VERY DEVALUED CURRENCY THESE DAYS. IT WAS ALL STAGED, EDIE. THE INTESTINES YOU THOUGHT WERE MINE WERE CHOPPED LIVER AND PLASTICINE.
BUT WHY. . . WHY WERE YOU PLAYING DEAD?
THAT DOESN'T MATTER. WHAT MATTERS IS. . .I'VE MISSED YOU. . .I'VE BEEN BURNING TO SEE YOU AGAIN.
I'VE MISSED YOU TOO, AX--
AGHHH!

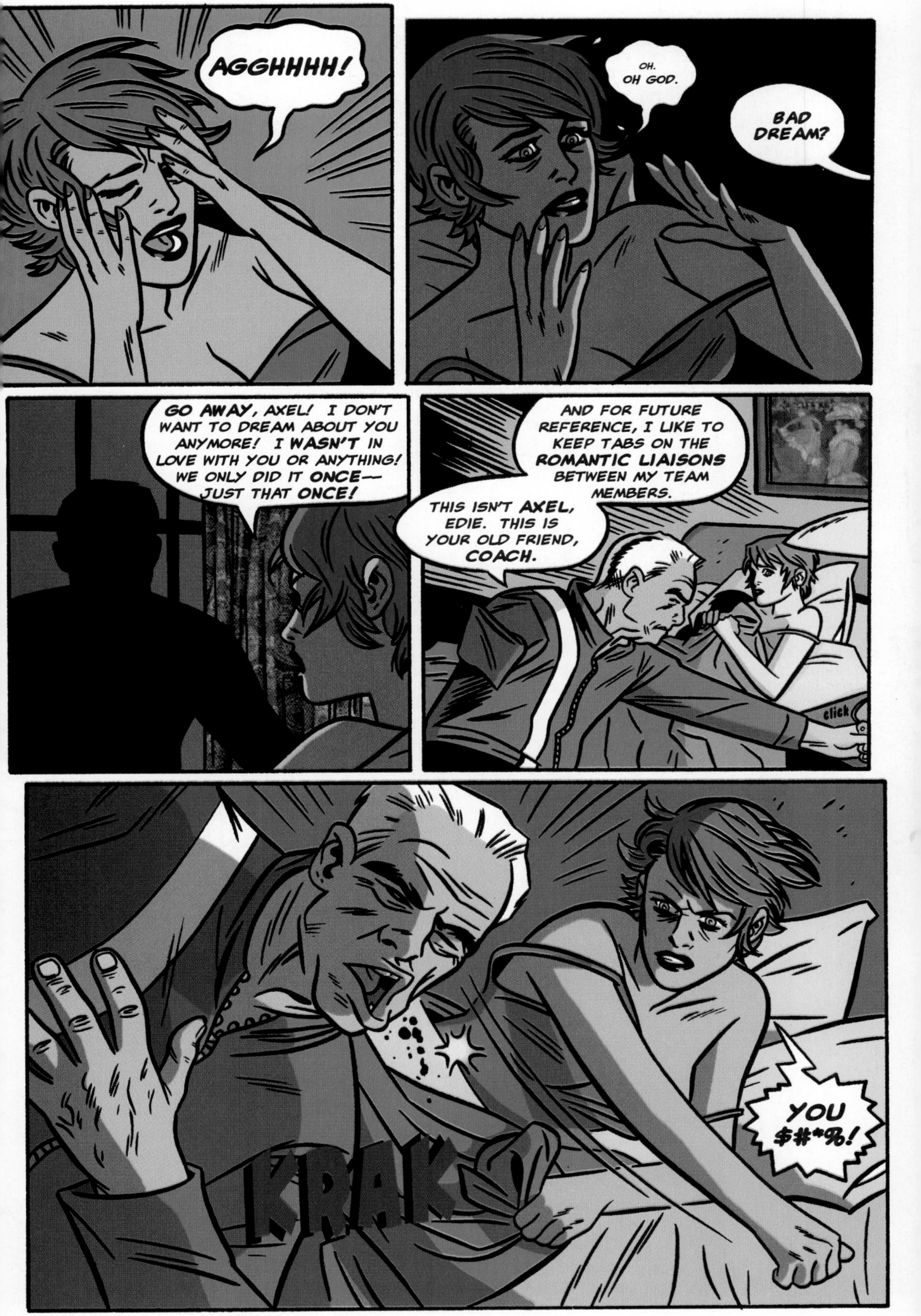
AGGHHHH!
OH.
OH GOD.
BAD DREAM?
GO AWAY, AXEL! I DON'T WANT TO DREAM ABOUT YOU ANYMORE! I WASN'T IN LOVE WITH YOU OR ANYTHING! WE ONLY DID IT ONCE— JUST THAT ONCE!
THIS ISN'T AXEL, EDIE. THIS IS YOUR OLD FRIEND, COACH.
AND FOR FUTURE REFERENCE, I LIKE TO KEEP TABS ON THE ROMANTIC LIAISONS BETWEEN MY TEAM MEMBERS.
click
KRAK
YOU $#*%!

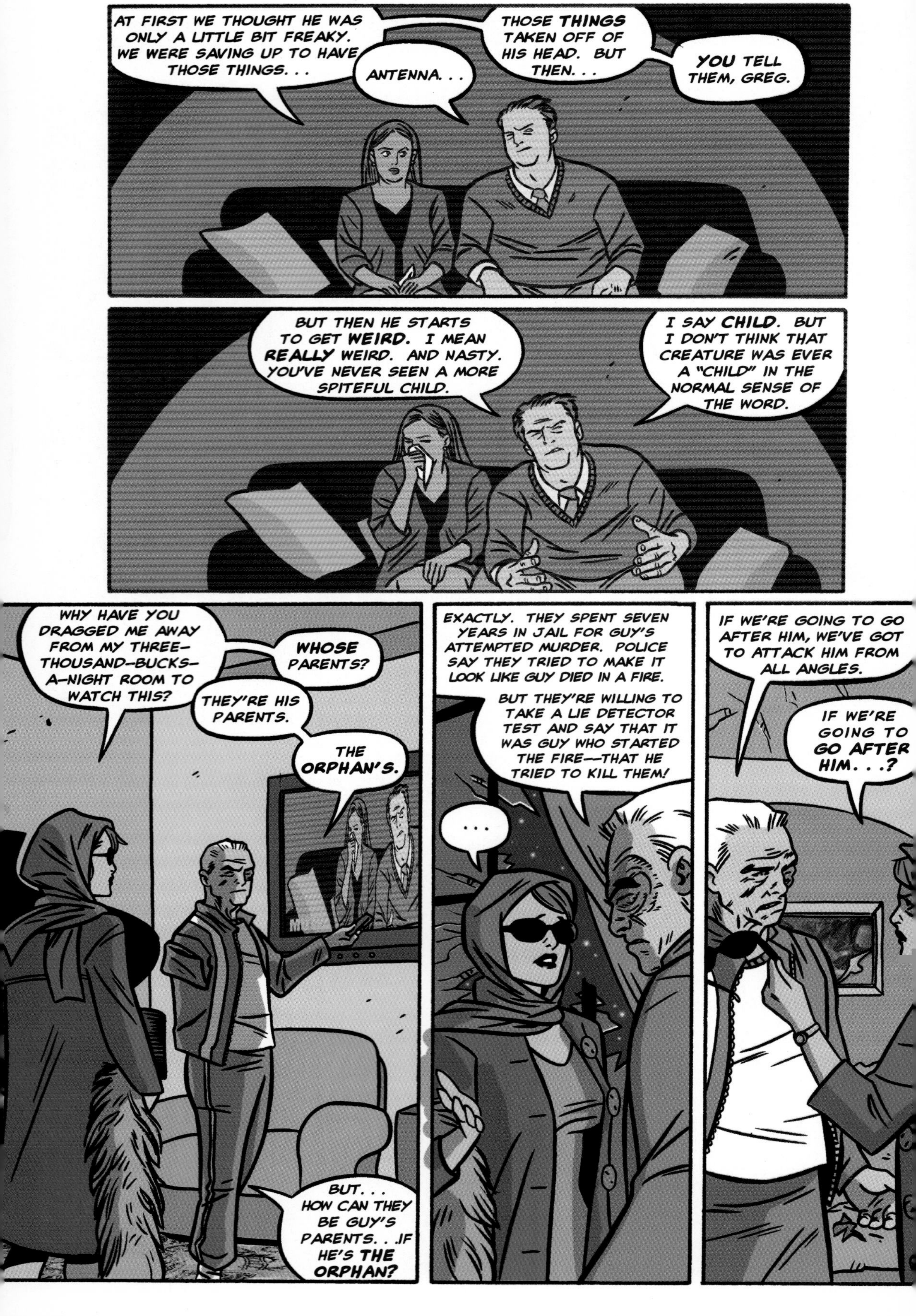

AT FIRST WE THOUGHT HE WAS ONLY A LITTLE BIT FREAKY. WE WERE SAVING UP TO HAVE THOSE THINGS. . .
ANTENNA. . .
THOSE THINGS TAKEN OFF OF HIS HEAD. BUT THEN. . .
YOU TELL THEM, GREG.
BUT THEN HE STARTS TO GET WEIRD. I MEAN REALLY WEIRD. AND NASTY. YOU'VE NEVER SEEN A MORE SPITEFUL CHILD.
I SAY CHILD. BUT I DON'T THINK THAT CREATURE WAS EVER A "CHILD" IN THE NORMAL SENSE OF THE WORD.
WHY HAVE YOU DRAGGED ME AWAY FROM MY THREE-THOUSAND-BUCKS-A-NIGHT ROOM TO WATCH THIS?
THEY'RE HIS PARENTS.
WHOSE PARENTS?
THE ORPHAN'S.
BUT. . . HOW CAN THEY BE GUY'S PARENTS. . .IF HE'S THE ORPHAN?
EXACTLY. THEY SPENT SEVEN YEARS IN JAIL FOR GUY'S ATTEMPTED MURDER. POLICE SAY THEY TRIED TO MAKE IT LOOK LIKE GUY DIED IN A FIRE.
BUT THEY'RE WILLING TO TAKE A LIE DETECTOR TEST AND SAY THAT IT WAS GUY WHO STARTED THE FIRE--THAT HE TRIED TO KILL THEM!
. . .
IF WE'RE GOING TO GO AFTER HIM, WE'VE GOT TO ATTACK HIM FROM ALL ANGLES.
IF WE'RE GOING TO GO AFTER HIM. . .?

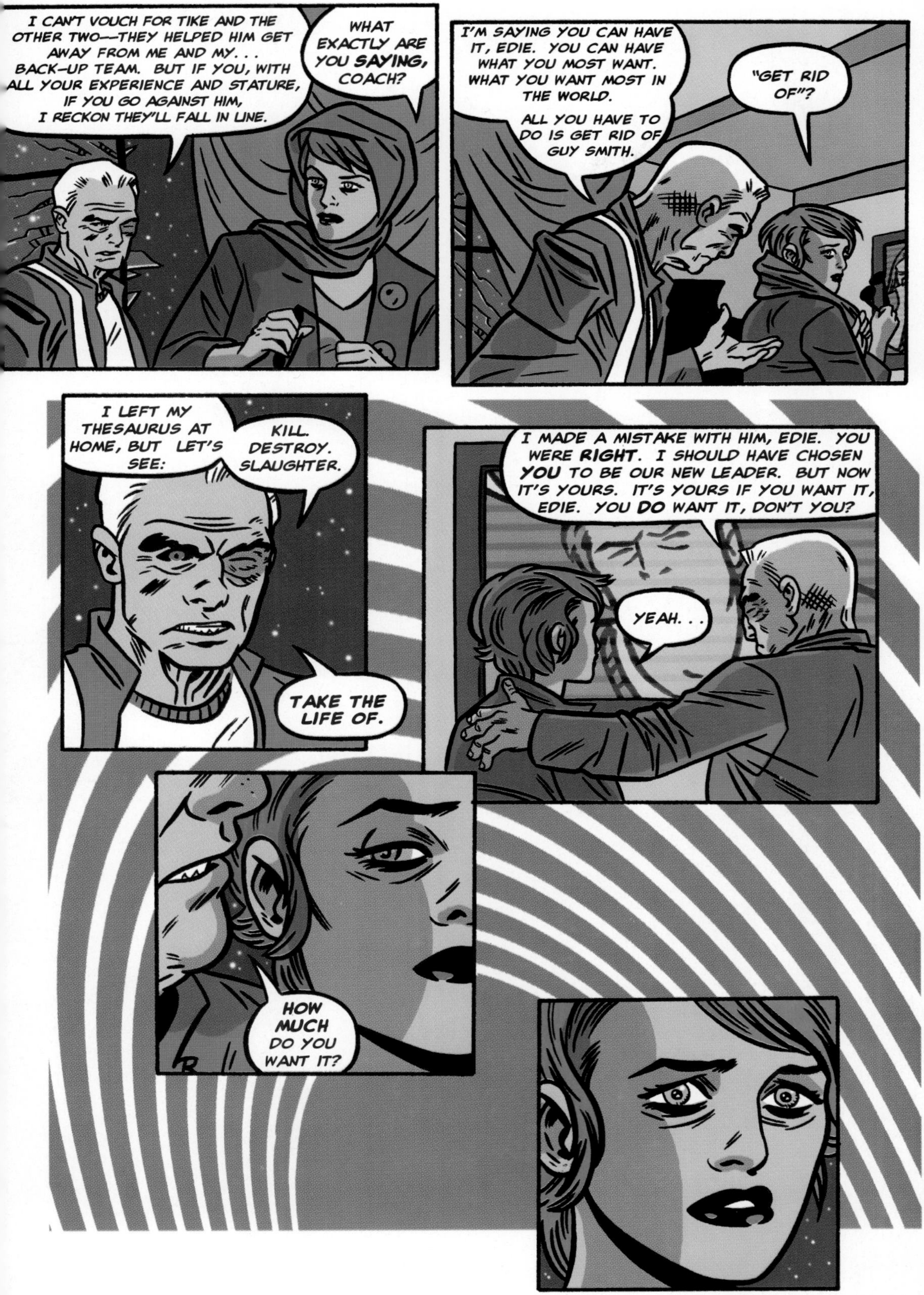
I CAN'T VOUCH FOR TIKE AND THE OTHER TWO--THEY HELPED HIM GET AWAY FROM ME AND MY... BACK-UP TEAM. BUT IF YOU, WITH ALL YOUR EXPERIENCE AND STATURE, IF YOU GO AGAINST HIM, I RECKON THEY'LL FALL IN LINE.
WHAT EXACTLY ARE YOU SAYING, COACH?
I'M SAYING YOU CAN HAVE IT, EDIE. YOU CAN HAVE WHAT YOU MOST WANT. WHAT YOU WANT MOST IN THE WORLD.
ALL YOU HAVE TO DO IS GET RID OF GUY SMITH.
"GET RID OF"?
I LEFT MY THESAURUS AT HOME, BUT LET'S SEE:
KILL. DESTROY. SLAUGHTER.
TAKE THE LIFE OF.
I MADE A MISTAKE WITH HIM, EDIE. YOU WERE RIGHT. I SHOULD HAVE CHOSEN YOU TO BE OUR NEW LEADER. BUT NOW IT'S YOURS. IT'S YOURS IF YOU WANT IT, EDIE. YOU DO WANT IT, DON'T YOU?
YEAH...
HOW MUCH DO YOU WANT IT?

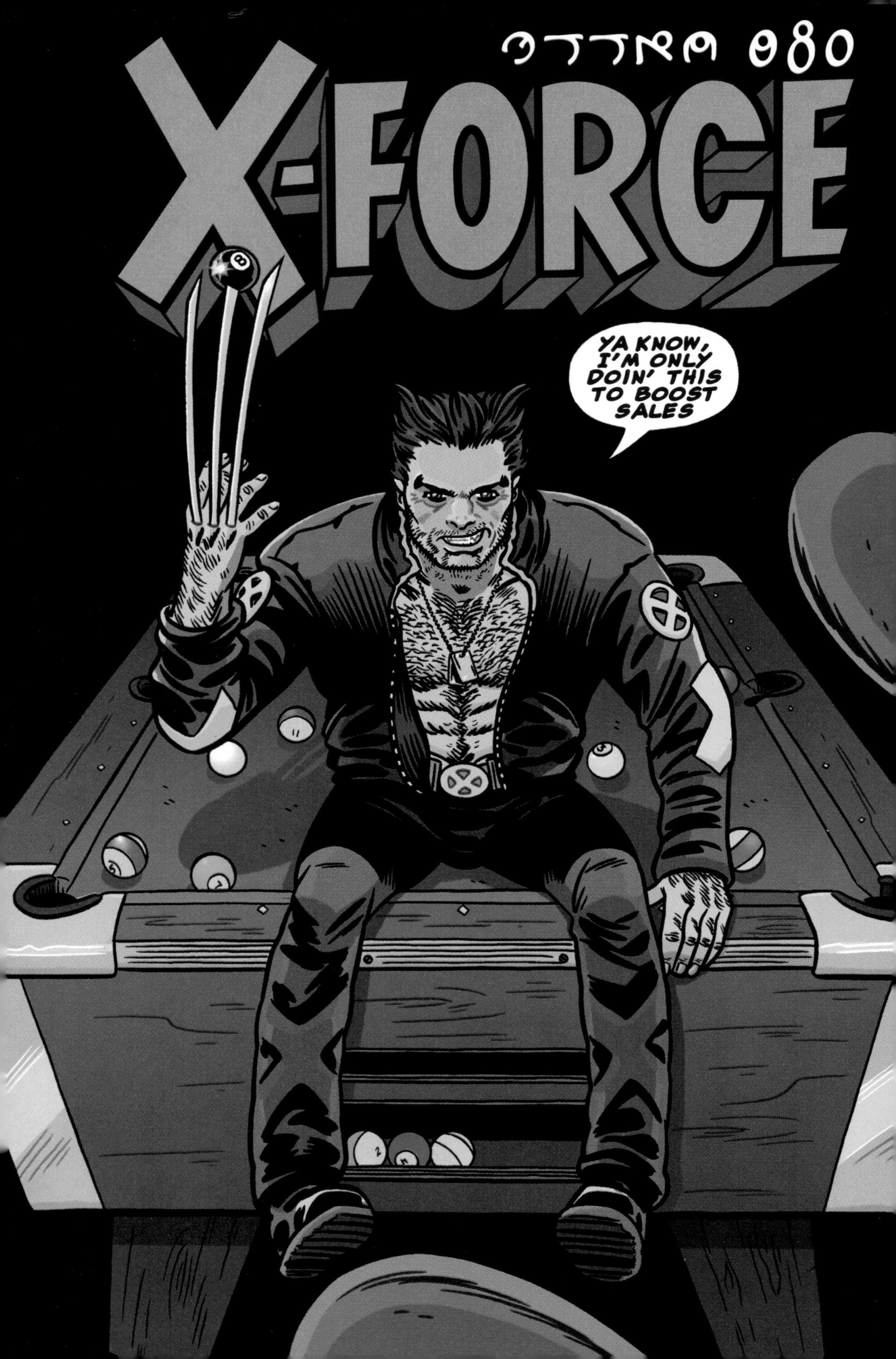
X-FORCE
YA KNOW, I'M ONLY DOIN' THIS TO BOOST SALES

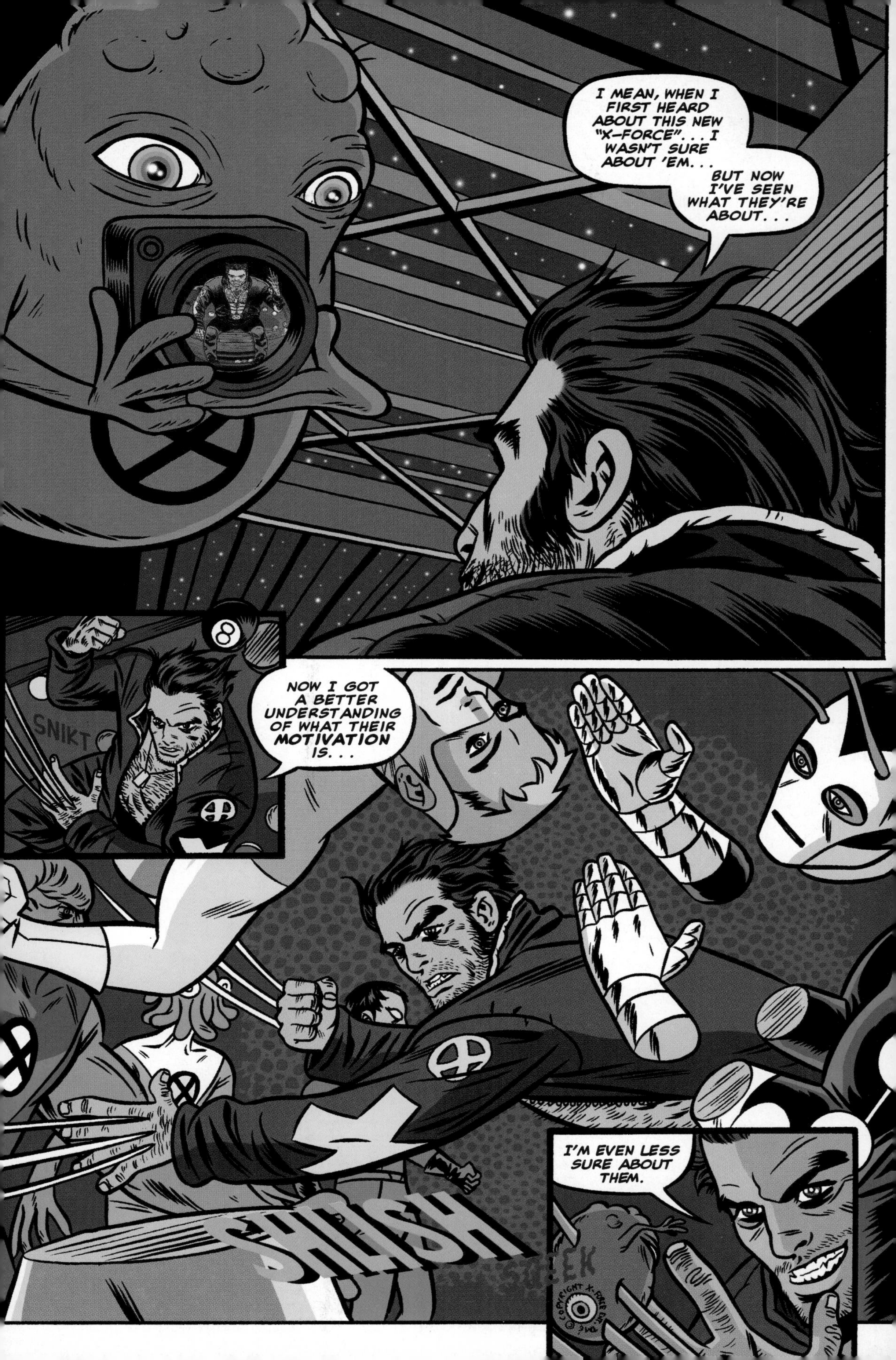
I MEAN, WHEN I FIRST HEARD ABOUT THIS NEW "X-FORCE"... I WASN'T SURE ABOUT 'EM...
BUT NOW I'VE SEEN WHAT THEY'RE ABOUT...
SNIKT
NOW I GOT A BETTER UNDERSTANDING OF WHAT THEIR **MOTIVATION** IS...
I'M EVEN LESS SURE ABOUT THEM.

HOW WAS THAT?

ᔕᎥᎧ ᎧᎯᎧ ᏰᎧᎧ ᎧᎧᏋᏰᎧ

NOT REALLY SURE IF I FOUND, YOU KNOW, MY "CENTER."

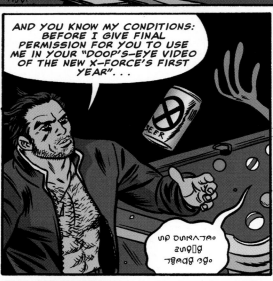

AND YOU KNOW MY CONDITIONS: BEFORE I GIVE FINAL PERMISSION FOR YOU TO USE ME IN YOUR "DOOP'S-EYE VIDEO OF THE NEW X-FORCE'S FIRST YEAR"...

ᎧᎯ ᎧᎧᎥᏒᎯᏠᎧ ᏕᎧᎧᏰᏸᎧ ᏽᏰᎧᏰᎧ ᎧᎧᎧ

I DON'T CARE **HOW** LONG WE'VE KNOWN EACH OTHER, I REALLY DON'T KNOW WHY YOU'RE STILL HANGIN' WITH THESE CLOWNS!

ᎧᎥᎯ ᏕᏪᎯᏒ ᎥᎯᏽᎧᎧᎧᏽᎧ ᎧᎯᎧᎧᎧ

EASY FOR **YOU** TO SAY.

BUT THE **COACH**, HE'S ONE MEAN SONOFA-GUN. AND AS FOR THAT **U-GO GIRL**...

WELL, WHAT I'D LIKE TO DO WITH HER PROBABLY WOULDN'T FIND ITS WAY ONTO YOUR LITTLE VIDEO DIARY.

SNIKT

ᏰᎧᏕᏽᎧ ᏰᎧᎧᏒ ᎧᏒ ᎧᎧᎧ

YA MEAN...?

ᎧᏠᎧᎧᏽᏕᏕᎧ

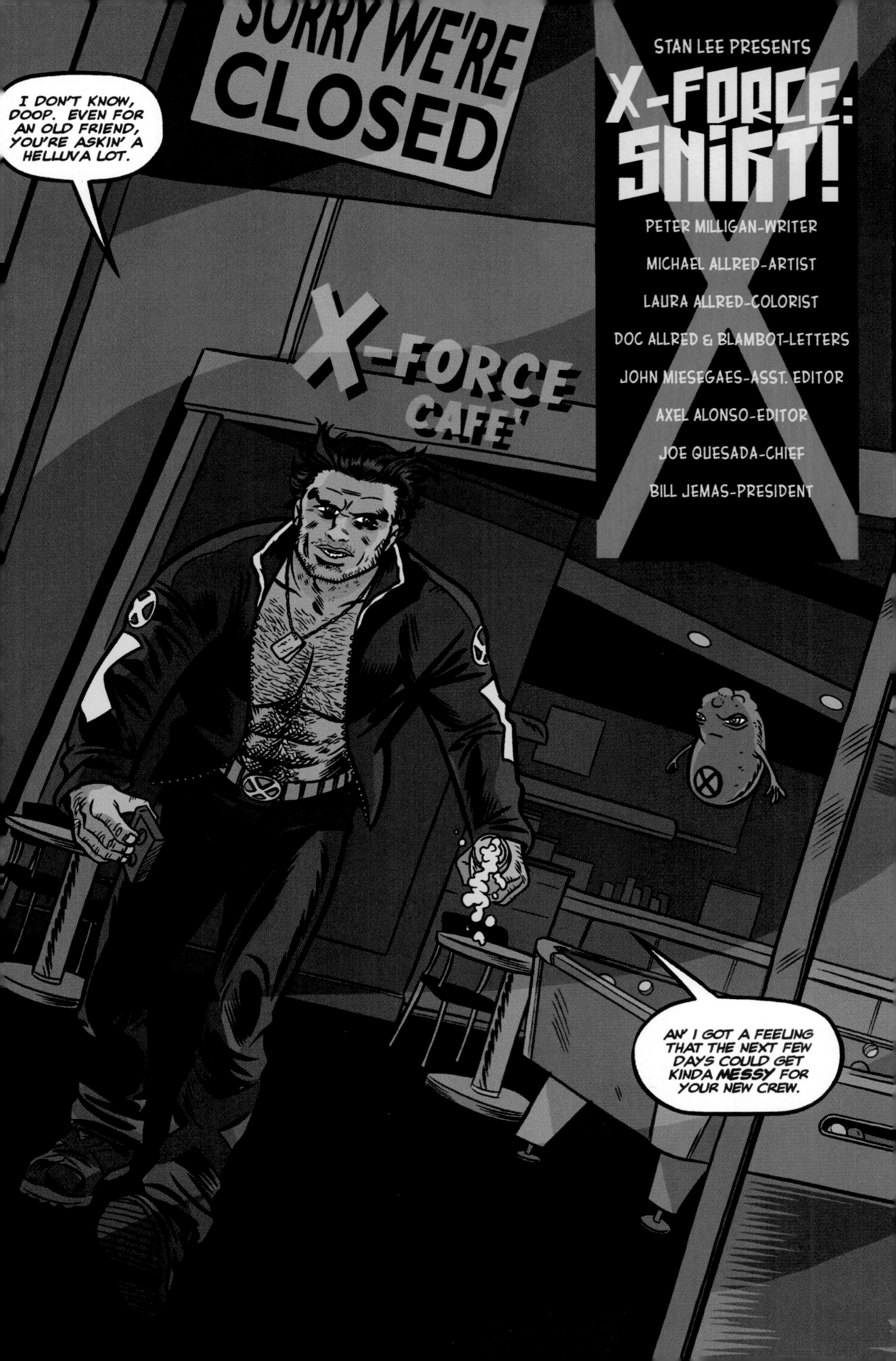
SORRY WE'RE CLOSED
I DON'T KNOW, DOOP. EVEN FOR AN OLD FRIEND, YOU'RE ASKIN' A HELLUVA LOT.
STAN LEE PRESENTS
X-FORCE: SNIKT!
PETER MILLIGAN-WRITER
MICHAEL ALLRED-ARTIST
LAURA ALLRED-COLORIST
DOC ALLRED & BLAMBOT-LETTERS
JOHN MIESEGAES-ASST. EDITOR
AXEL ALONSO-EDITOR
JOE QUESADA-CHIEF
BILL JEMAS-PRESIDENT
X-FORCE CAFE'
AN' I GOT A FEELING THAT THE NEXT FEW DAYS COULD GET KINDA MESSY FOR YOUR NEW CREW.

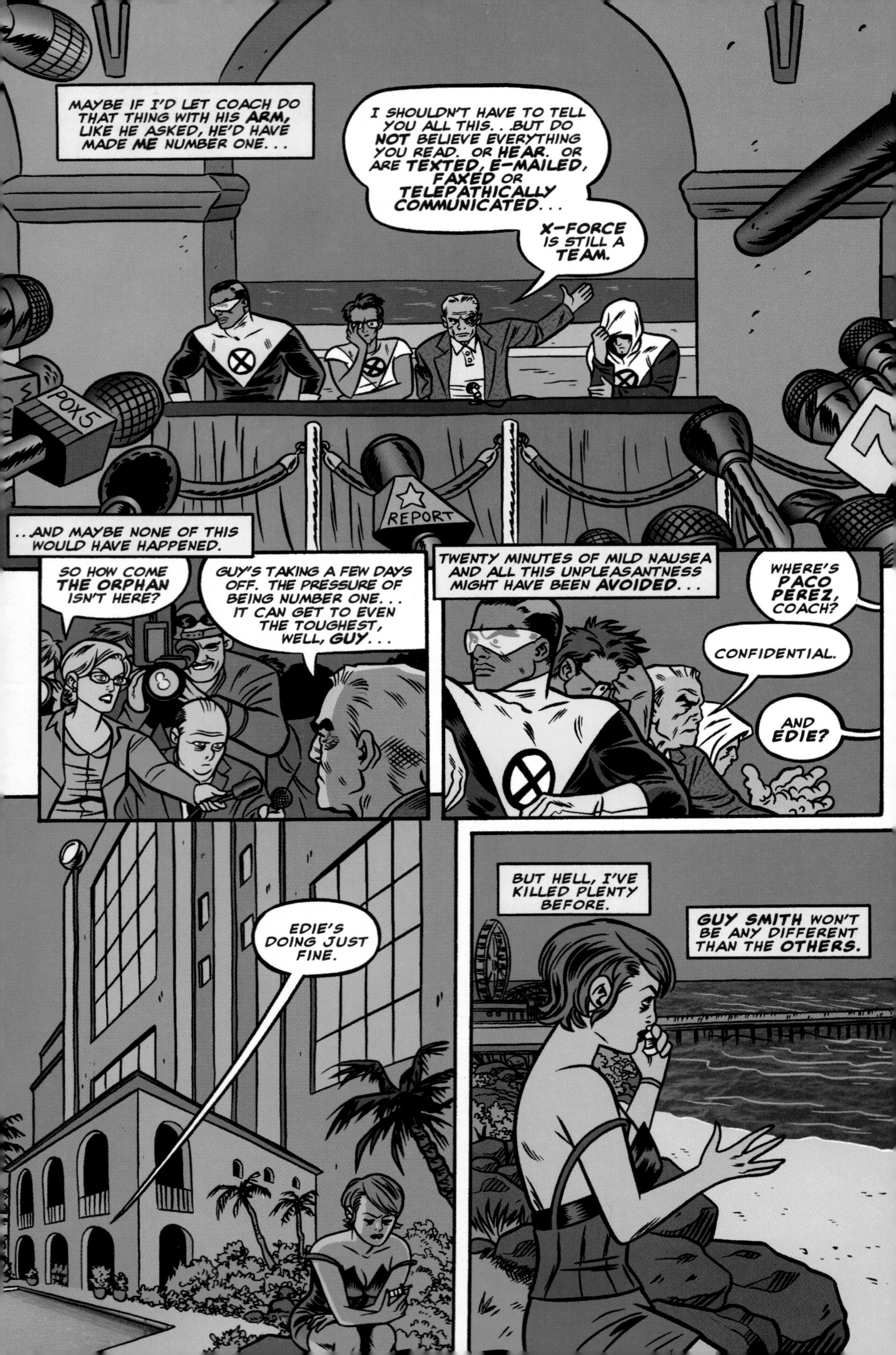

MAYBE IF I'D LET COACH DO THAT THING WITH HIS ARM, LIKE HE ASKED, HE'D HAVE MADE ME NUMBER ONE. . .
I SHOULDN'T HAVE TO TELL YOU ALL THIS. . .BUT DO NOT BELIEVE EVERYTHING YOU READ. OR HEAR. OR ARE TEXTED, E-MAILED, FAXED OR TELEPATHICALLY COMMUNICATED. . .
X-FORCE IS STILL A TEAM.
FOX5
REPORT
. . .AND MAYBE NONE OF THIS WOULD HAVE HAPPENED.
SO HOW COME THE ORPHAN ISN'T HERE?
GUY'S TAKING A FEW DAYS OFF. THE PRESSURE OF BEING NUMBER ONE. . . IT CAN GET TO EVEN THE TOUGHEST, WELL, GUY. . .
TWENTY MINUTES OF MILD NAUSEA AND ALL THIS UNPLEASANTNESS MIGHT HAVE BEEN AVOIDED. . .
WHERE'S PACO PEREZ, COACH?
CONFIDENTIAL.
AND EDIE?
EDIE'S DOING JUST FINE.
BUT HELL, I'VE KILLED PLENTY BEFORE.
GUY SMITH WON'T BE ANY DIFFERENT THAN THE OTHERS.

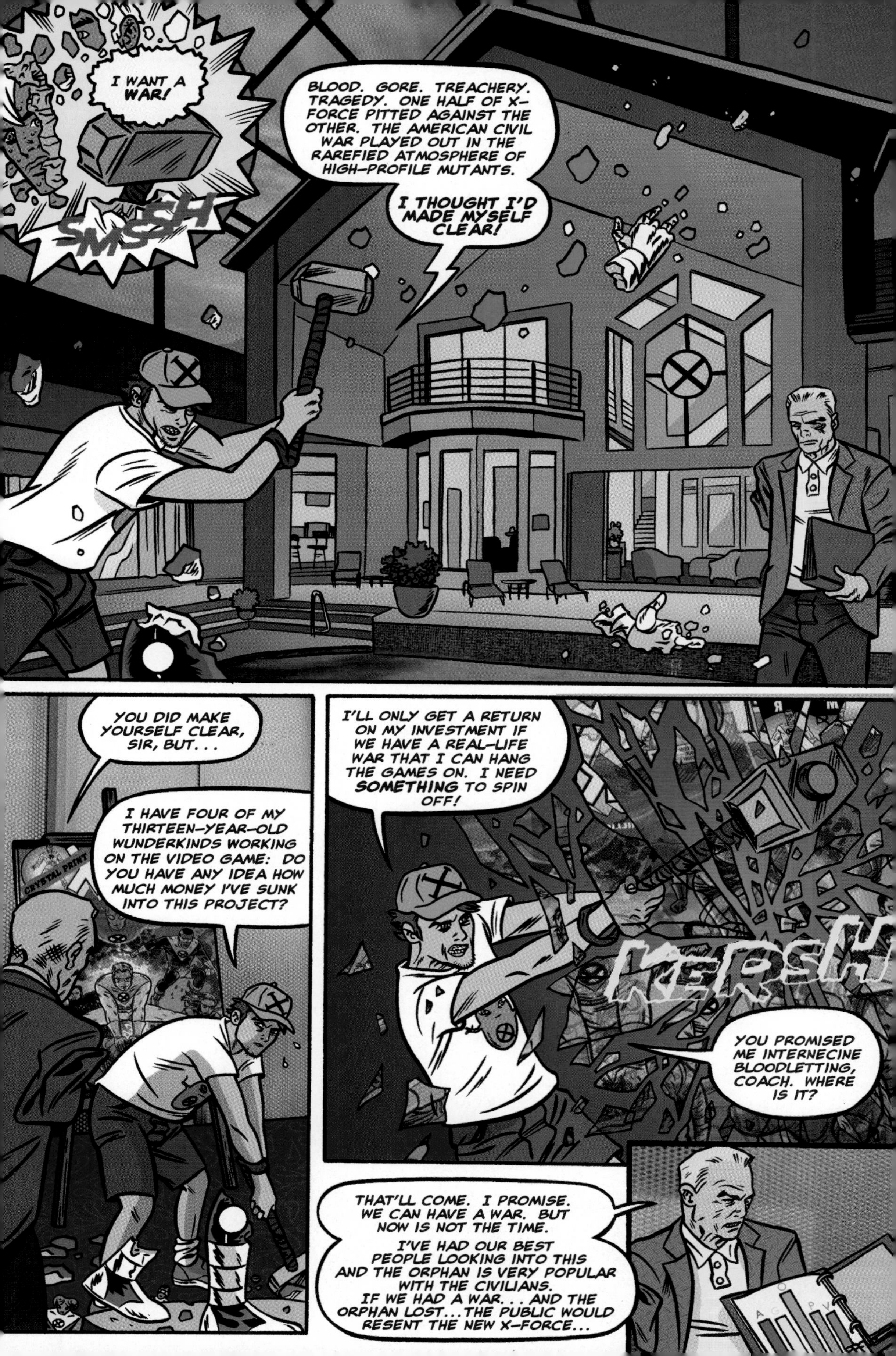
I WANT A WAR!
SMSSH
BLOOD. GORE. TREACHERY. TRAGEDY. ONE HALF OF X-FORCE PITTED AGAINST THE OTHER. THE AMERICAN CIVIL WAR PLAYED OUT IN THE RAREFIED ATMOSPHERE OF HIGH-PROFILE MUTANTS.
I THOUGHT I'D MADE MYSELF CLEAR!
YOU DID MAKE YOURSELF CLEAR, SIR, BUT...
I HAVE FOUR OF MY THIRTEEN-YEAR-OLD WUNDERKINDS WORKING ON THE VIDEO GAME: DO YOU HAVE ANY IDEA HOW MUCH MONEY I'VE SUNK INTO THIS PROJECT?
CRYSTAL PRINT
I'LL ONLY GET A RETURN ON MY INVESTMENT IF WE HAVE A REAL-LIFE WAR THAT I CAN HANG THE GAMES ON. I NEED SOMETHING TO SPIN OFF!
KERSH
YOU PROMISED ME INTERNECINE BLOODLETTING, COACH. WHERE IS IT?
THAT'LL COME. I PROMISE. WE CAN HAVE A WAR. BUT NOW IS NOT THE TIME.
I'VE HAD OUR BEST PEOPLE LOOKING INTO THIS AND THE ORPHAN IS VERY POPULAR WITH THE CIVILIANS.
IF WE HAD A WAR... AND THE ORPHAN LOST... THE PUBLIC WOULD RESENT THE NEW X-FORCE...

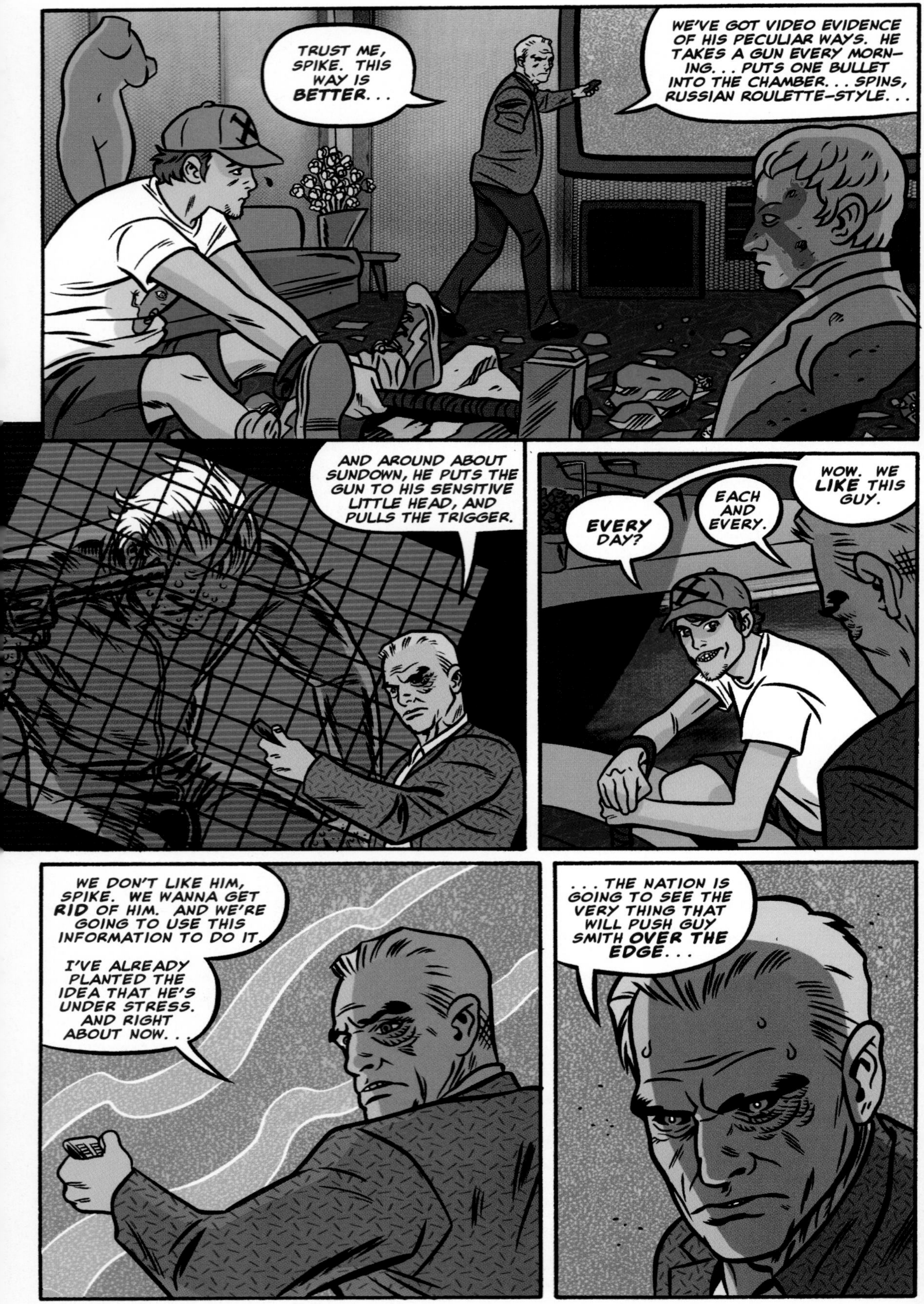
TRUST ME, SPIKE. THIS WAY IS BETTER...
WE'VE GOT VIDEO EVIDENCE OF HIS PECULIAR WAYS. HE TAKES A GUN EVERY MORNING... PUTS ONE BULLET INTO THE CHAMBER... SPINS, RUSSIAN ROULETTE-STYLE...
AND AROUND ABOUT SUNDOWN, HE PUTS THE GUN TO HIS SENSITIVE LITTLE HEAD, AND PULLS THE TRIGGER.
EVERY DAY?
EACH AND EVERY.
WOW. WE LIKE THIS GUY.
WE DON'T LIKE HIM, SPIKE. WE WANNA GET RID OF HIM. AND WE'RE GOING TO USE THIS INFORMATION TO DO IT.
I'VE ALREADY PLANTED THE IDEA THAT HE'S UNDER STRESS. AND RIGHT ABOUT NOW...
... THE NATION IS GOING TO SEE THE VERY THING THAT WILL PUSH GUY SMITH OVER THE EDGE...

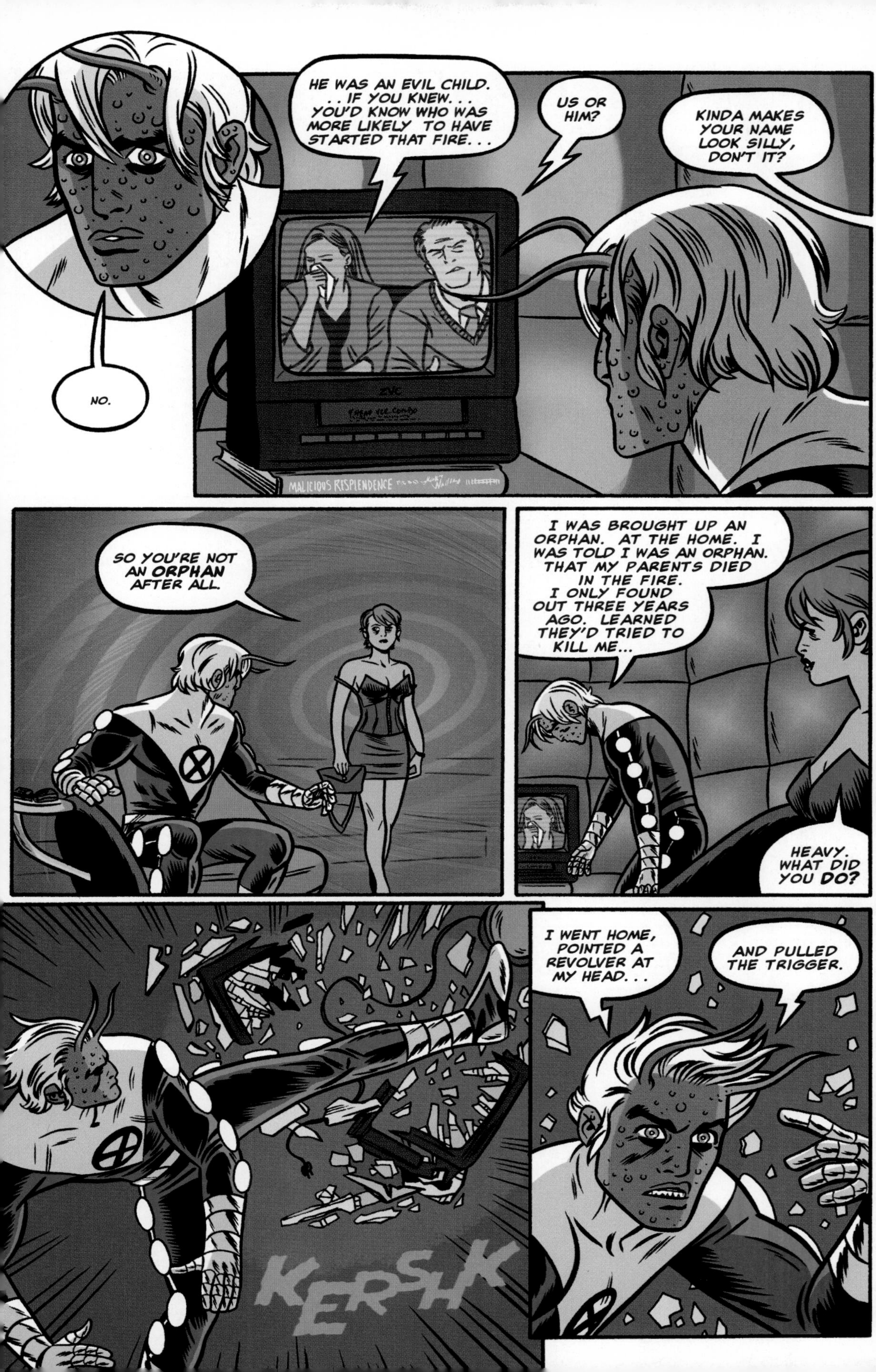
NO.
HE WAS AN EVIL CHILD. . . IF YOU KNEW. . . YOU'D KNOW WHO WAS MORE LIKELY TO HAVE STARTED THAT FIRE. . .
US OR HIM?
KINDA MAKES YOUR NAME LOOK SILLY, DON'T IT?
ZVC
MALICIOUS RISPLENDENCE
SO YOU'RE NOT AN **ORPHAN** AFTER ALL.
I WAS BROUGHT UP AN ORPHAN. AT THE HOME. I WAS TOLD I WAS AN ORPHAN. THAT MY PARENTS DIED IN THE FIRE. I ONLY FOUND OUT THREE YEARS AGO. LEARNED THEY'D TRIED TO KILL ME...
HEAVY. WHAT DID YOU **DO?**
KERSHK
I WENT HOME, POINTED A REVOLVER AT MY HEAD. . .
AND PULLED THE TRIGGER.

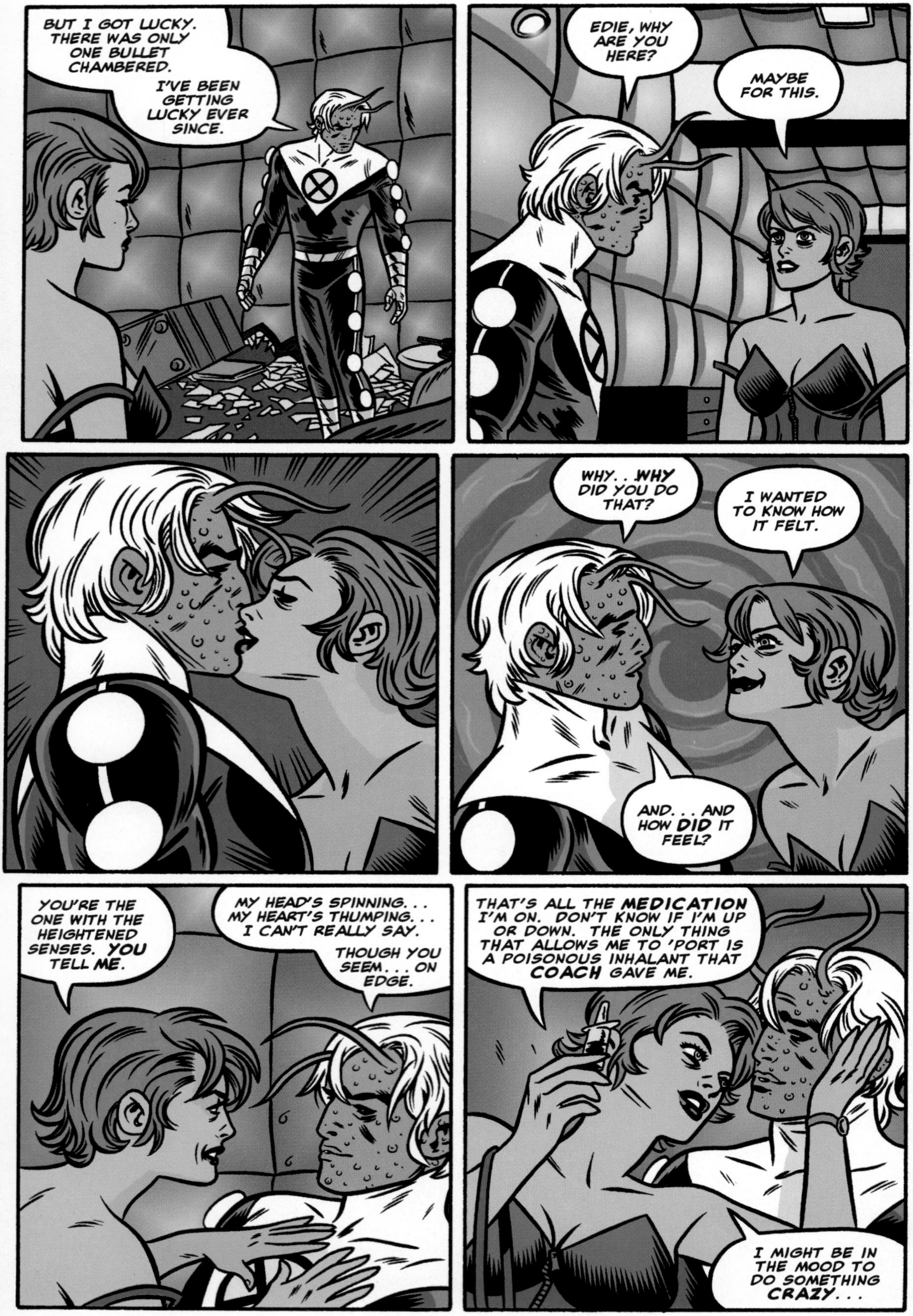
BUT I GOT LUCKY. THERE WAS ONLY ONE BULLET CHAMBERED.
I'VE BEEN GETTING LUCKY EVER SINCE.
EDIE, WHY ARE YOU HERE?
MAYBE FOR THIS.
WHY. . WHY DID YOU DO THAT?
I WANTED TO KNOW HOW IT FELT.
AND. . . AND HOW DID IT FEEL?
YOU'RE THE ONE WITH THE HEIGHTENED SENSES. YOU TELL ME.
MY HEAD'S SPINNING. . . MY HEART'S THUMPING. . . I CAN'T REALLY SAY.
THOUGH YOU SEEM. . . ON EDGE.
THAT'S ALL THE MEDICATION I'M ON. DON'T KNOW IF I'M UP OR DOWN. THE ONLY THING THAT ALLOWS ME TO 'PORT IS A POISONOUS INHALANT THAT COACH GAVE ME.
I MIGHT BE IN THE MOOD TO DO SOMETHING CRAZY. . .

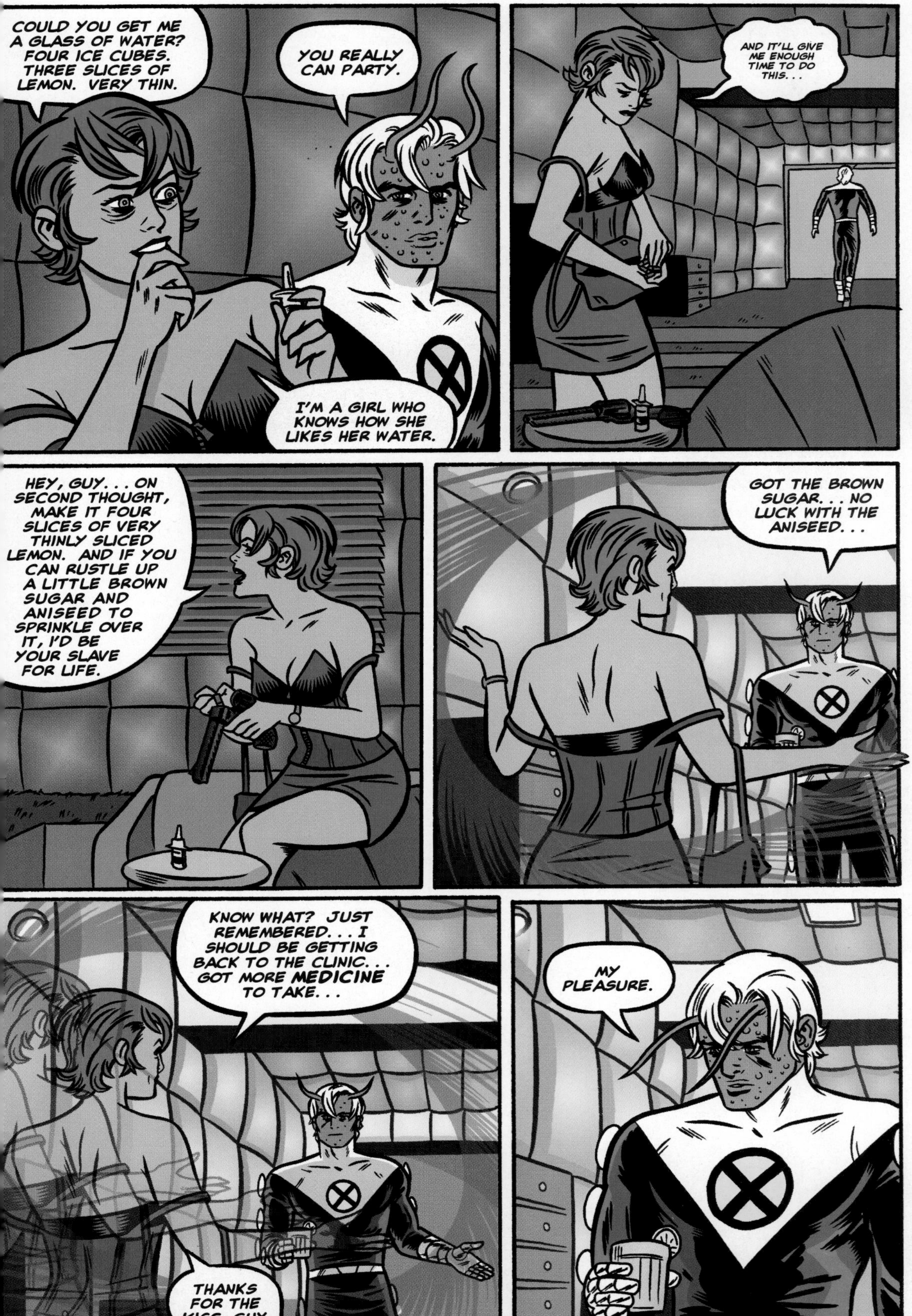

COULD YOU GET ME A GLASS OF WATER? FOUR ICE CUBES. THREE SLICES OF LEMON. VERY THIN.
YOU REALLY CAN PARTY.
I'M A GIRL WHO KNOWS HOW SHE LIKES HER WATER.
AND IT'LL GIVE ME ENOUGH TIME TO DO THIS...
HEY, GUY... ON SECOND THOUGHT, MAKE IT FOUR SLICES OF VERY THINLY SLICED LEMON. AND IF YOU CAN RUSTLE UP A LITTLE BROWN SUGAR AND ANISEED TO SPRINKLE OVER IT, I'D BE YOUR SLAVE FOR LIFE.
GOT THE BROWN SUGAR... NO LUCK WITH THE ANISEED...
KNOW WHAT? JUST REMEMBERED... I SHOULD BE GETTING BACK TO THE CLINIC... GOT MORE MEDICINE TO TAKE...
THANKS FOR THE KISS, GUY.
MY PLEASURE.

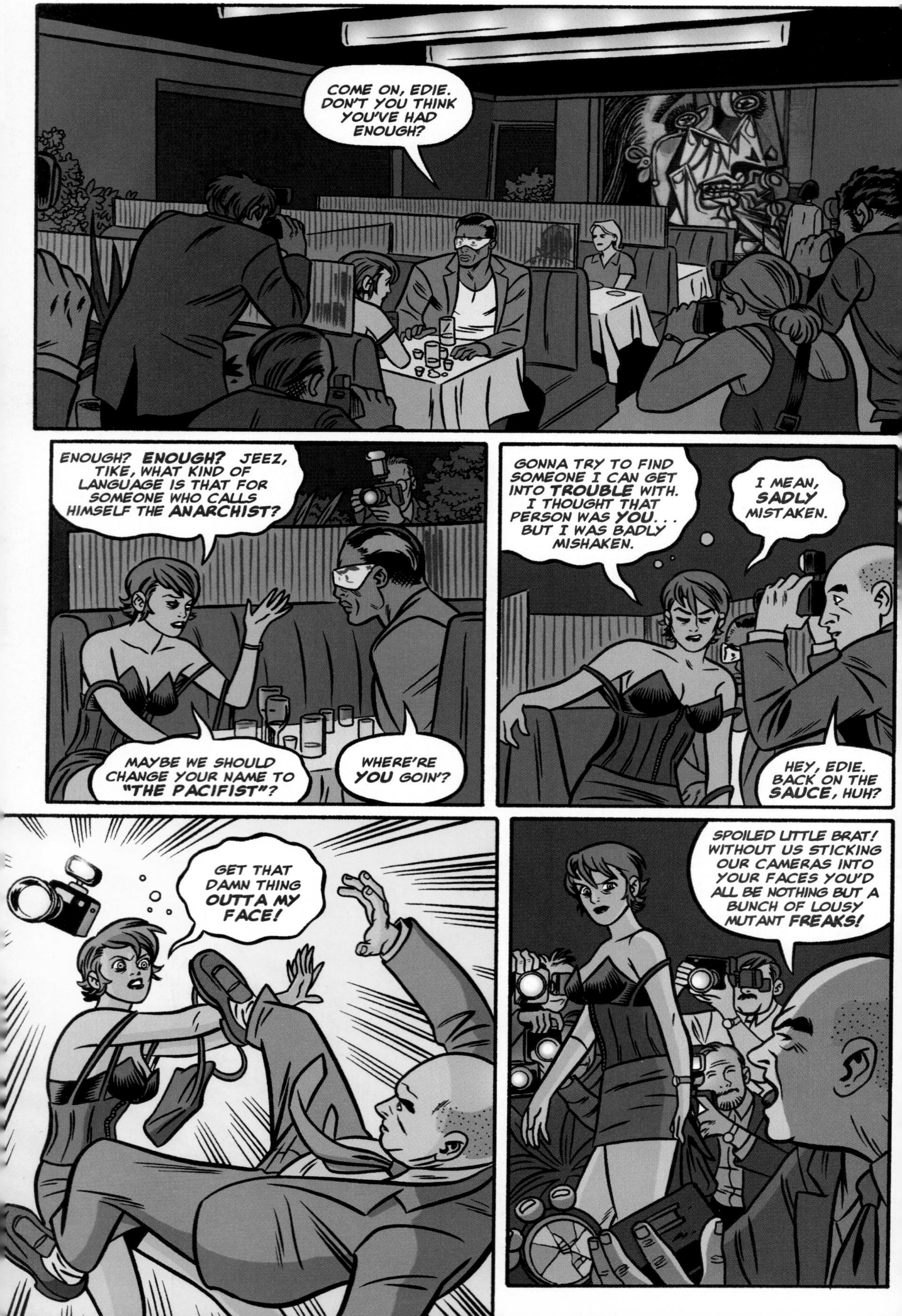
COME ON, EDIE. DON'T YOU THINK YOU'VE HAD ENOUGH?
ENOUGH? **ENOUGH?** JEEZ, TIKE, WHAT KIND OF LANGUAGE IS THAT FOR SOMEONE WHO CALLS HIMSELF THE **ANARCHIST**?
MAYBE WE SHOULD CHANGE YOUR NAME TO **"THE PACIFIST"**?
WHERE'RE **YOU** GOIN'?
GONNA TRY TO FIND SOMEONE I CAN GET INTO **TROUBLE** WITH. I THOUGHT THAT PERSON WAS **YOU**. . . BUT I WAS BADLY MISHAKEN.
I MEAN, **SADLY** MISTAKEN.
HEY, EDIE. BACK ON THE **SAUCE**, HUH?
GET THAT DAMN THING **OUTTA MY FACE!**
SPOILED LITTLE BRAT! WITHOUT US STICKING OUR CAMERAS INTO YOUR FACES YOU'D ALL BE NOTHING BUT A BUNCH OF LOUSY MUTANT **FREAKS!**

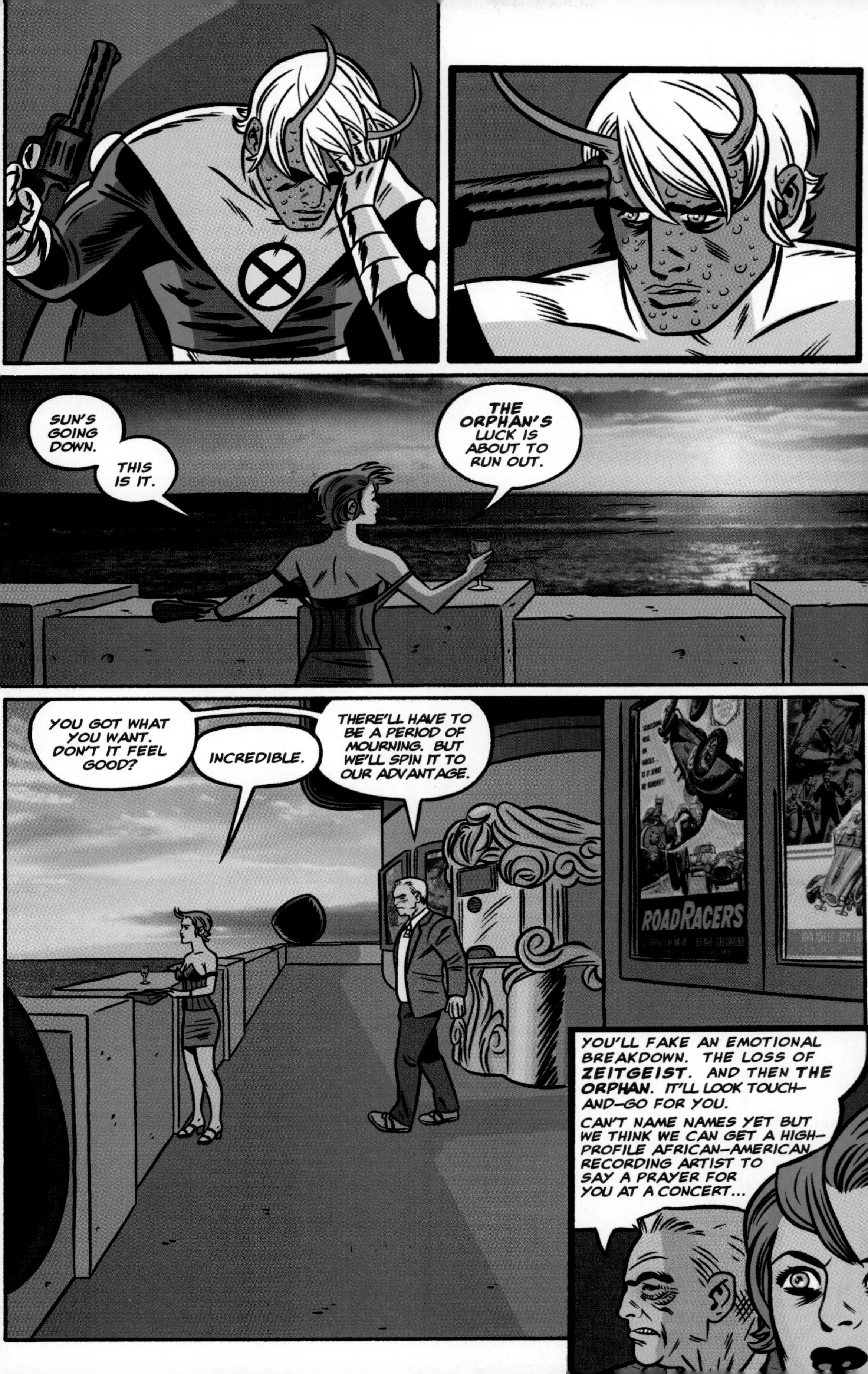
SUN'S GOING DOWN.
THIS IS IT.
THE ORPHAN'S LUCK IS ABOUT TO RUN OUT.
YOU GOT WHAT YOU WANT. DON'T IT FEEL GOOD?
INCREDIBLE.
THERE'LL HAVE TO BE A PERIOD OF MOURNING. BUT WE'LL SPIN IT TO OUR ADVANTAGE.
ROADRACERS
YOU'LL FAKE AN EMOTIONAL BREAKDOWN. THE LOSS OF ZEITGEIST. AND THEN THE ORPHAN. IT'LL LOOK TOUCH-AND-GO FOR YOU.
CAN'T NAME NAMES YET BUT WE THINK WE CAN GET A HIGH-PROFILE AFRICAN-AMERICAN RECORDING ARTIST TO SAY A PRAYER FOR YOU AT A CONCERT...

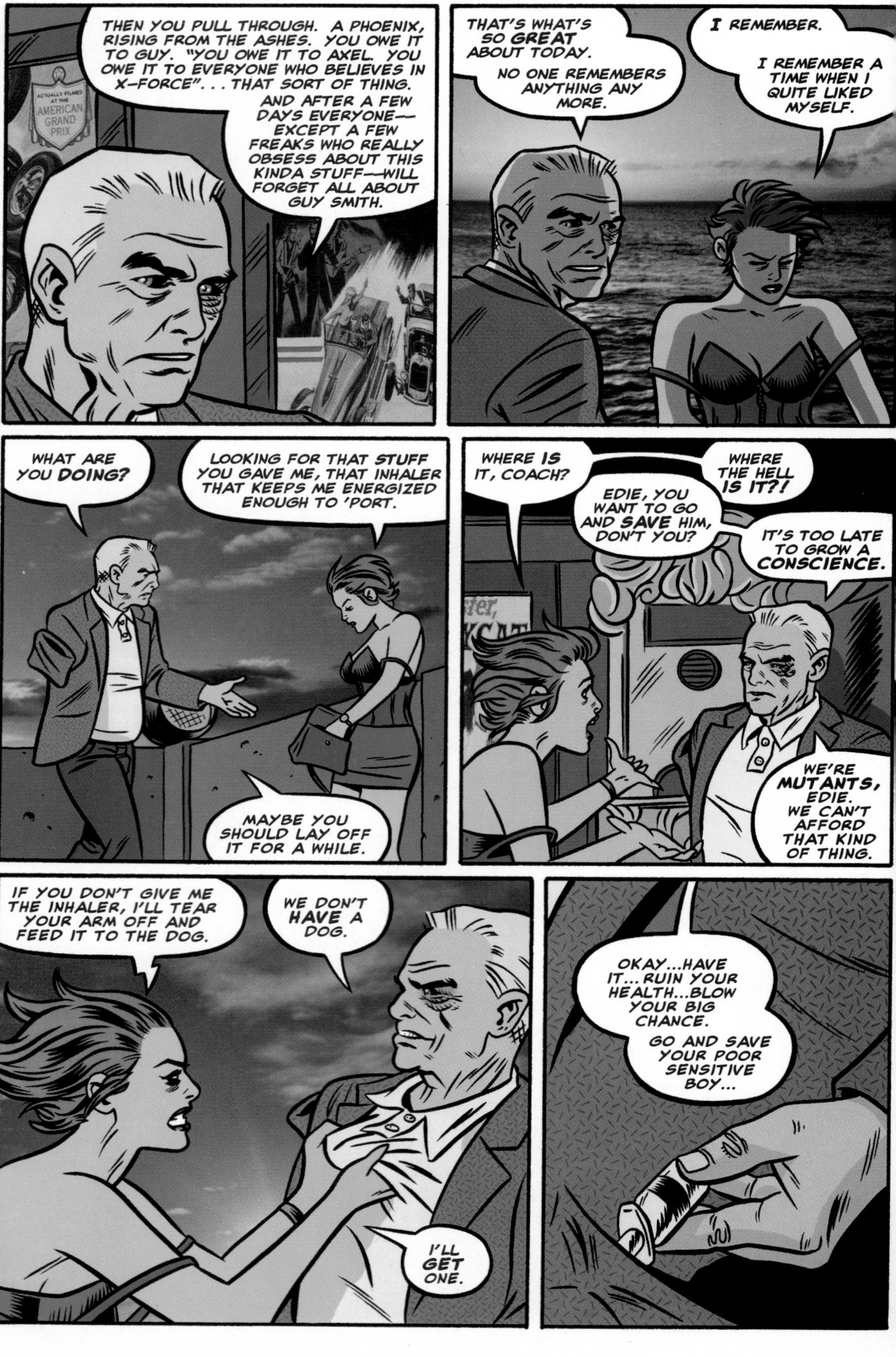
THEN YOU PULL THROUGH. A PHOENIX, RISING FROM THE ASHES. YOU OWE IT TO GUY. "YOU OWE IT TO AXEL. YOU OWE IT TO EVERYONE WHO BELIEVES IN X-FORCE"... THAT SORT OF THING.
AND AFTER A FEW DAYS EVERYONE—EXCEPT A FEW FREAKS WHO REALLY OBSESS ABOUT THIS KINDA STUFF—WILL FORGET ALL ABOUT GUY SMITH.
ACTUALLY FILMED AT THE AMERICAN GRAND PRIX
THAT'S WHAT'S SO **GREAT** ABOUT TODAY.
NO ONE REMEMBERS ANYTHING ANY MORE.
I REMEMBER.
I REMEMBER A TIME WHEN I QUITE LIKED MYSELF.
WHAT ARE YOU **DOING?**
LOOKING FOR THAT **STUFF** YOU GAVE ME, THAT INHALER THAT KEEPS ME ENERGIZED ENOUGH TO 'PORT.
MAYBE YOU SHOULD LAY OFF IT FOR A WHILE.
WHERE **IS** IT, COACH?
WHERE THE HELL **IS IT?!**
EDIE, YOU WANT TO GO AND **SAVE** HIM, DON'T YOU?
IT'S TOO LATE TO GROW A **CONSCIENCE.**
WE'RE **MUTANTS,** EDIE. WE CAN'T AFFORD THAT KIND OF THING.
IF YOU DON'T GIVE ME THE INHALER, I'LL TEAR YOUR ARM OFF AND FEED IT TO THE DOG.
WE DON'T **HAVE** A DOG.
I'LL **GET** ONE.
OKAY...HAVE IT... RUIN YOUR HEALTH...BLOW YOUR BIG CHANCE.
GO AND SAVE YOUR POOR SENSITIVE BOY...

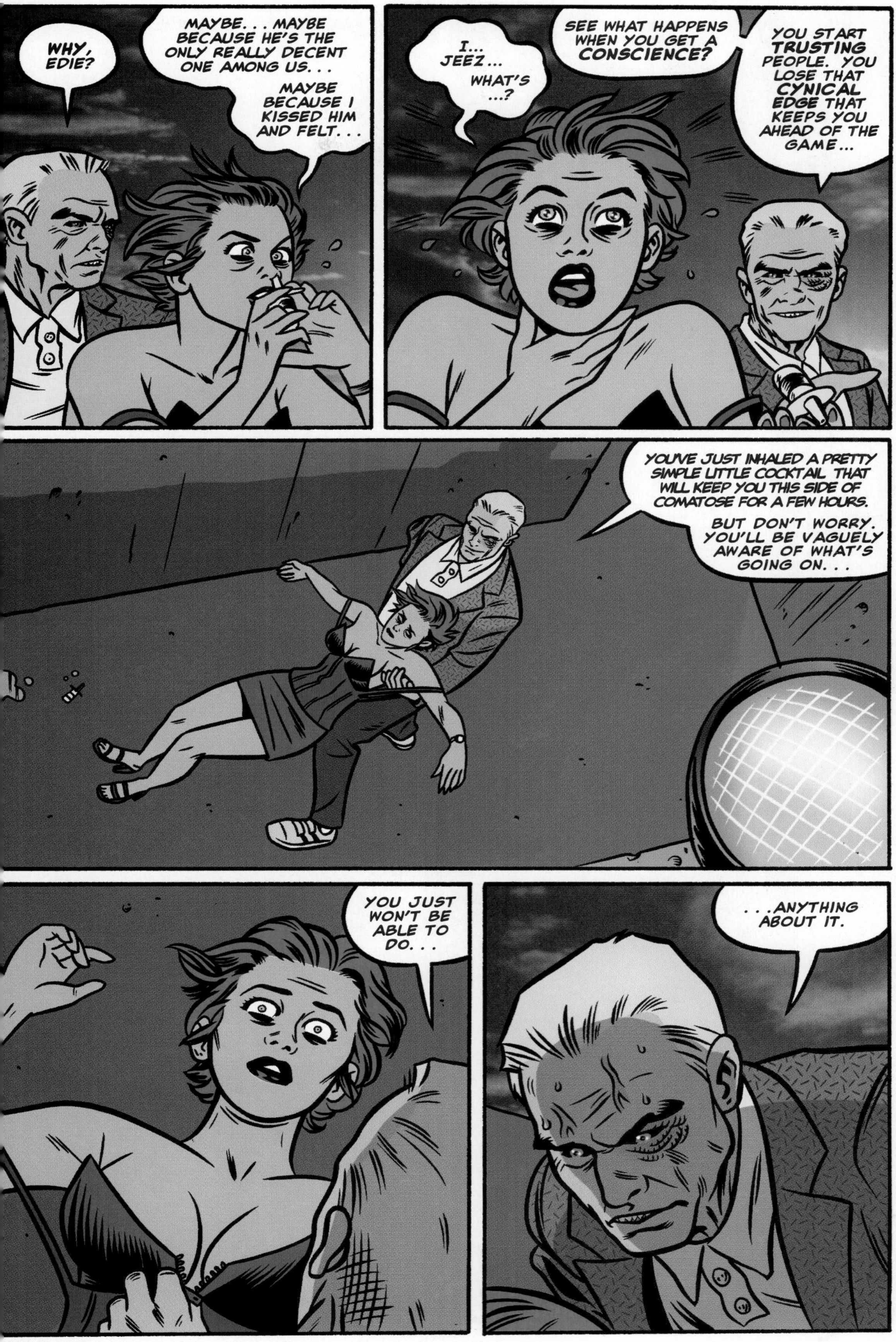

WHY, EDIE?
MAYBE. . . MAYBE BECAUSE HE'S THE ONLY REALLY DECENT ONE AMONG US. . .
MAYBE BECAUSE I KISSED HIM AND FELT. . .
I... JEEZ...
WHAT'S ...?
SEE WHAT HAPPENS WHEN YOU GET A CONSCIENCE?
YOU START TRUSTING PEOPLE. YOU LOSE THAT CYNICAL EDGE THAT KEEPS YOU AHEAD OF THE GAME...
YOU'VE JUST INHALED A PRETTY SIMPLE LITTLE COCKTAIL THAT WILL KEEP YOU THIS SIDE OF COMATOSE FOR A FEW HOURS.
BUT DON'T WORRY. YOU'LL BE VAGUELY AWARE OF WHAT'S GOING ON. . .
YOU JUST WON'T BE ABLE TO DO. . .
. . .ANYTHING ABOUT IT.

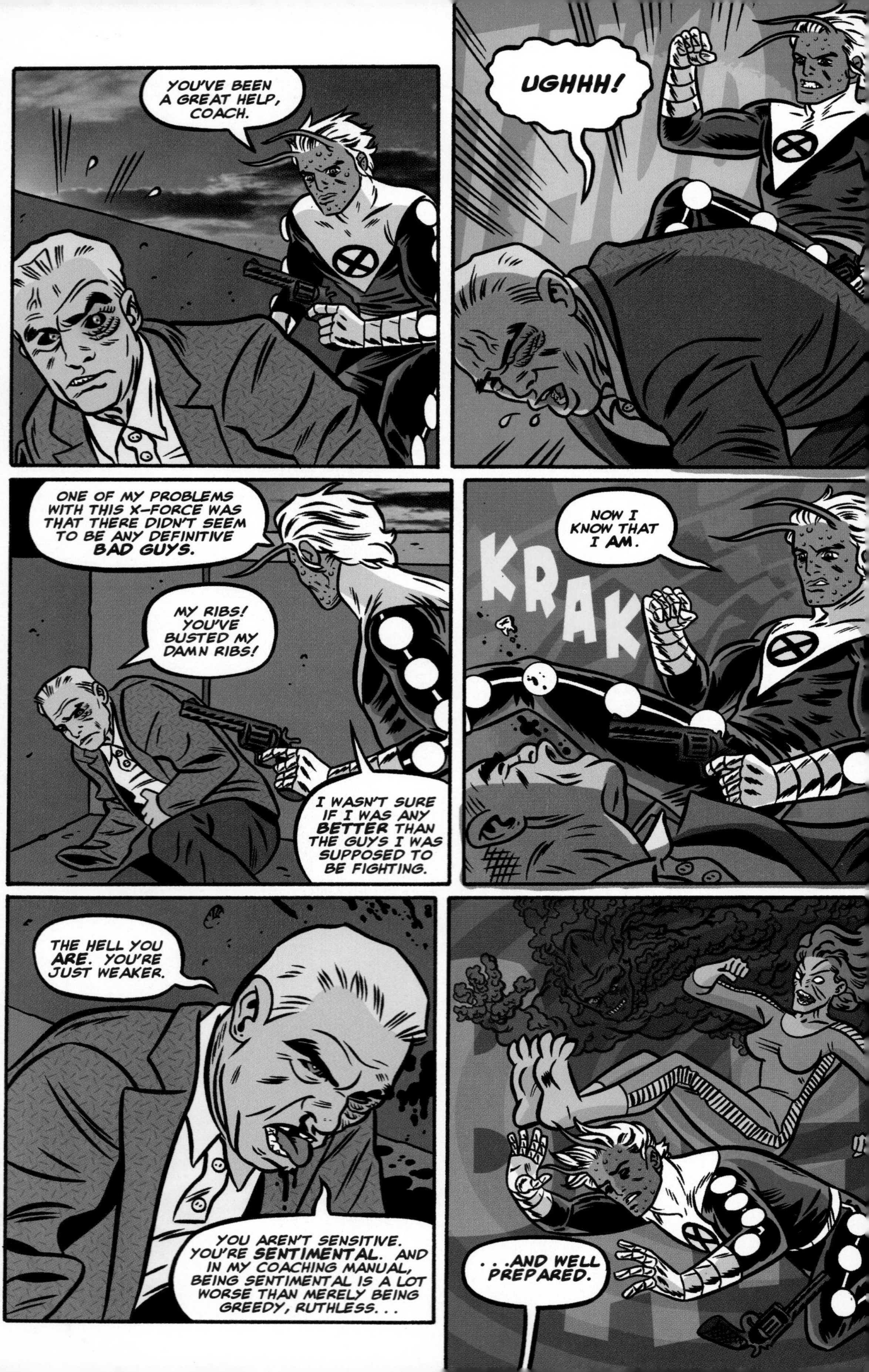
YOU'VE BEEN A GREAT HELP, COACH.
UGHHH!
ONE OF MY PROBLEMS WITH THIS X-FORCE WAS THAT THERE DIDN'T SEEM TO BE ANY DEFINITIVE BAD GUYS.
MY RIBS! YOU'VE BUSTED MY DAMN RIBS!
I WASN'T SURE IF I WAS ANY BETTER THAN THE GUYS I WAS SUPPOSED TO BE FIGHTING.
KRAK
NOW I KNOW THAT I AM.
THE HELL YOU ARE. YOU'RE JUST WEAKER.
YOU AREN'T SENSITIVE. YOU'RE SENTIMENTAL. AND IN MY COACHING MANUAL, BEING SENTIMENTAL IS A LOT WORSE THAN MERELY BEING GREEDY, RUTHLESS...
...AND WELL PREPARED.

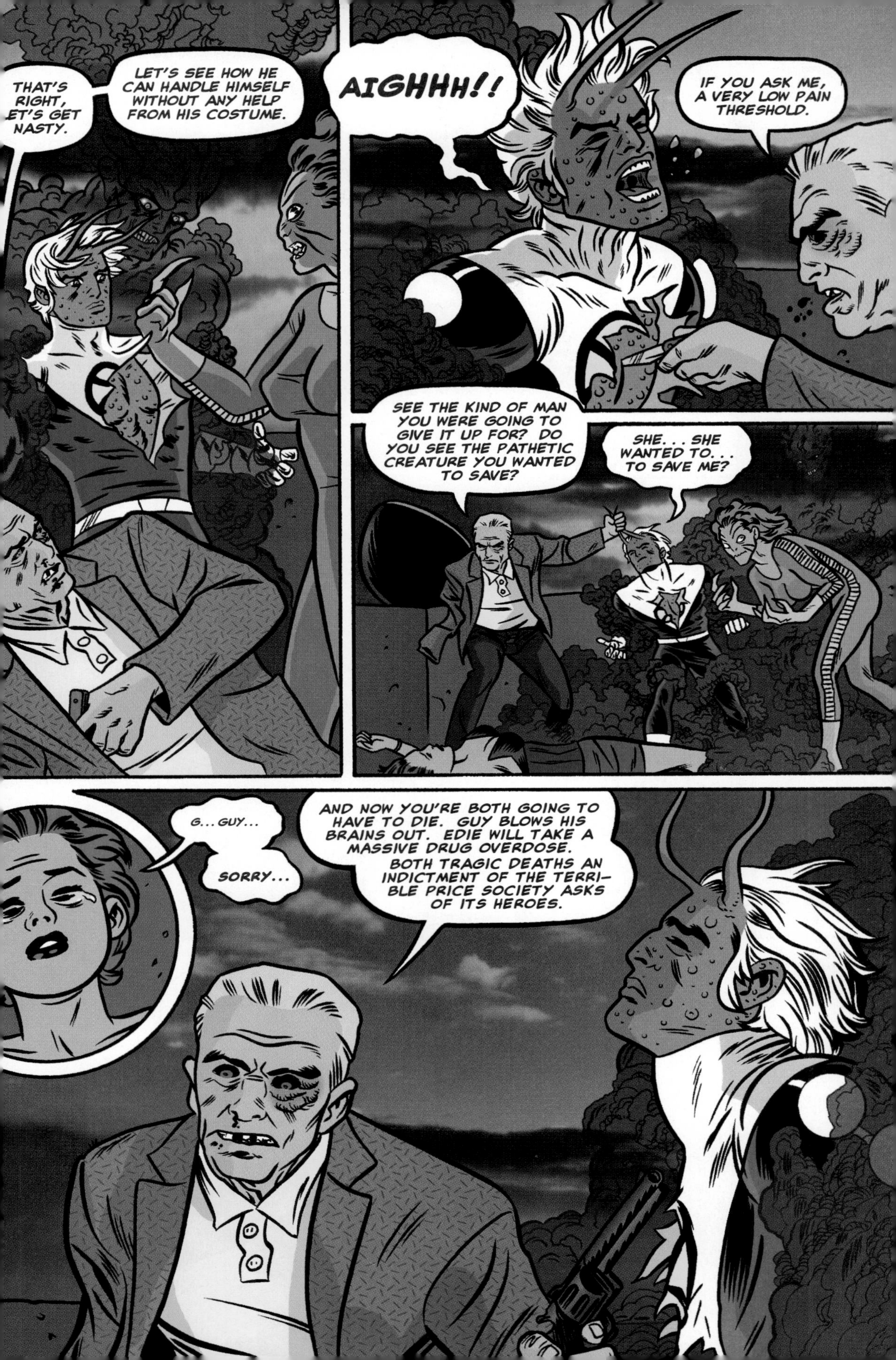

THAT'S RIGHT, LET'S GET NASTY.
LET'S SEE HOW HE CAN HANDLE HIMSELF WITHOUT ANY HELP FROM HIS COSTUME.
AIGHHH!!
IF YOU ASK ME, A VERY LOW PAIN THRESHOLD.
SEE THE KIND OF MAN YOU WERE GOING TO GIVE IT UP FOR? DO YOU SEE THE PATHETIC CREATURE YOU WANTED TO SAVE?
SHE... SHE WANTED TO... TO SAVE ME?
G... GUY...
SORRY...
AND NOW YOU'RE BOTH GOING TO HAVE TO DIE. GUY BLOWS HIS BRAINS OUT. EDIE WILL TAKE A MASSIVE DRUG OVERDOSE.
BOTH TRAGIC DEATHS AN INDICTMENT OF THE TERRIBLE PRICE SOCIETY ASKS OF ITS HEROES.

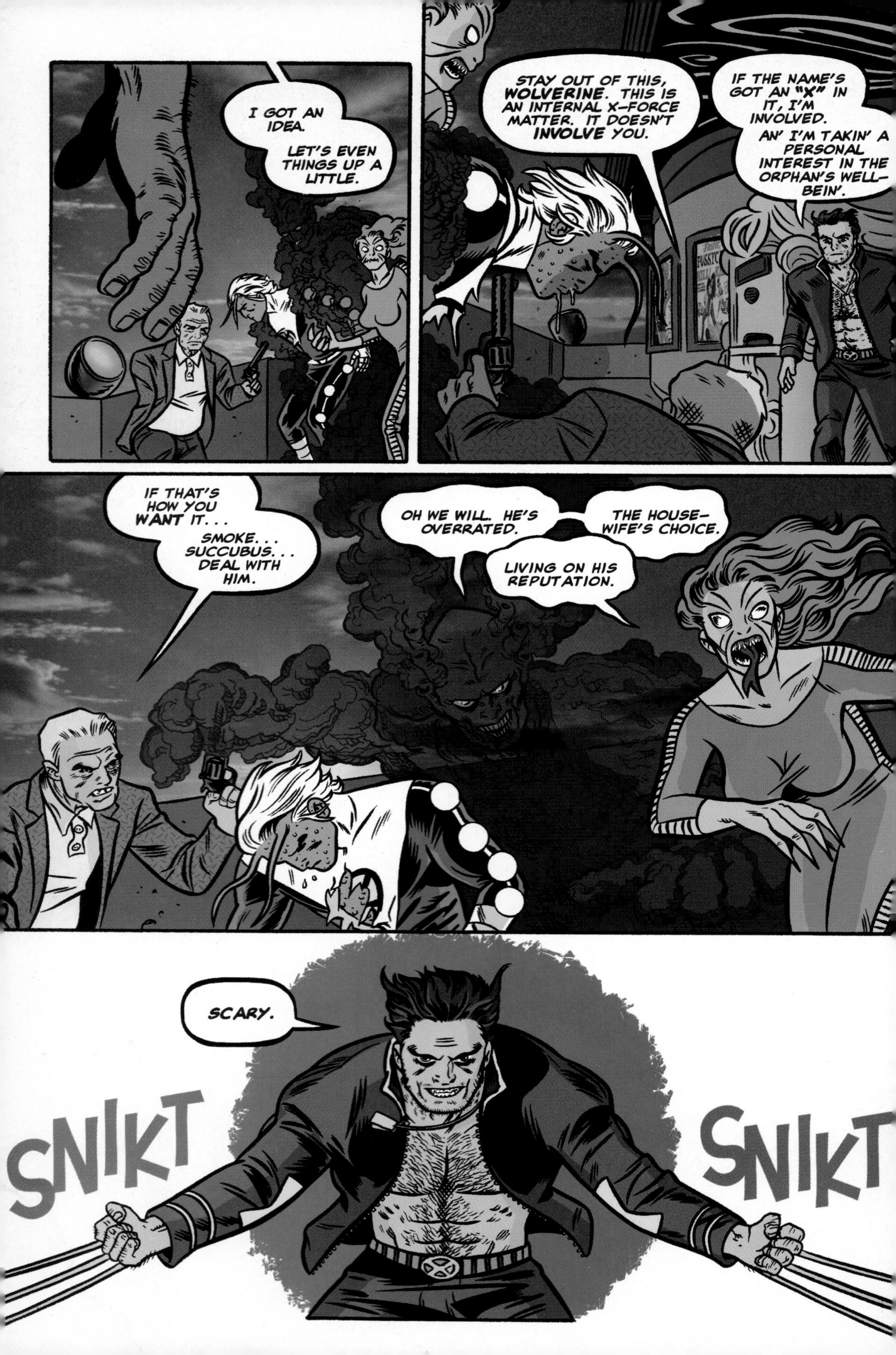
I GOT AN IDEA.
LET'S EVEN THINGS UP A LITTLE.
STAY OUT OF THIS, WOLVERINE. THIS IS AN INTERNAL X-FORCE MATTER. IT DOESN'T INVOLVE YOU.
IF THE NAME'S GOT AN "X" IN IT, I'M INVOLVED.
AN' I'M TAKIN' A PERSONAL INTEREST IN THE ORPHAN'S WELL-BEIN'.
IF THAT'S HOW YOU WANT IT...
SMOKE... SUCCUBUS... DEAL WITH HIM.
OH WE WILL. HE'S OVERRATED.
THE HOUSE-WIFE'S CHOICE.
LIVING ON HIS REPUTATION.
SCARY.
SNIKT
SNIKT

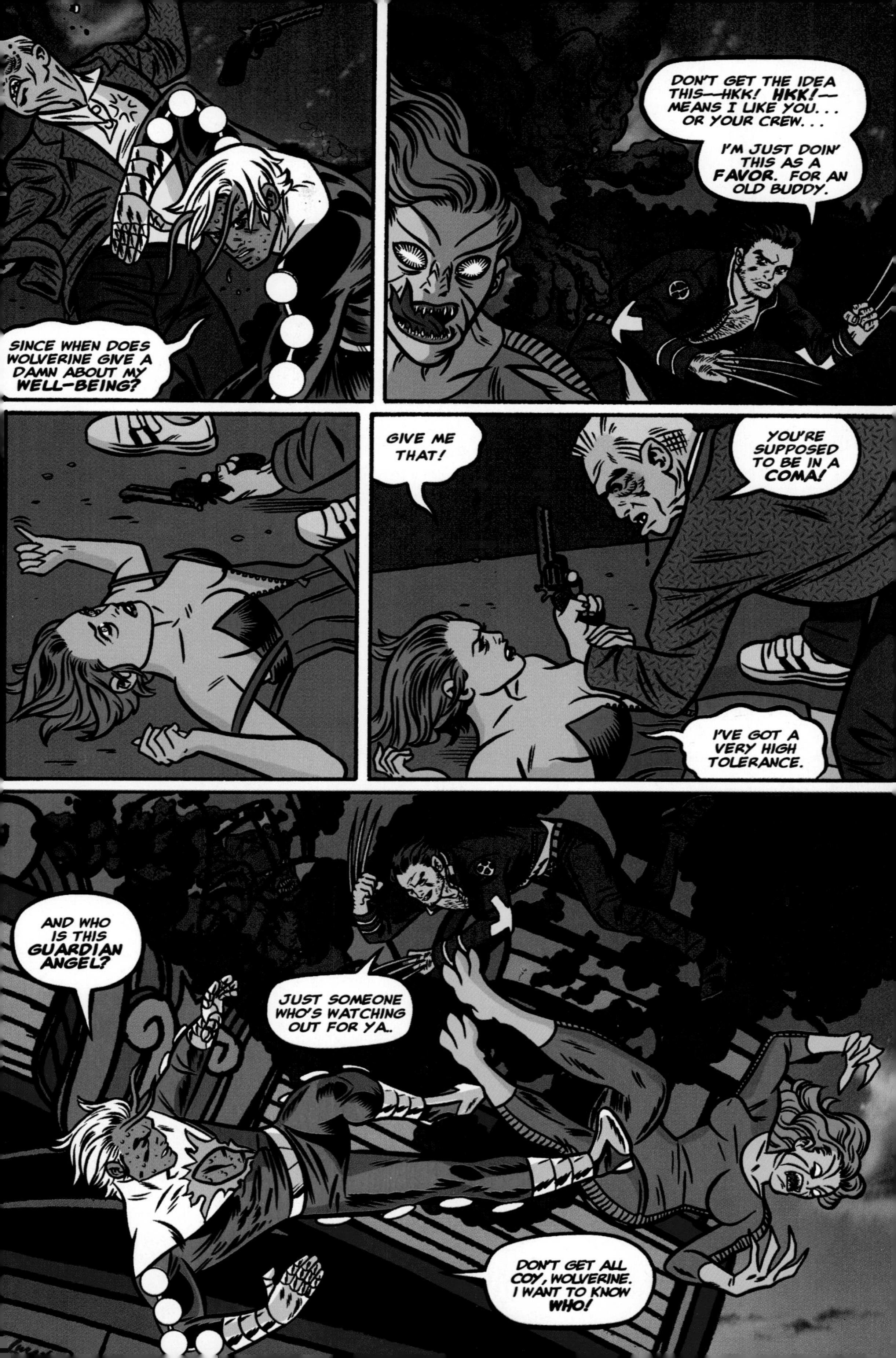
SINCE WHEN DOES WOLVERINE GIVE A DAMN ABOUT MY WELL-BEING?
DON'T GET THE IDEA THIS—HKK! HKK!— MEANS I LIKE YOU... OR YOUR CREW...
I'M JUST DOIN' THIS AS A FAVOR. FOR AN OLD BUDDY.
GIVE ME THAT!
YOU'RE SUPPOSED TO BE IN A COMA!
I'VE GOT A VERY HIGH TOLERANCE.
AND WHO IS THIS GUARDIAN ANGEL?
JUST SOMEONE WHO'S WATCHING OUT FOR YA.
DON'T GET ALL COY, WOLVERINE. I WANT TO KNOW WHO!

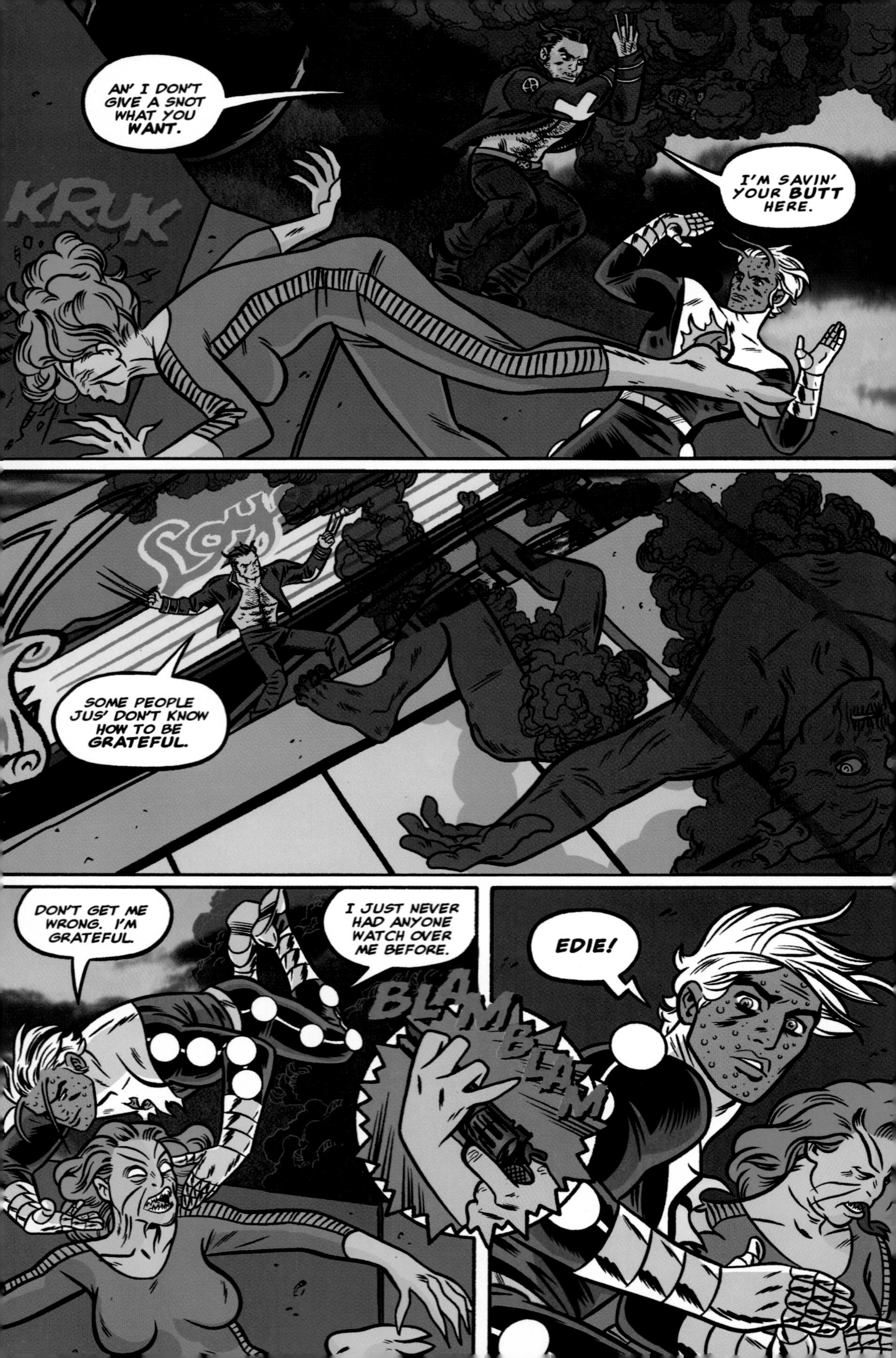

AN' I DON'T GIVE A SNOT WHAT YOU WANT.
KRUK
I'M SAVIN' YOUR BUTT HERE.
SOME PEOPLE JUS' DON'T KNOW HOW TO BE GRATEFUL.
DON'T GET ME WRONG. I'M GRATEFUL.
I JUST NEVER HAD ANYONE WATCH OVER ME BEFORE.
BLAM
BLAM
BLAM
EDIE!

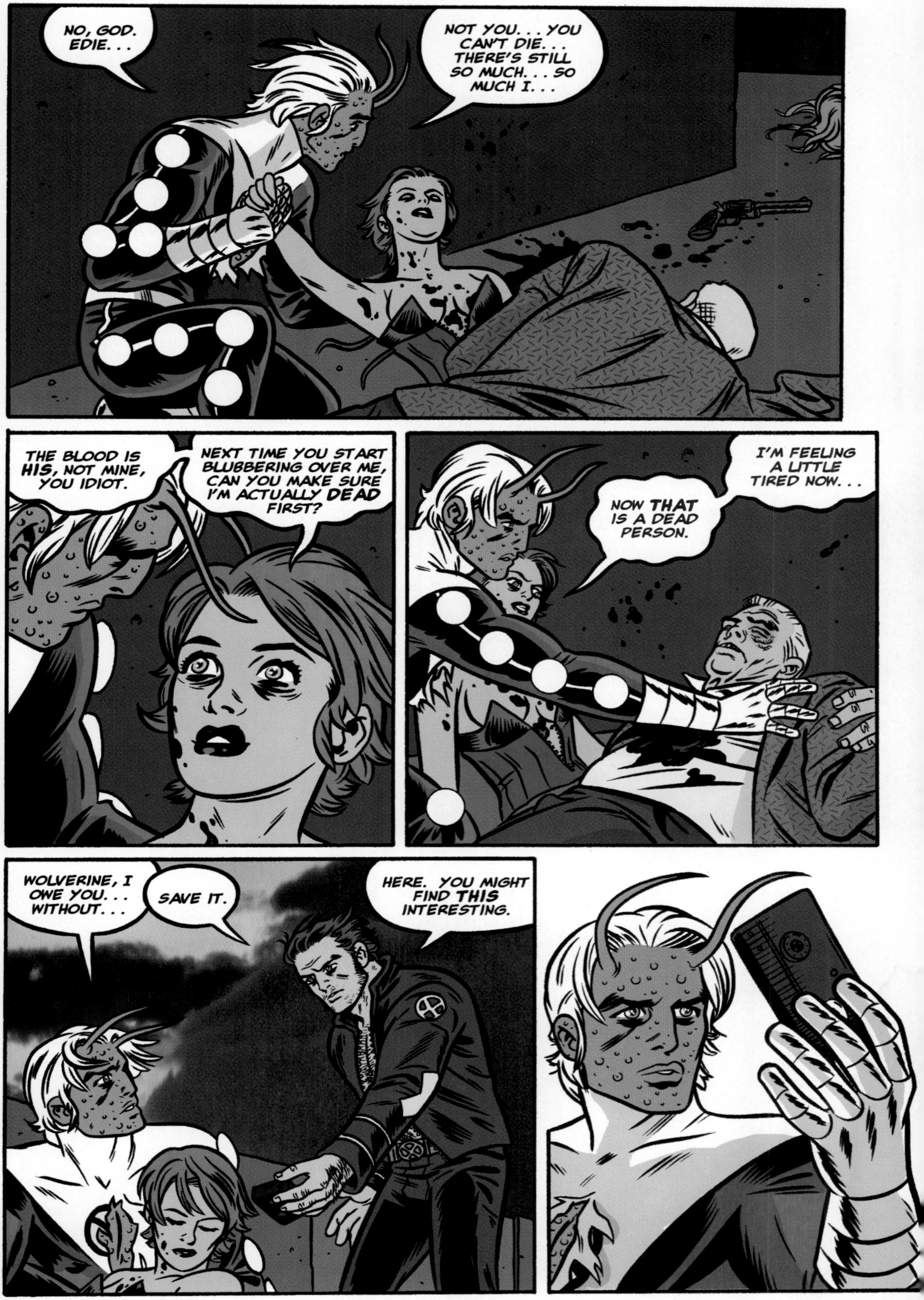
NO, GOD. EDIE...
NOT YOU... YOU CAN'T DIE... THERE'S STILL SO MUCH... SO MUCH I...
THE BLOOD IS HIS, NOT MINE, YOU IDIOT.
NEXT TIME YOU START BLUBBERING OVER ME, CAN YOU MAKE SURE I'M ACTUALLY DEAD FIRST?
NOW THAT IS A DEAD PERSON.
I'M FEELING A LITTLE TIRED NOW...
WOLVERINE, I OWE YOU... WITHOUT...
SAVE IT.
HERE. YOU MIGHT FIND THIS INTERESTING.

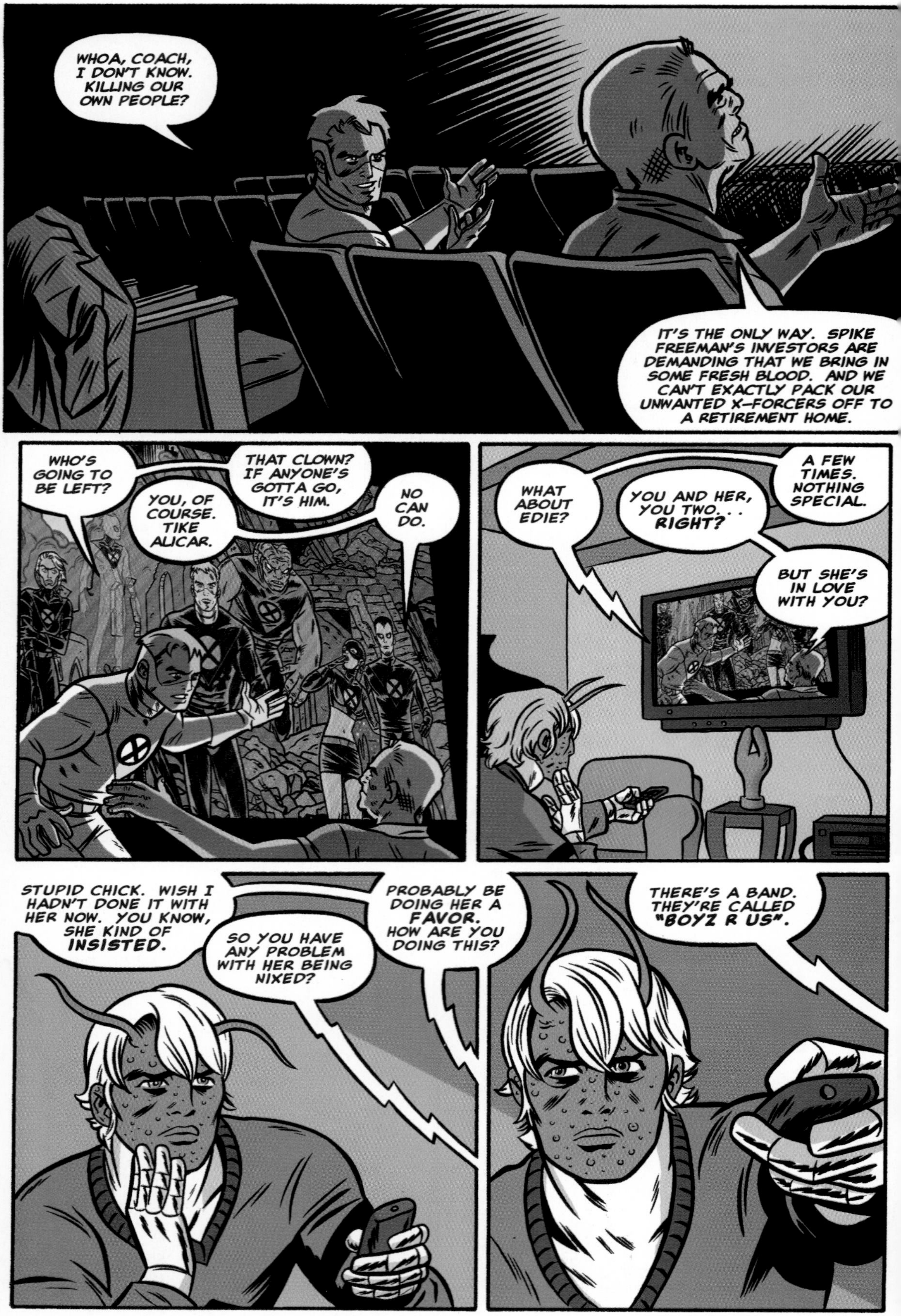

WHOA, COACH, I DON'T KNOW. KILLING OUR OWN PEOPLE?
IT'S THE ONLY WAY. SPIKE FREEMAN'S INVESTORS ARE DEMANDING THAT WE BRING IN SOME FRESH BLOOD. AND WE CAN'T EXACTLY PACK OUR UNWANTED X-FORCERS OFF TO A RETIREMENT HOME.
WHO'S GOING TO BE LEFT?
YOU, OF COURSE. TIKE ALICAR.
THAT CLOWN? IF ANYONE'S GOTTA GO, IT'S HIM.
NO CAN DO.
WHAT ABOUT EDIE?
YOU AND HER, YOU TWO. . . RIGHT?
A FEW TIMES. NOTHING SPECIAL.
BUT SHE'S IN LOVE WITH YOU?
STUPID CHICK. WISH I HADN'T DONE IT WITH HER NOW. YOU KNOW, SHE KIND OF INSISTED.
SO YOU HAVE ANY PROBLEM WITH HER BEING NIXED?
PROBABLY BE DOING HER A FAVOR. HOW ARE YOU DOING THIS?
THERE'S A BAND. THEY'RE CALLED "BOYZ R US".

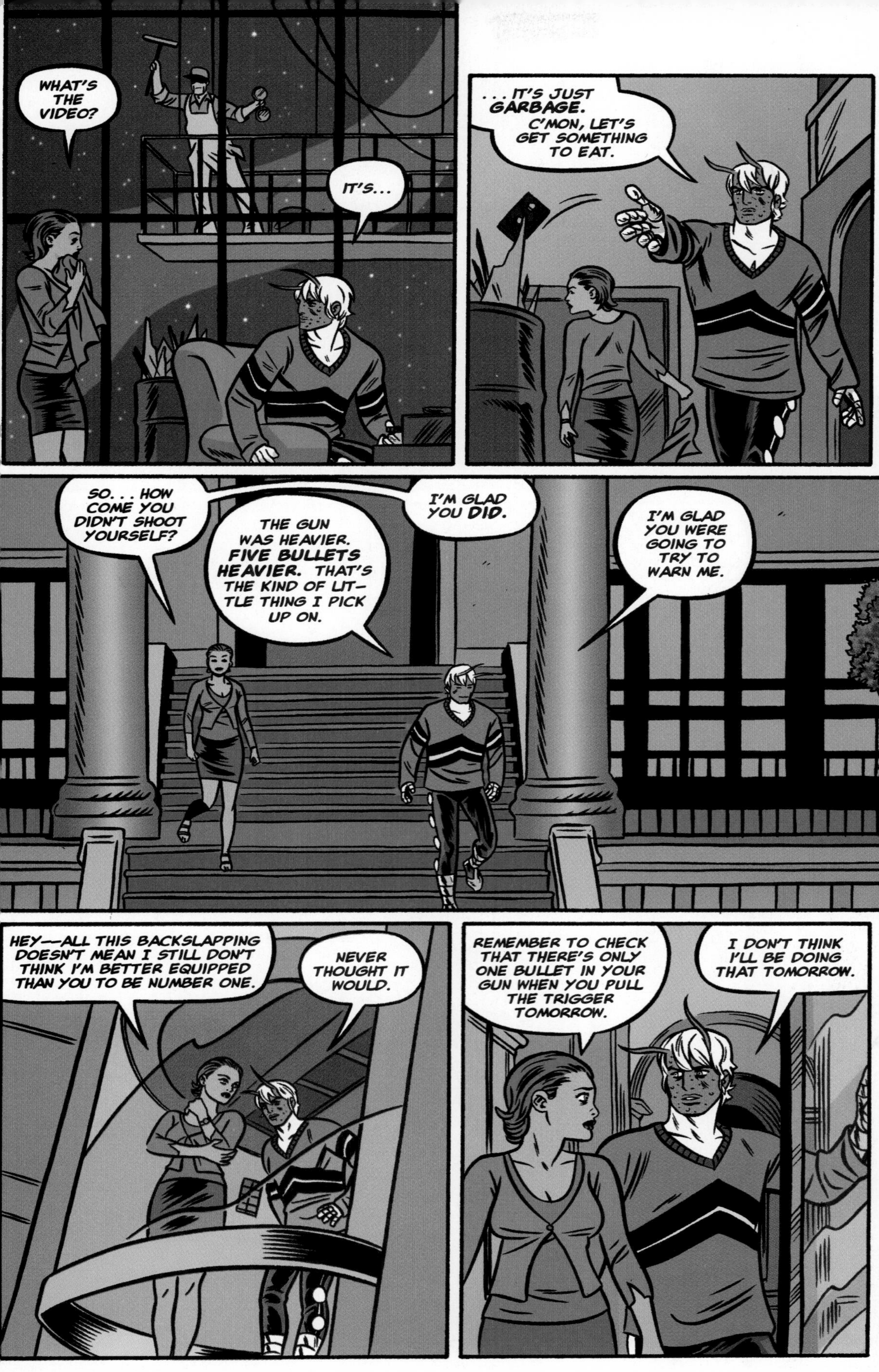
WHAT'S THE VIDEO?
IT'S...
. . . IT'S JUST GARBAGE.
C'MON, LET'S GET SOMETHING TO EAT.
SO. . . HOW COME YOU DIDN'T SHOOT YOURSELF?
THE GUN WAS HEAVIER. FIVE BULLETS HEAVIER. THAT'S THE KIND OF LIT-TLE THING I PICK UP ON.
I'M GLAD YOU DID.
I'M GLAD YOU WERE GOING TO TRY TO WARN ME.
HEY—ALL THIS BACKSLAPPING DOESN'T MEAN I STILL DON'T THINK I'M BETTER EQUIPPED THAN YOU TO BE NUMBER ONE.
NEVER THOUGHT IT WOULD.
REMEMBER TO CHECK THAT THERE'S ONLY ONE BULLET IN YOUR GUN WHEN YOU PULL THE TRIGGER TOMORROW.
I DON'T THINK I'LL BE DOING THAT TOMORROW.

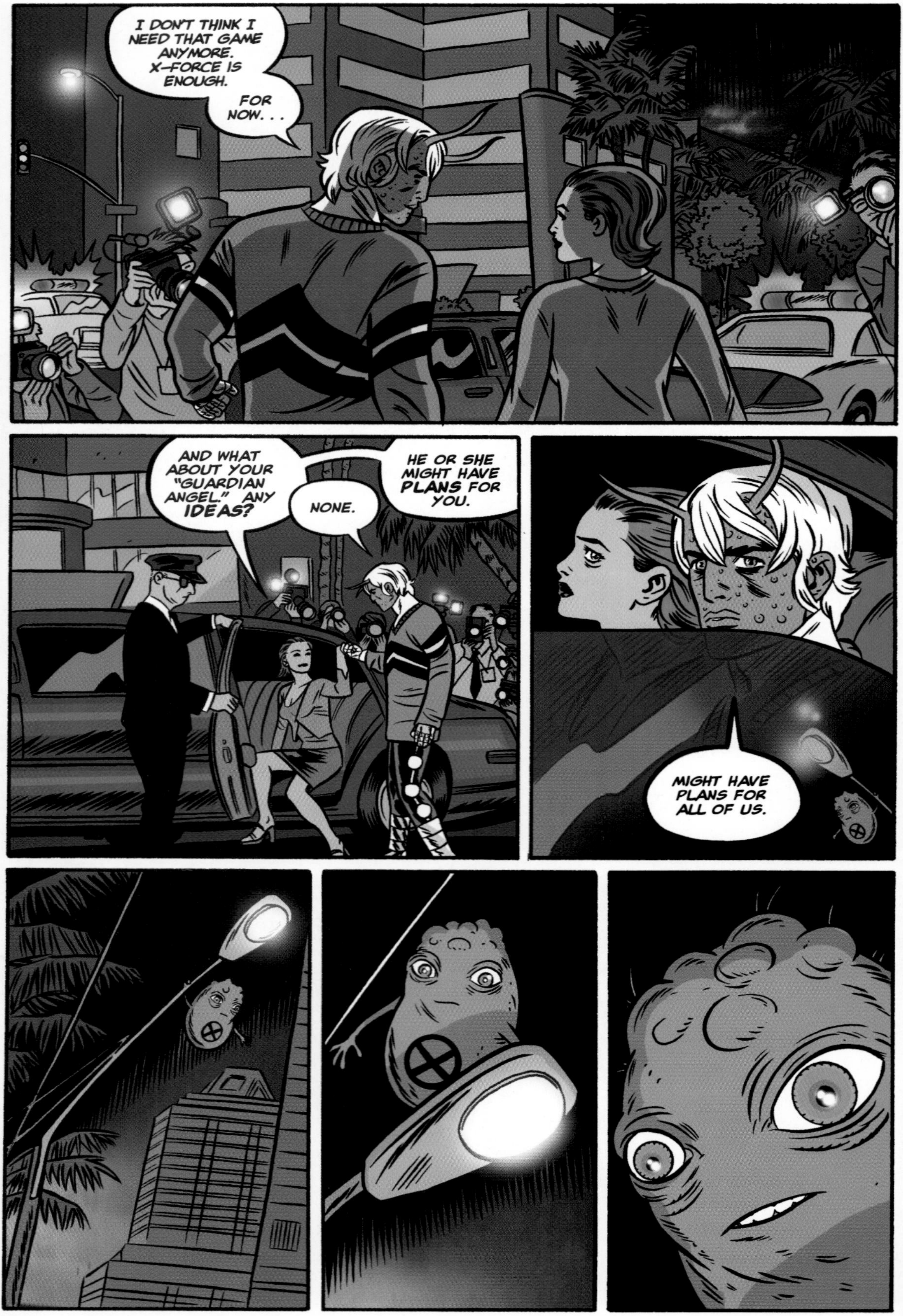
I DON'T THINK I NEED THAT GAME ANYMORE. X-FORCE IS ENOUGH.
FOR NOW. . .
AND WHAT ABOUT YOUR "GUARDIAN ANGEL." ANY IDEAS?
NONE.
HE OR SHE MIGHT HAVE PLANS FOR YOU.
MIGHT HAVE PLANS FOR ALL OF US.

X-FORCE®

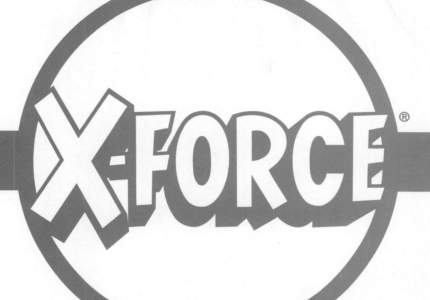

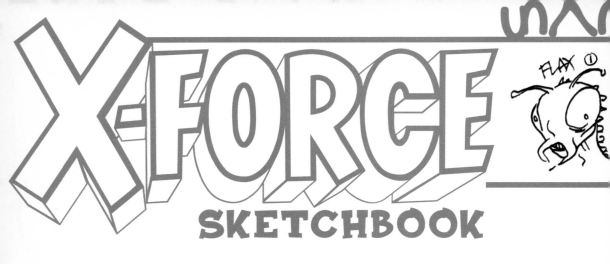

X-FORCE SKETCHBOOK

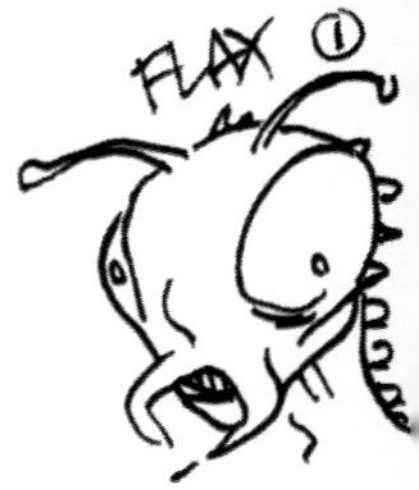
FLAX ①

THE FOLLOWING GALLERY SHOWS EARLY CHARACTER DESIGNS AND CONCEPTUAL SKETCHES BY MIKE ALLRED.

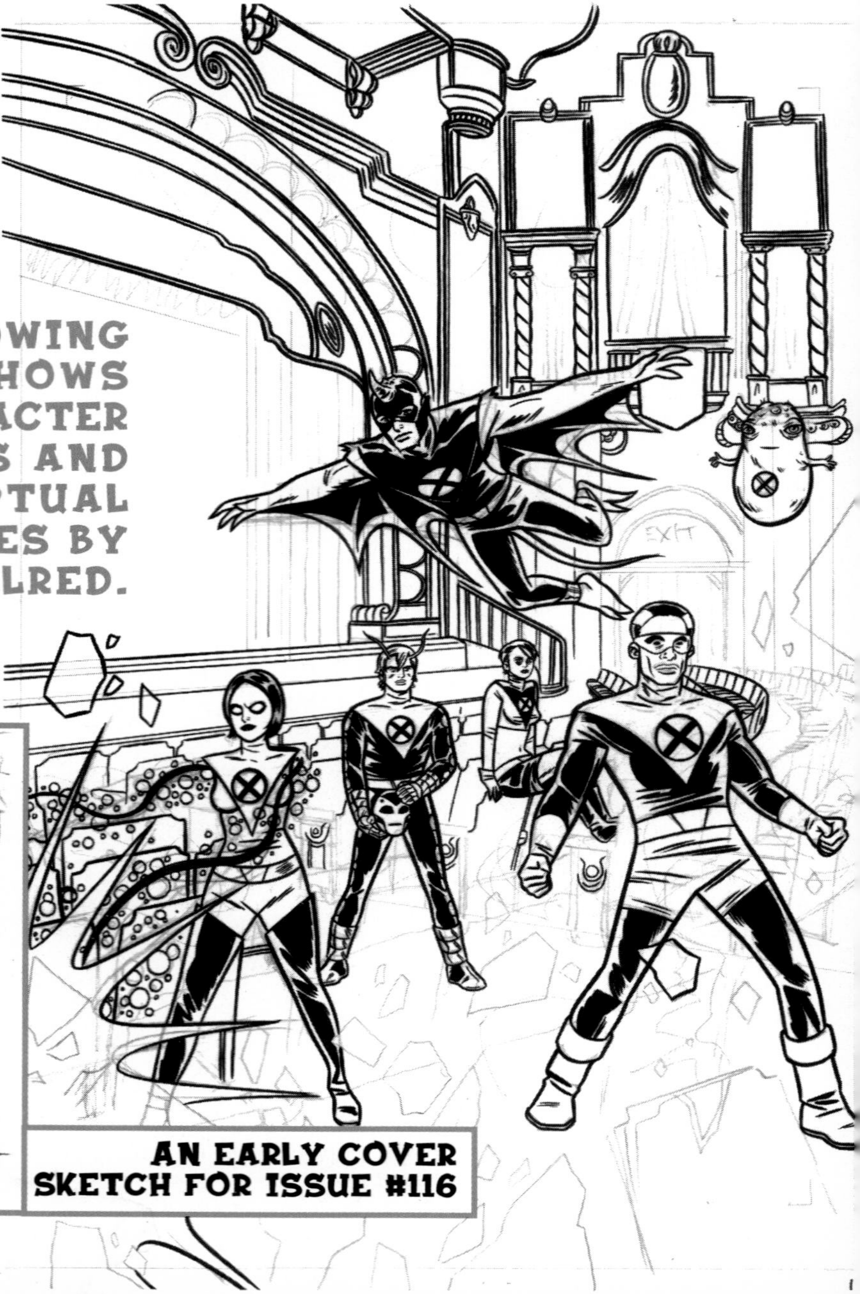
EXIT

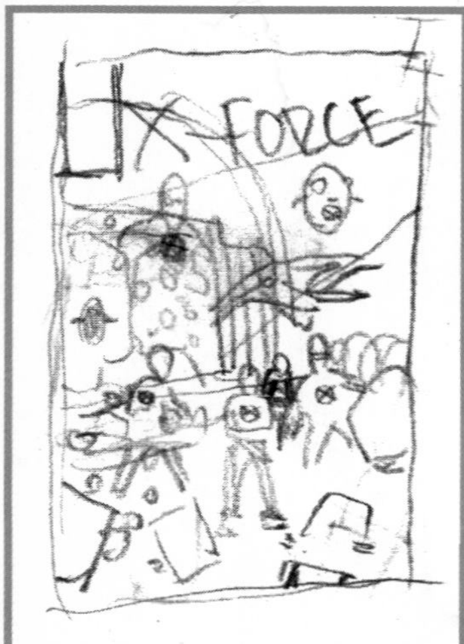

AN EARLY COVER SKETCH FOR ISSUE #116

THESE THREE UNPUBLISHED COVER "SKETCHES" ARE EXAMPLES OF MIKE ALLRED "THINKING OUT LOUD ON PAPER." ALL THREE WERE COMPLETED PRIOR TO PETER MILLIGAN COMPLETING THE FIRST SCRIPT.

THIS COVER SKETCH, HEAVILY INFLUENCED BY COMICS VISIONARY JIM STERANKO, WAS THE FIRST FULL SKETCH OF THE ORIGINAL X-FORCE TEAM. BLOKE WAS LATER REPLACED BY BATTERING RAM. ▶

◀ THIS COVER SKETCH IS THE FIRST CONCEPTUAL SKETCH FOR THE X-FORCE TEAM HEADQUARTERS. ALSO PICTURED ARE THE HORN (TOP) AND VENUS DEE MILO (BELOW DOOP).

THIS PIN-UP OF THE ORIGINAL X-FORCE LINEUP WAS PRINTED IN WIZARD'S X-MEN PREVIEW. ▶

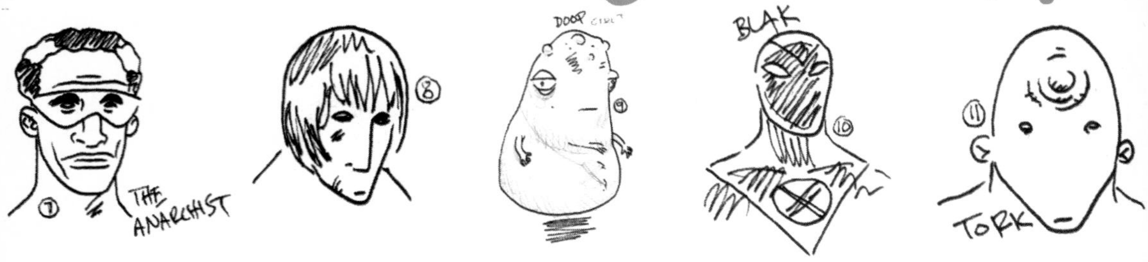
7
THE ANARCHIST
8
DOOP
9
BLAK
10
11
TORK

THIS UNPUBLISHED COVER "SKETCH" SHOWS THE TEAM IN ACTION WEARING THEIR NIGHTTIME BATTLE GEAR. IN THE FOREGROUND IS VENUS DEE MILO, A FUTURE TEAM MEMBER

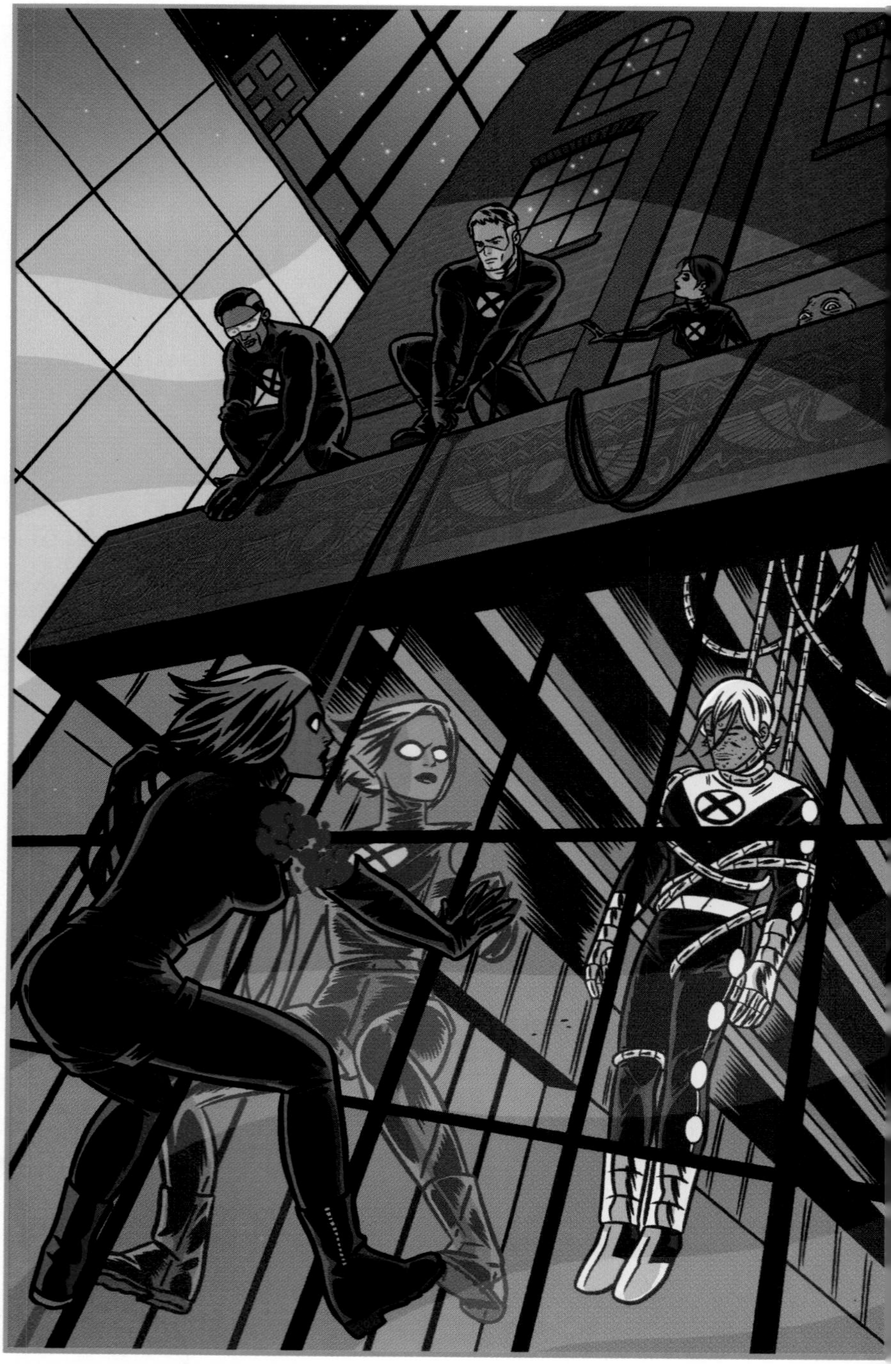

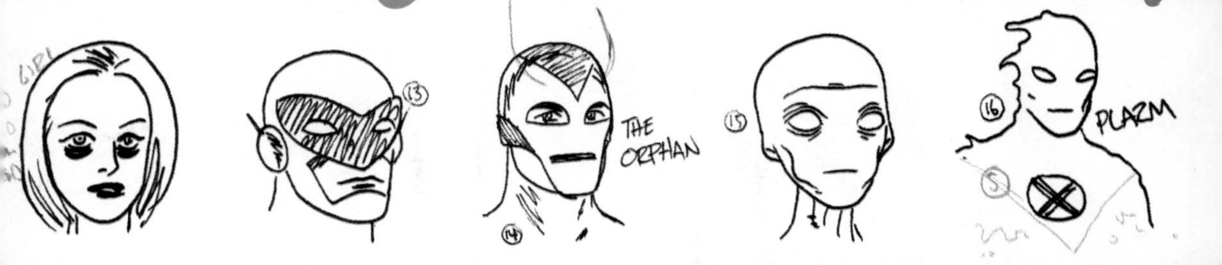
13
THE ORPHAN
14
15
16
PLAZM
5

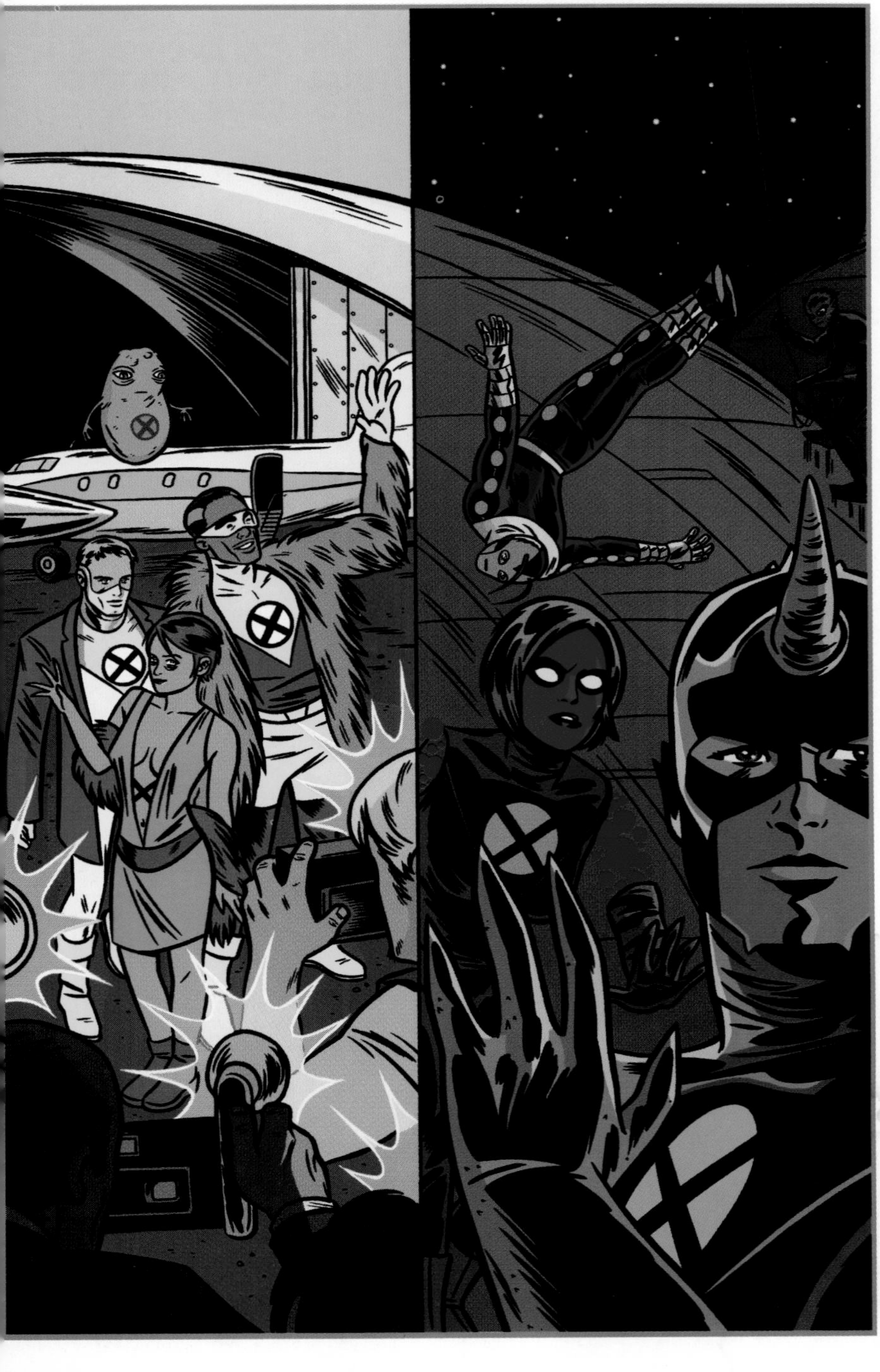

THIS NEVER-BEFORE-SEEN SPLIT COVER "SKETCH" SHOWS THE TEAM AT PLAY AND AT WORK.

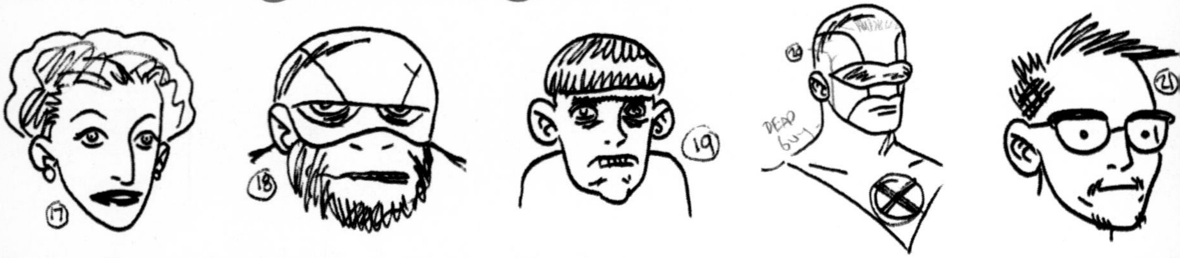
17
18
19
DEAD GUY
20
21

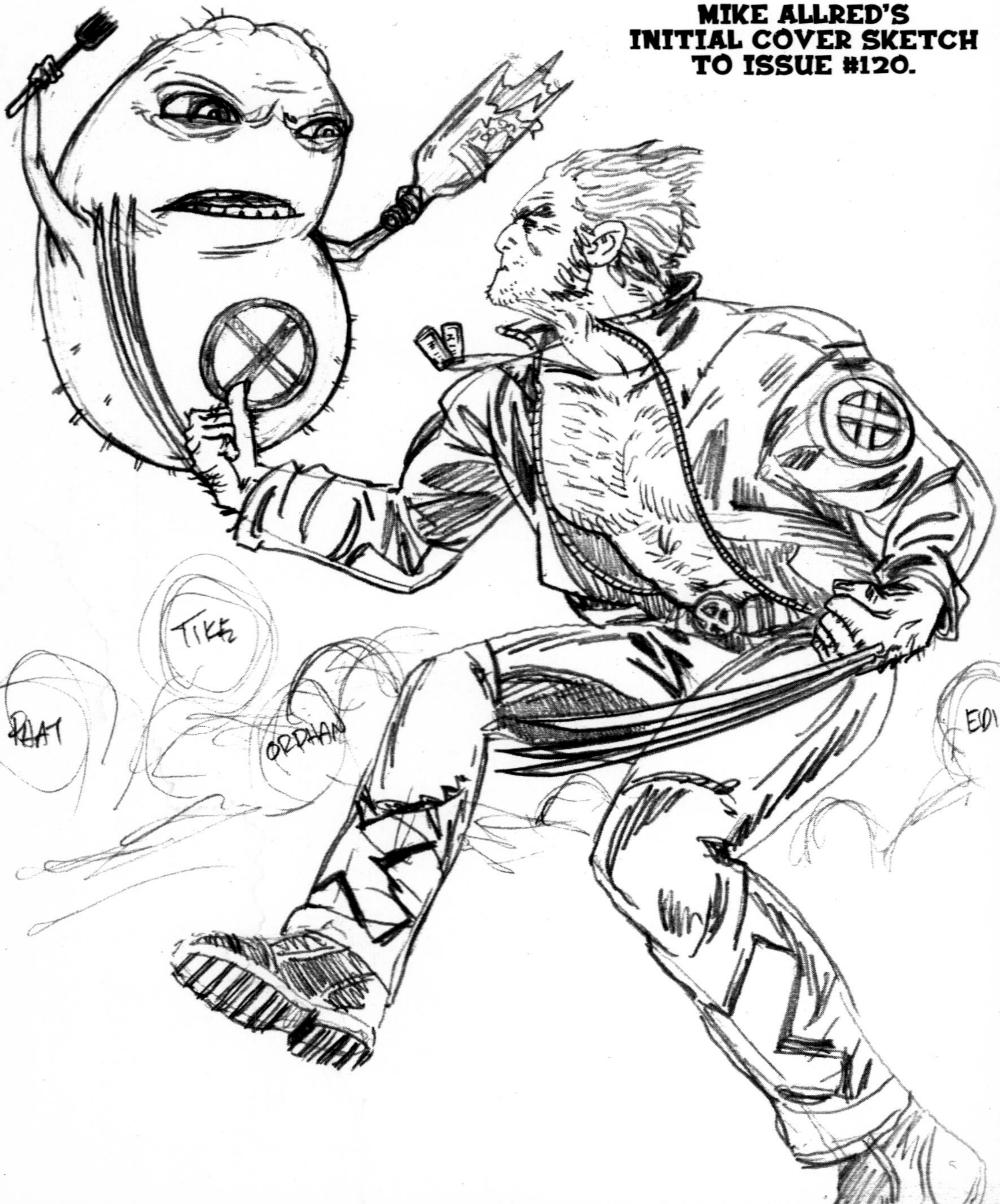
TIKE
PLAT
ORPHAN
EDIE

MIKE ALLRED'S INITIAL COVER SKETCH TO ISSUE #120.

 JELLYFISH

 HOOK

GUY SMITH A.K.A. THE ORPHAN (FORMERLY MR. SENSITIVE)

"FRANK" SKIN

PALE BLUE OR WHITE SKIN

RED HAIR

BLUE

GREEN TURQUOISE

6 OR 60

RED ?

BLUE METAL WHITE

THE ORPHAN

DARK RED

YELLOW

PURPLE AND SKIN

YELLOW BAND

TIKE ALLEY

THE ANARCHIST

TRYING YOGA TO CHILL HOT TJAPLA

EDIE SAWYER A.K.A. U-GO GIRL

TIKE ALICOR A.K.A. THE ANARCHIST

EARLY VERSIONS OF THE

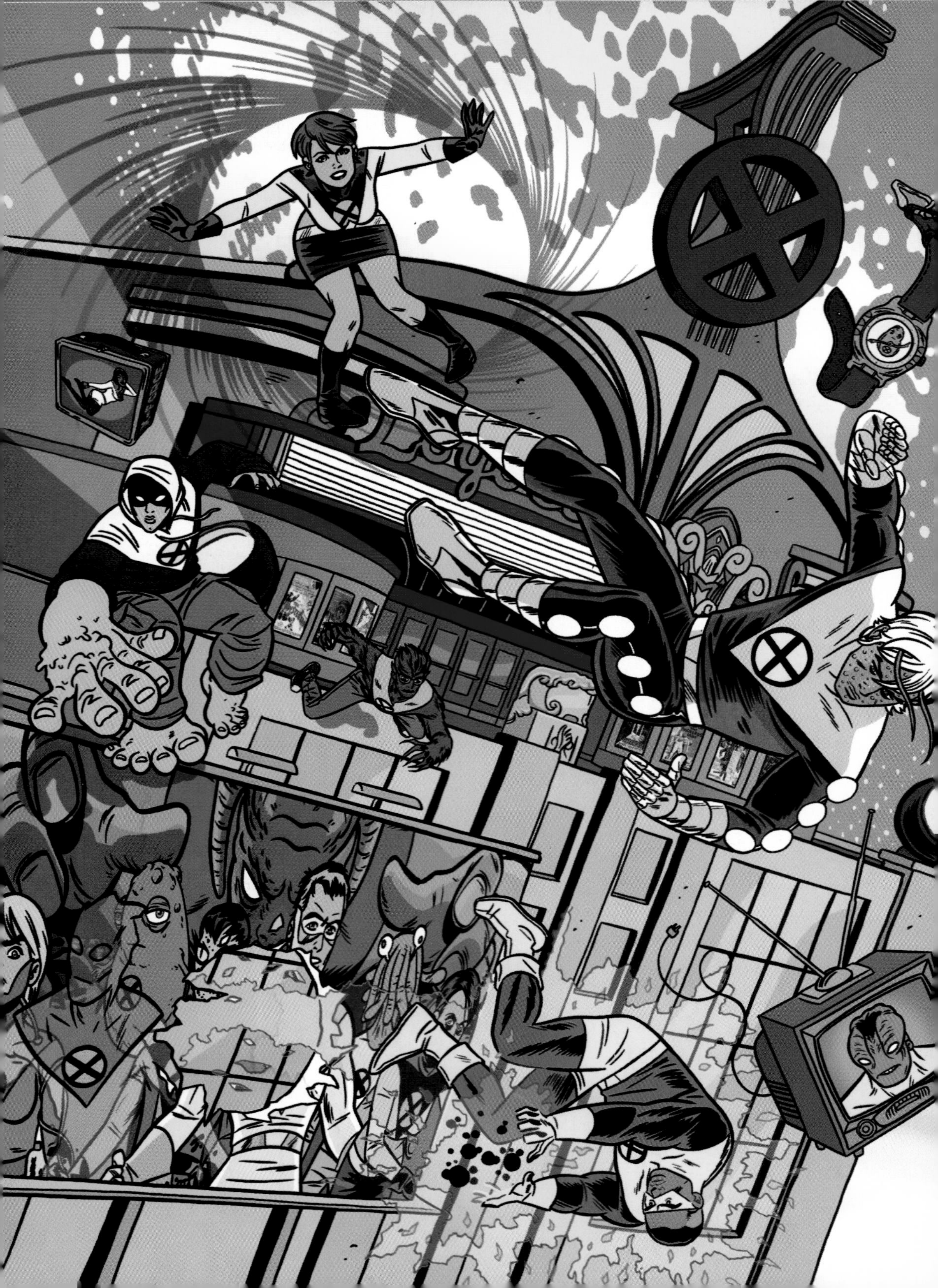

TRADE PAPERBACK COVER

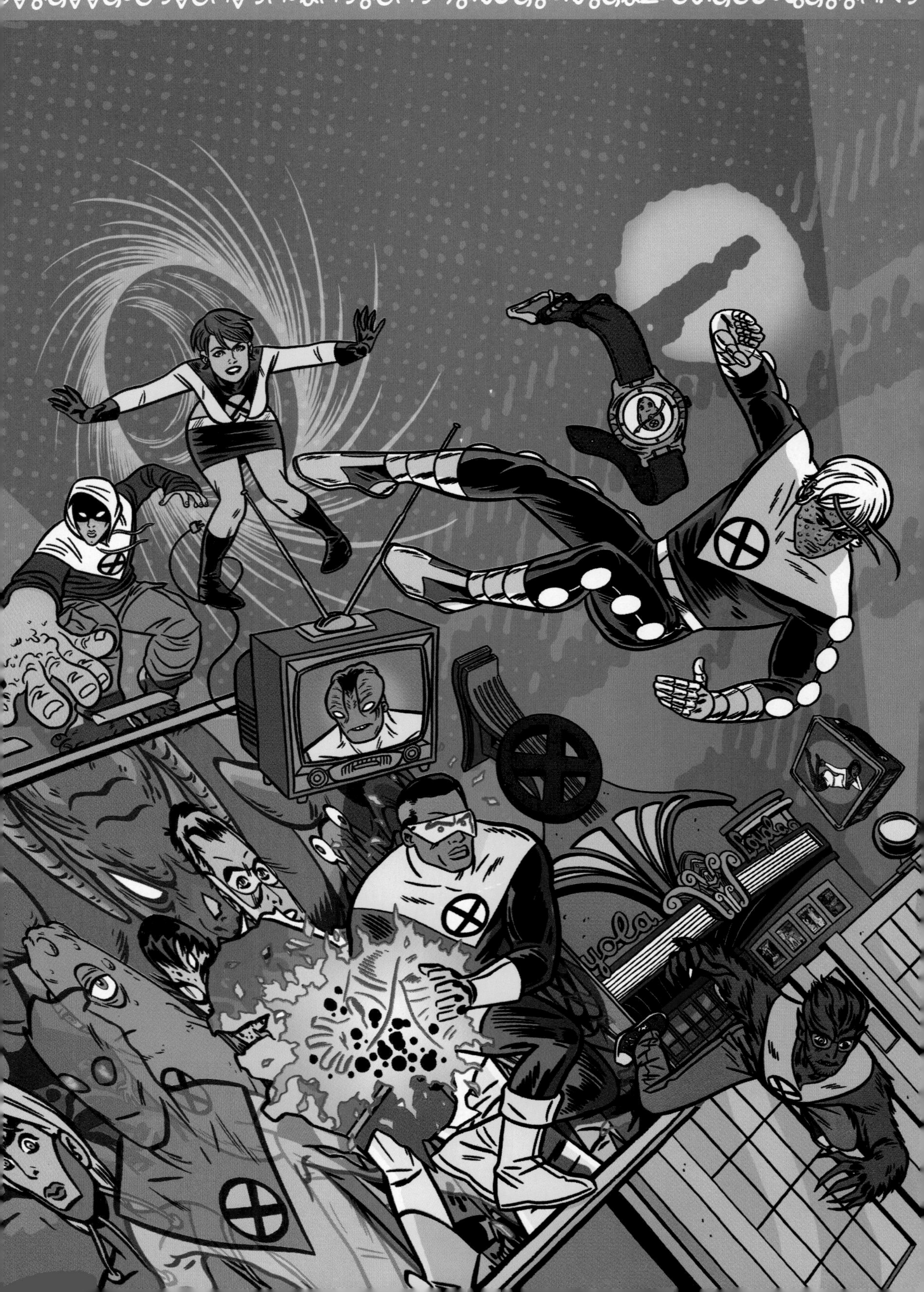